HOW SMART MACHINES THINK

HOW SMART MACHINES THINK

SEAN GERRISH
Foreword by Kevin Scott, CTO, Microsoft

The MIT Press
Cambridge, Massachusetts
London, England

This book was set in Bembo Std by Westchester Publishing Services.
Printed and bound in the United States of America.

Library of Congress Cataloging-in-Publication Data is available.
Names: Gerrish, Sean, author.
Title: How smart machines think / Sean Gerrish.
Description: Cambridge, MA : MIT Press, [2018] | Includes bibliographical references and index.
Identifiers: LCCN 2017059862 | ISBN 9780262038409 (hardcover : alk. paper)
Subjects: LCSH: Neural networks (Computer science) | Machine learning. | Artificial intelligence.
Classification: LCC QA76.87 .G49 2018 | DDC 006.3--dc23 LC record available at https://lccn.loc.gov/2017059862

10 9 8 7 6 5 4 3 2 1

This book is for the engineers and researchers who conceived of and then built these smart machines.

CONTENTS

FOREWORD

I met Sean over a decade ago. I was then leading the teams at Google responsible for many of the large-scale machine learning systems powering Google's search ads business. Sean, one of the top engineers in my group, was working on a set of challenging problems at the frontier of what was possible with machine learning at the time. Since we first began working together, the type of artificial intelligence embodied in the techniques of statistical machine learning has gone from a relatively inaccessible, arcane art and the exclusive domain of researchers and the highest of high-tech companies, to an increasingly approachable and highly useful set of tools and techniques that deserves to be in every software developer's bag of tricks.

The rapid progress being made at the moment in machine learning is being driven in part by an explosion in data; a renaissance in high performance computer architecture; cloud providers competing to build scalable AI platforms for developers and researchers; and a rush to embed real-time intelligence into mobile devices, cars, consumer electronics, and the increasingly ubiquitous computing devices connected at the edge of the cloud. Even though this rapid progress has included achievements that have surprised many onlookers as machines have approached or exceeded human capabilities in a number of narrow domains—such as labeling objects in images, recognizing speech, playing strategy games, and translating between human languages—we are still in the early days of the development of these technologies with decades of innovation and discovery ahead of us.

Understanding how machine learning works is a smart career bet for developers and researchers alike. Expertise in these technologies is already in high demand at the world's biggest technology companies. Many of

these same companies—Microsoft, Amazon, Google, Apple, Baidu—
provide APIs, toolkits, and cloud computing infrastructure to put machine
learning development in the hands of tens of millions of developers across
the world. Over the coming years it is highly likely that most developers
will need at least a little machine learning in their repertoire as more and
more applications incorporate "intelligent" functionality. And that's where
this book will prove to be an invaluable asset.

How Smart Machines Think was borne out of Sean's desire to understand
what makes modern machine learning tick. And in describing the essence
of these systems in a clear, approachable way, Sean leverages over a decade
of experience in industry and academia solving some of the toughest
problems that machine learning has to offer. Given that machine-learning
systems are sometimes able to reproduce aspects of human intelligence,
poetic license can be stretched near its breaking point. Sean's careful, pragmatic descriptions of these technologies reflect his years in the trenches,
where one learns through a sometimes-painful process of trial and error
that machine learning isn't magic. It's an extremely useful tool when you
understand how to apply it, and where its limits lie, and near worthless
when you don't.

Sean makes the concepts of modern machine learning accessible by
motivating techniques with real-world examples and by avoiding unnec-
essary jargon. *How Smart Machines Think* assumes relatively little background in machine learning or computer science, and hence is entirely
approachable to a broader audience. Given the lively contemporary dia-
logue around machine learning–based artificial intelligence and the
impacts that these technologies might have on our future, it behooves anyone wanting to get involved in that conversation to get as educated as
they can. With the paucity of approachable, technically sound introductions
to machine learning, this book is an ideal way to bootstrap your understanding of the underlying technologies, and to help you make better
determinations about what to believe and what to discard as hyperbolic
nonsense.

Kevin Scott
CTO, Microsoft

The seed for this book was planted in an AI research lab on the top floor of a computer science department one night in 2010. Having attended some recent talks about self-driving cars, and curious about how they worked, I did a few web searches. The best explanations I could find were the original academic papers written by some of the researchers at Carnegie Mellon University and Stanford. I looked at them for a few minutes, gained a superficial understanding of how self-driving cars worked, and eventually moved on.

But over time, I found myself repeating this process again and again. Whenever I saw another breakthrough in artificial intelligence or machine learning hit the press, I came back to the same question: *How does it work?* The curious thing to me was that I'd spent countless hours studying and practicing machine learning in academia and industry, and yet I still couldn't consistently answer that question. Perhaps I didn't know AI and machine learning as well as I should, I thought, or perhaps college courses didn't teach us the right material. Most college courses on these topics usually just teach the building blocks behind these breakthroughs—not how these building blocks should be put together to do interesting things.

But there was another, more fundamental reason I couldn't figure out how they worked: most of these breakthroughs really did involve groundbreaking research; we simply didn't know how to build them until a group of researchers figured it out and wrote about the process or built a prototype. That's why researchers have been writing about these breakthroughs in peer-reviewed journals: precisely because they're novel, impactful, and non-obvious (and peer-reviewed). But it still didn't help that the details behind these breakthroughs, once published, were spread out, haphazardly, across many different sources.

Eventually I realized that I should share what I was learning during my own research with other people, so they wouldn't need to jump through the same hoops to understand the same things. In other words: I wrote this book because it was a book I wanted to read.

I've written *How Smart Machines Think* with the hope that it will be helpful for tech enthusiasts young and old who are curious about science and technology in general, or to industry leaders who hope to learn more about whether machine learning and artificial intelligence might be useful for their companies. This book is meant to be accessible to a broad audience—from a curious high school student to a retired mechanical engineer. Although it will help if you know a little computer science, the only real prerequisites for this book are curiosity and a bit of an attention span. And I have intentionally kept the math in this book to a minimum to communicate the core ideas without alienating casual readers.

Experts in the robotics, AI, and machine learning communities will often know the implementation details of some of the algorithms I will describe; but the remaining narrative and the design of entire systems will still probably be new to many of them (except when that is their area of research). My hope is that there is something new in this book for everyone.

ACKNOWLEDGMENTS

It would have been impossible to write *How Smart Machines Think* without the hard work of the many researchers and engineers behind the breakthroughs in the following pages, as well as the journalists who have covered many of the more "human" details of their efforts. In some sense, this book was easy for me to write, because these researchers have already done most of the hard work. They've spent thousands of person-years on experiments, research, and documenting their findings. My role in writing this book has primarily been to collate and organize the results of their research into a more digestible form.

Many people and organizations have been helpful in the development of this book. My family has provided invaluable support through the process. This includes my wife, Sarah, who read more drafts than she would have liked, and my parents and brothers for their role in introducing me to computers in the first place. Teza Technologies was very generous for finding a way to accommodate my desire to write this book (during nights and weekends) while working at the company. From Teza, Michael Tucker reviewed the entire manuscript and provided helpful feedback. MIT Press's editorial staff, including Marie Lufkin Lee, Marcy Ross, and Christine Savage, have also been extremely collegial and helpful through the process, and anonymous reviewers who read early drafts provided helpful feedback. Mary Bagg additionally provided many helpful suggestions, comments, and corrections to the manuscript, and South Park Commons provided a nice community as I added the finishing touches to the book.

Many friends have also offered their ideas, time, and introductions, including Eric Jankowski, Andrew Cowitt, and Ricky Wong. Daniel Duckworth provided especially thorough feedback on the *Jeopardy* chapters, and my dad, Gary Gerrish, provided helpful feedback on the first half of the manuscript. David Churchill, Ben Weber, Jie Tang, James Fan, and Chris Volinsky have also graciously lent their time to answer questions about some of their work that I've discussed in this book, and to provide feedback on chapter drafts. Jason Yosinski and his colleagues also kindly allowed me to use their images of what neural networks see in chapter 9, the first full chapter about deep learning, and Alex Krizhevsky gave me permission to use an image of AlexNet (in the end I used a variant of that image).

Finally, I am fortunate to have had guidance from various mentors, formal or not, who have shown me many of these ideas throughout the years, before I began work on this book.

1 THE SECRET OF THE AUTOMATON

THE FLUTE PLAYER

In the year 1737, at the dawn of the Industrial Revolution, the French mechanical genius Jacques de Vaucanson completed a masterpiece: a statue that could create music from a flute like a real human. Holding a real flute up to its mouth, the life-sized statue would blow into the instrument with its mechanical lungs to produce a note. By moving its lips and adjusting how hard it blew, and by moving its fingers precisely over the holes, the statue could produce a sequence of notes to form a complete song "as perfectly as any human being."[1] Vaucanson, not content with a statue that could play just a single song on its flute, endowed the statue with the ability to play 12 different songs.[2]

The public had seen devices like the Flute Player before, although this one was special. They knew such machines as *automata*, and they simply couldn't get enough of them. Commissioning such devices had become a hobby among the wealthy elite throughout Europe.[3] For a little while Vaucanson charged the equivalent of a week's salary for each member of a small audience to see his strange device. Its natural movement and the complexity of its behavior were simply unknown at the time. Eventually Vaucanson toured this and several of his other automata around other parts of Europe.

But how did it work? Was it dark magic? A church official had ordered a decade earlier that one of Vaucanson's workshops be destroyed, because he considered it profane; so Vaucanson was sure to steer clear of doing anything that might look too much like magic. Was it a hoax? Just a few years before the Flute Player, an automaton that could apparently play the harpsichord had enchanted the French king Louis XV. The king, insisting on learning how the device worked, discovered that it was just a puppet, with a five-year-old girl inside.[4] But Vaucanson, keenly aware of this hoax, eagerly showed his audiences the inner mechanics of his Flute Player. It moved so fluidly and naturally, yet, as he showed them, it was apparently just following a sequence of instructions encoded into its mechanical bowels.

To further legitimize his invention, Vaucanson presented the automaton to the French Academy of Sciences, offering a dissertation titled "Mechanism of the Automaton Flute Player." In his dissertation, Vaucanson explained precisely how the fantastic machine worked. The statue was constructed of wood and cardboard, painted to look like marble, with leather on its fingertips to form a tight seal with the flute's holes. The mechanical drivers of the automaton were two rotating axles. To produce the statue's breath, one of these axles—the crankshaft—pumped three sets of bellows, which produced flows of air at three different pressures: low, medium, and high. These three streams combined into a single artificial trachea that fed into the statue's mouth. The other axle of the device slowly rotated a drum covered with small studs. As the drum rotated, these studs pressed against fifteen spring-loaded levers. Via chains and cables, these levers actuated various parts of the automaton. Some of the levers controlled the movement of the fingers and lips.[5] The remaining levers determined which of the three pressure ranges should be used to blow into the flute, as well as which position the device's tongue should take to modify the airflow. By placing the studs onto the correct positions on the rotating drum, Vaucanson could program the statue to play virtually any song he wanted; it was little more than a gigantic—albeit sophisticated—music box. The academy accepted his dissertation with a glowing review.[6]

Vaucanson's masterpiece was just one of many automata developed by the inventors of that century, over the course of decades. The automaton was popular precisely because it was fully autonomous and because it appeared to replicate human intelligence. The Flute Player and others like it were the artificially intelligent harbingers of the Industrial Revolution: as the materials and inventions that would enable it became available over the course of decades, the technologists and hobbyists of the time used them in their uniquely human quest to replicate our bodies and minds.

TODAY'S AUTOMATA

Fast-forward to the present day. Real-life self-driving cars now cruise around the cities of Silicon Valley day and night. We've trained computer programs to play Atari games far better than humans can by offering them treats, the same way you would train a dog to sit or to rollover. A computer program managed somehow to defeat two world champions at the game of *Jeopardy!* We've developed a computer program that can beat the best humans at the ancient game of Go. Meanwhile, the artificial intelligence behind these breakthroughs has been improving at a rate that's astonishing even to experts in the field.

It's hard to overstate this last point. The team that created Watson to play *Jeopardy* said it wasn't yet possible to create a program that could beat the world's best players, just before they embarked on a system that did just that. Many experts thought that it would take another decade to create a computer program that could play Go competitively up until they were proven wrong by AlphaGo, a program trained over the course of months to beat a leading world champion. Within 20 months, AlphaGo's creators developed another version of the program that taught itself thousands of years' worth of accumulated knowledge about the game within the course of three days; this version of AlphaGo defeated the previous version in 100 out of 100 matches with a 10th of the computing power. This was in part due to advances in artificial neural networks, the technology underlying AlphaGo and the focus of intensive research over the past decade. These networks don't just play games: they now have an ability to recognize images in photographs and spoken text that rivals humans' abilities.

As these breakthroughs have continued to make headlines, they naturally pique our curiosity: *How do they work?* Just as 18th-century Europeans wondered about the Flute Player and other automata of the time, this question often lingers unanswered, always beneath the surface, when we talk about these new automata.

Fortunately, and comparable to the way Vaucanson presented his dissertation to the French Academy of Sciences, the creators of many of these recent advances have documented in precise detail how to build these smart computer programs. That detail is spread across many different places; so in this book I have attempted to organize it, and to explain in simple terms, how these smart machines think.

Unlike the hoax automaton with the five-year-old girl hidden inside, the breakthroughs we'll look at in this book are legitimate scientific advances. Although they might look like magic, academic communities have vetted them all carefully, just like the Academy of Sciences vetted the Flute Player. Also like the Flute Player, they're examples of automata. An automaton is a self-moving machine. It appears to operate independently, often like a person or an animal, as if it could think for itself. But by definition, automata follow programs. These programs are predetermined sequences of instructions, like the programs Vaucanson developed for the Flute Player to play its songs.

As we'll see, it turns out that technologists haven't changed much over the past few centuries. They're still building and programming automata to replicate the human mind and body, and they sometimes still create hoax automata. The only difference is that now they've upgraded their tool chest to the levers, gears, and engines of the 21st century: computers and the software that runs on them.

THE SWING OF A PENDULUM

The automata of the 18th century sometimes used the cutting edge of precision technology at the time—mechanical clockwork—to carry out their programs. They were powered with mechanical energy: a hefty weight lifted high or a wound-up coil turned by a key. Their creators were often watchmakers, and the automata's technological ancestors were clocks that performed elaborate and entertaining mechanical sequences at the strike of an hour. These kept the time and performed their feats by drawing from potential energy stored within them before they were set in motion. Their clockwork enabled them to carry out their programs, step by step, by releasing this stored energy in small increments.

Mechanical clocks keep time with the swing of a pendulum. The pendulum swings with such regular frequency that it was the best method for timekeeping until the 1930s.[7] With each swing, a series of latches and gears registers the passage of another epoch, releasing a bit of stored energy so the clock can do something interesting, and to give the pendulum a small push to keep it swinging. And then the process repeats itself. A mechanical watch works on a similar principle: a finely coiled spring spins a circular disk back and forth around its center. With each twist of the disk, a gear moves one or two teeth at a time, so that the rest of the clockwork can do something interesting.

To a first approximation, this is the same machinery that enables electronic computers to run their programs. Computers use the principle of latches and gears; but instead of the quiet swing of a clock's pendulum, they use the swing of electrons, as they silently whoosh from one part of the circuit to another and back again. When the electrons are halfway to their destination at either extreme, they keep their momentum as they flow through another part of the circuit: a coiled piece of wire, for example (an electromagnet); or even the elastic swing of a crystalline tuning fork (a lab-grown and precisely cut piece of sand) whose vibrations at millions of times per second offers the circuit an extraordinarily precise resonant frequency. These crystal oscillators replaced physical pendula because they were stable—resistant to external forces like earthquakes, temperature changes, and the acceleration of airplanes and submarines—and because they were fast (millions of swings-per-second fast).

Each time these electrons swing from one part of the circuit to the other, electronic latches—analogous to the physical latches of a mechanical clock or watch—register the passage of another epoch in which to carry out another instruction in the program. Then the instruction counter moves forward, the clockwork waits for the electrons to swing back (or for new electrons to take their place), and the process repeats itself.

AUTOMATA WE'LL DISCUSS IN THIS BOOK

The swing of these electrons, and the intelligent behavior they enable, will be the focus of this book. In this book we won't ever look at the low-level instructions of these programs—that is, the variable and function names that the programmers wrote down to create their programs or the machine code generated by their programs. But we will look at the intermediate building blocks that make up these automata—basically the "statistical gears and bellows" one level higher. By understanding the building blocks that make up these automata, my hope is that you'll be better prepared to understand how *other* modern automata work. For example, now that you know how Vaucanson's Flute Player worked, you could probably make some educated guesses at how parts of his famous Digesting Duck worked. This automaton could flap its wings, quack, eat, digest, and (apparently) defecate.[8]

Vaucanson's automata couldn't react to the world. The automata of his day followed simple, predefined sequences of steps. Our modern-day automata can react to a changing environment because they have an ability to *perceive*. They can react not only to the press of a button on a keyboard, but also to the sight of cars and pedestrians passing through a crowded intersection, or to the subtle clues laid out in a *Jeopardy* question. Today's automata can do these things in ways that would have left Vaucanson and his contemporaries in awe.

I've written this book for anyone interested in how these devices work. You won't need to have a college degree in computer science to understand this book, although I'll assume that you're familiar with some basic facts about computers, such as that they follow explicit instructions encoded by humans, that images are represented by computers based on the amount of red, green, and blue they have in each pixel, and so on. And if you're already familiar with artificial intelligence or robotics, some parts of this book will probably still be new to you. Although you might have learned about the building blocks of these devices in your classes—the elements of machine learning and artificial intelligence—there's still a good chance that you haven't learned about how these building blocks have been put together to create these breakthroughs, because these topics aren't all typically taught in a single place. And finally, I've written this book so that you can usually jump straight to the topic that most interests you if you don't feel like reading all the way through. You shouldn't need to backtrack more than a couple of chapters to catch up on the machine learning and artificial intelligence background you need to know.

What are machine learning and artificial intelligence, anyway? Artificial intelligence (AI) is a broad field of study devoted to giving computers the ability to do intelligent things. There's no promise in AI that computers will do these things the way humans do them, and as we'll see, they often do things very differently than humans would do them. AI simply addresses *how* they can do intelligent things, and usually it addresses this question for very narrow domains, like finding a path through a maze. Machine learning is a closely related field devoted to enabling machines to do smart things by learning from data. As we'll see in this book, neither AI nor machine learning on their own can do everything. There will be cases where we'll need algorithms that can dumbly brute-force their way to intelligent solutions without using any data whatsoever; and there will be cases where we need to design algorithms that can learn from billions of data points but are still useless until we combine them with the dumb, brute-forced solutions. We'll need to combine algorithms of both types to do interesting things.

I've already mentioned some of the wonderful advances in machine learning and AI that we'll explore in *How Smart Machines Think*. In the first half of the book, I'll outline some of the key ideas that enable intelligent machines to perceive and interact with the world. We'll see what enables self-driving cars to stay on the road and to navigate through crowded urban environments. We'll see how neural networks can enable these cars—and other machines—to perceive the world around them, and we'll see how they can recognize objects in pictures or words in a recording of human speech. I'll also outline how one of the best movie-recommendation engines in the world worked, both because the story behind it is so fascinating and because many of the core ideas from that system permeate the other machines we'll look at in this book. Then I'll tell you how we can train computers to perform certain behaviors by feeding them treats and how they can perceive the world with artificial neural networks. Later in this book we'll look more closely at how computers can play a variety of games. Specifically, we'll take a look at AlphaGo and Deep Blue, which beat reigning world champions Lee Sedol and Garry Kasparov at the strategy games of (respectively) Go and chess; as well as IBM's Watson, which beat *Jeopardy* champions Ken Jennings and Brad Rutter.

Throughout this book, we'll follow the stories behind how these breakthroughs have occurred. We'll meet many of the researchers involved, and we'll see the factors beyond their technology and methodology that made these advances possible. One recurring theme, for example, is that a competitive research community can help to focus efforts and to catalyze progress. This is what thrust the field of self-driving cars into the public imagination and into its modern form: hundreds of research teams competed in a contest to build self-driving robot cars that could travel for miles in the desert, without human drivers. And that's where our story begins—on a cool morning in the Mojave Desert, as some of these teams prepared their cars for the race.

Most things worth doing aren't easy, and they aren't fast. You play with what
you got, and how things turn out, that's the way they are supposed to be. The
right thing to do is choose something you love, go after it with everything you
got, and that's what life is about.
—William "Red" Whittaker, leader of the Red Team[1]

THE $1 MILLION RACE IN THE DESERT

The first robot car race began in the Mojave Desert on a cool Thursday
morning in 2004. As the sun began to rise, a desert tortoise poked its head
out of its burrow, hoping to spend the day basking on the quickly warm-
ing road. Today he found himself trapped near his burrow, unable to move
far in any direction. Some twenty biologists had put barriers around this
and similar burrows to protect endangered species from the fleet of robot
cars that was about to drive down the nearby highway.[2] They anticipated
(correctly) that the cars wouldn't be able to stay on the roads, let alone
avoid tortoises in the middle of them.

Expectations about the cars' ability to finish the race varied wildly.
The race manager unblinkingly claimed a winner would finish the 142-
mile span in under 10 hours.[3] Others—including many in the robotics
community—doubted that any contestants would finish the race at all.[4]

A $1 million prize was at stake. Among those who wanted that prize was
Chris Urmson, design lead for a team of researchers developing a self-
driving Humvee.

Chris was tall and thin, with messy blond hair. Under the mentorship
of the legendary roboticist William "Red" Whittaker, Chris was working
his way toward a PhD at Carnegie Mellon University (CMU). Singularly

dedicated to his research, he had spent nearly two months in the desert running tests on the team's Humvee, staying up for nearly 40 hours straight at one point.[5] During one of its long-running tests he watched till near midnight, huddled under heavy blankets, as the Humvee drove in circles.[6] With its headlights visible through the thin fog, the Humvee suddenly veered off-course into a chain-link fence.[7] In another experiment the Humvee rolled over when it attempted a sharp turn, throwing its sensors off for weeks. Chris knew it was better to have these accidents before the race than during it.

A self-driving motorcycle was (of course) the media darling for the race. Its designers had attached gyroscopes to it so that it could remain upright by counter-turning just enough to stay balanced. It was among more than 100 submissions from researchers and hobbyists throughout the country.[8] A gyroscopic motorcycle was clever, but everyone knew that if any team were to win the race it would likely be Chris and William's team from CMU. Researchers from Carnegie Mellon had been leading the field for the past two decades, putting a rudimentary self-driving car onto Pittsburgh's streets as far back as 1991. No one could deny the CMU researchers' electromechanical chops. And their generous funding by military grants probably didn't hurt.[9]

The day of the race, the Humvee designed by Chris and his team zoomed by the tortoise's burrow, peppered with sensors and followed closely by another car. The Humvee had been driving for about 25 minutes. It wasn't driving fast—it averaged a little over 15 miles per hour for the 7 miles it had traveled—but it was still faring better than the other submissions that day. Its windshield obscured by a large CAT logo, the robot car hummed along confidently. But suddenly its vision gave out as it followed a switchback curving sharply to the left. Unable to see the road, the car was driving blind.

HOW TO BUILD A SELF-DRIVING CAR

How did the Humvee drive on its own for seven miles? You might have heard that self-driving cars use machine learning—specifically "deep neural networks"—to drive themselves. But when Chris and his colleagues described their Humvee after the race, they didn't mention machine learning or neural networks at all. This was 2004, nearly a decade before we had figured out how to train neural networks to reliably "see" objects. So what did these early self-driving cars use instead? In the next few chapters, I'll answer this question, explaining some of the bare minimum algorithms that enable cars to drive autonomously. I'll start by explaining how a car can drive for miles on a remote desert road without any traffic, when it has been given a list of locations to visit. Then I'll work my way up over the next few chapters to describe the algorithms that enable these cars to "see" the world around them and to reason about driving in an urban environment well enough to obey California traffic laws. But before we get into those details—all of which are part of a self-driving car's software—let's take a quick look at the way a computer controls the hardware of the car.

When Vaucanson created the Flute Player we saw in the last chapter, he programmed it to play specific songs by carefully placing studs at specific locations on the rotating drum. These studs then pressed levers that controlled its lips, the airflow in its breath, and its fingers. If Vaucanson wanted to create a new song, he just needed to create a new drum with its studs placed at different locations. And if he wanted to change the way the statue moved its lips or fingers, while keeping his library of 12 songs, he just needed to adjust the levers, chains, and joints of the physical device. He had separated the development of his automaton into two parts—the rotating drum and the rest of the system—which made improving it and reasoning about it much easier. We can do the same thing with a self-driving car.

Let's just focus on its speed for now. At its simplest, the car needs to turn a number the computer gives to it—such as "25"—into something concrete: the car's driving speed. The thing that makes this more difficult than it sounds is that the physical engine has no concept of what "25" means. For example, even if you knew that applying 250 volts to an electric engine would make the car drive at 25 miles per hour, you couldn't expect that by simply scaling the voltage up or down you'd get the speed you want. If you wanted the car to drive at one mile per hour, you couldn't expect that applying 10 volts to the engine would do the job. It wouldn't move at all at that voltage.

Vaucanson's contemporaries solved this problem by using a device called a centrifugal governor, which creates a feedback loop to control the engine's speed. A centrifugal governor is the "spinny" device with two metal balls—as shown in figure 2.1—that you might associate with steam engines and the mechanical workshops of the Enlightenment. As the

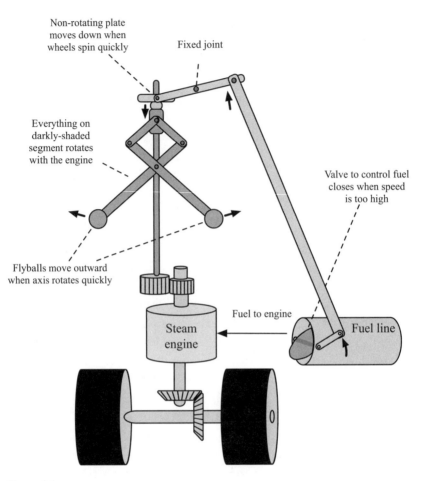

Non-rotating plate moves down when wheels spin quickly

Fixed joint

Everything on darkly-shaded segment rotates with the engine

Valve to control fuel closes when speed is too high

Flyballs move outward when axis rotates quickly

Fuel to engine

Steam engine

Fuel line

Figure 2.1
A centrifugal governor, the precursor to electronic control systems. As the engine runs more quickly, the rotating axis with the "flyballs" spins more rapidly, and the flyballs are pulled outward by centrifugal force. Through a series of levers, this causes the valve to the engine to close. If the engine is running too slowly, the valve will allow more fuel through.

engine runs faster, the governor spins more quickly, and the metal balls are pulled outward by centrifugal force. Through a series of levers, a valve closes on the fuel line feeding into the engine, slowing it back down. If the engine is running too slowly, the device increases fuel to the steam engine, speeding it back up. By adjusting the fuel to the engine, the governor keeps the engine's speed consistent.

The downside to this governor is that it only knows how to keep the engine running at a single speed. Modern self-driving cars use a similar feedback loop, except that they can run at whatever target speed is dictated by the computer program. You can see such a feedback loop in figure 2.2. Your target speed—say, 25 miles per hour—is an input to this feedback loop, and the loop uses an electronic speed sensor instead of a spinny device to gauge how far the wheel speed is from the target speed.

The intuitive behavior we want out of a speed control algorithm is that it will increase the power to the motor when the car is driving too slowly and decrease it when the car is driving too fast. One popular way to adjust the power to the motor is called *proportional control*, so-called because the adjustments we make to the power are equal to the difference between the target and current speed, multiplied by a fixed number. Proportional control isn't perfect—if the car is driving uphill or driving against strong winds, it will tend to drive more slowly than we want. So usually a couple of other adjustments are made to the control algorithm—so that, for example, if the car is consistently too slow, the power to the engine will get a little boost.

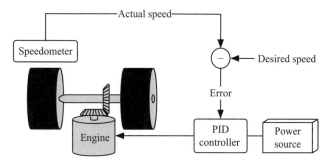

Figure 2.2
The control loop for a PID controller, the three-rule controller described in the text. The controller uses feedback from the speedometer to adjust inputs to the engine, such as power.

The most common control algorithm is a set of three simple rules like this that reliably get the car to its target speed. It was this three-rule controller (experts call it a PID controller) that was used in many of the self-driving cars we'll cover in the next few chapters.[10]

Now that we have a rough sense for how to control the hardware, we don't need to think a whole lot more about these messy details. Creating the hardware is certainly important, but we can assume that it's a separate challenge, maybe a topic for a different book. To control speed and steering from our perspective, we just need to write software that tells the car what speed to drive at, and how much it should turn its wheels. We've turned driving a car from a hardware problem into a software problem, and now we can focus exclusively on that software problem.

PLANNING A PATH

When the Humvee drove in the race, it didn't just drive for 25 minutes in a random direction; it drove along a path toward a specific destination. It did this because the car had a piece of software that told it where to go. This planning component is the most important part of the self-driving car: it determines the priorities for the rest of the system. Everything else the car does—such as steering to stay on the path and not crashing into rocks—is done to further the goal of following that path.

The organizers of the robot car race gave the contestants an electronic map of the route a mere two hours before the race started because they didn't want the contestants to peek at the route. This map outlined—with global positioning system (GPS) coordinates—where the car could go on its way from the beginning of the race to the end of the race. So Chris and his team outfitted their car with a GPS sensor to detect where it was. In theory, the car simply needed to navigate from one spot on the map to another, using their GPS sensor to turn this way and that to stay close to the route.

Chris's team, which called itself the Red Team, knew that GPS was the most important part of navigation, but they also knew that it wasn't enough. Obstacles like fences and rocks would be in the way. So the Red Team also created a massive map in advance, which they called "the best map in the world," to augment the one they would receive the morning of the race.[11] In the weeks before the race began, they studied satellite images from 54,000 square miles of desert to identify where the obstacles were located.

Then, during the two-hour window in which they had the route's GPS coordinates before the race started, fourteen humans hurried (with the help of a couple dozen computers) to manually annotate the terrain along the route.[12]

As these human workers annotated the map, a computer continuously searched for the best route from the start of the race to the end of it, sending updates back to the workers so they could prioritize their research. Chris and his team planned to upload this pre-computed path to their self-driving Humvee just before the race started.

PATH SEARCH

When you were a child, you may have played a game in which you pretended that the floor in your living room was hot lava. The point of this game was to find a path through the room that avoided the floor—that is, the lava—whenever possible. The Humvee needed to do the same thing to get from its current position to the next goal point in the map, except that instead of avoiding lava, it needed to avoid dangerous parts of the desert.

But we can't simply tell the Humvee, "Find a good path." Remember, when Vaucanson created the Flute Player, he had to provide the statue with instructions for every little movement it would need to make to play the flute. Similarly, when we program a computer to find a good path, we need to give it a clear sequence of steps it must follow to figure out that path on its own. These steps are like a recipe, except that we must be explicit about the most minute of details.

If we were to formalize the process you went through to find a path through your hot-lava living room, it probably went something like this. First, without thinking about it, you assigned a cost in your mind to taking a step on different surfaces or items in the room, perhaps like this:

Table 2.1

Terrain type	"Cost" of one step
Carpet (lava)	1
Table	0.5 (Mom will get mad, but it's not lava)
Couch	0
Sleeping dog or cat	10

Then you planned your path through the room by estimating which sequence of steps would get you to the other side of the room *for the least possible cost.* Notice that we framed the problem of searching for a good path as minimizing some function (the cost of a path). This is important, because we framed the problem in terms of something computers are good at. They're bad at open-ended planning in complex environments, but they're good at minimizing functions. We will see this idea again and again in this book.

The Humvee was in a timed race, so the Red Team assigned a cost to each meter-by-meter cell in their map to reflect the time they expected the Humvee would take to safely drive one meter, on a six-point scale. Difficult terrain received a higher cost than easy terrain since the Humvee would need to drive more slowly on it. The team added extra penalties for regions of the map that were unpaved, lacked GPS data, or had uneven or steep ground, or for cells that were too far from the center of the race corridor described by their GPS coordinates. Once they had a map with costs assigned to each square cell, they needed to estimate their path through the map.

In one popular path-finding process called Dijkstra's algorithm, the computer searches for a path by growing a search "frontier" out from the start point.[13] The program runs a loop, pushing the frontier out a small amount each time it runs through the loop until eventually the frontier reaches the final destination. As the program grows the frontier, it slowly increases the cost it's willing to "pay" to get to any point within the frontier; so any time it stretches the frontier to include another point, that new point is just at the cusp of what it's willing to pay. The benefit of stretching the frontier like this is that the frontier can search along the most promising routes— such as smooth roads, which have a low cost—long before it bothers searching far into the more difficult routes—such as rough, off-road terrain.

By the time this frontier reaches the goal point—the destination, in the case of the self-driving car—the computer knows a path exists, and it knows the cost of that path. As long as the computer kept track of how it spread the frontier through the map, it can then quickly backtrack to find the shortest path to the goal point. You can see what such a shortest path looks like—as well as what the search frontier looks like—in figure 2.3.

Computer scientists and roboticists have spent years studying algorithms like this, and they know how to find the lowest-cost path in large maps in

A

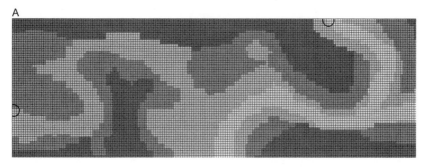

Figure 2.3a
An example map. Darker shades indicate a higher travel cost.

B

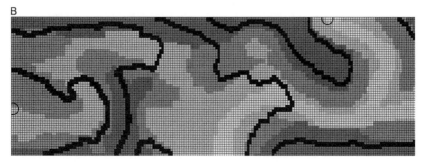

Figure 2.3b
The search "frontier" at different iterations of Dijkstra's algorithm.

C

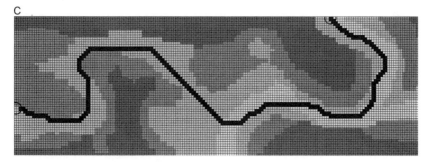

Figure 2.3c
An optimal path through this map.

(a) A map with four different types of terrain. Each cell in the grid represents a square meter and takes one of four colors, indicating the type of terrain. Darker shades have a higher cost and cannot be traversed as easily. Start and end positions are respectively marked on the left and at the top. From lightest to darkest grey, the time to pass over a cell are 1.0, 3.0, 9.0, and 18.0 seconds / meter. (b) Some search algorithms run by growing a search "frontier" out from the start point. Each frontier is represented by a contour line; these represent how far the car could travel in 175, 350, 525, and 700 seconds. (c) Once the algorithm has completed, it has mapped an optimal path through the cost grid. In this case, the path tends to prefer to stay on light-colored terrain, on which the car can drive more quickly.

a fraction of a second. When the path doesn't need to be the best possible path—just a good-enough path—they can estimate it in even less time. After the Red Team's computers planned the Humvee's path with such an algorithm, the Humvee was ready to begin the race.

NAVIGATION

To find its position on the map, the Humvee used a GPS sensor that Chris's team had strapped to it. GPS sensors use signals from a constellation of dozens of carefully calibrated satellites put into orbit by the US Department of Defense. At any given time, a handful of these satellites—not always the same ones—will be visible to a GPS sensor; it uses four of the visible ones to triangulate its current time (t) and its position (x, y, z) up to a few meters.

GPS alone isn't enough for a self-driving car, however. First, GPS measurements aren't consistently accurate: a good GPS system might be accurate up to centimeters, but some systems can be hundreds of meters off in the worst cases. There might also be gaps in GPS measurements from hardware hiccups, when passing through a tunnel, or even from disturbances of the satellites' signals as the signals pass through the earth's ionosphere. GPS also couldn't tell the robot car its orientation: the Humvee might lose its bearings if its wheels slipped on the dusty road, for example. Having a way to navigate *without* GPS was therefore critical for the Humvee.

So the Red Team also put accelerometers onto the Humvee to measure its acceleration in three dimensions, which the Humvee accumulated to estimate the car's velocity and position. They also attached gyros, which are accelerometers that measure rotation, so the Humvee could keep track of its orientation.

The car combined measurements from these accelerometers and GPS sensors using a Kalman filter, a mathematical model discovered in 1960. A Kalman filter is a method for tracking an object over time—the position of a submarine in the ocean or a robot Humvee, for example—by distilling a collection of measurements of the object into an estimate of its position. The core idea behind a Kalman filter is that we never really know an object's true position and speed: we can only take imperfect snapshots, like blips on sonar. Some blips might be wrong, and we don't want that to throw off the estimate—maybe it's a reflection off of an orca or a piece of seaweed, for example—but a Kalman filter can smooth out these outliers.

In fact, a Kalman filter doesn't expect *any* of its measurements to be correct; it just expects them to be correct *on average*. And with enough observations, it can approximate an object's true position and velocity extraordinarily well: a Kalman filter taking in measurements from accelerometers, gyros, and GPS, combined with measurements from the wheels, can enable a self-driving car to estimate its position, even during a two-minute GPS outage, with an error of mere centimeters.[14]

But even with these precise measurements, the Humvee might still run into fences, boulders, or other things along the road that might not have been visible in the Red Team's map, so the team also added a gigantic "eye" to the Humvee. They planned for this giant eye to scan the ground in the Humvee's path to find obstacles that weren't already encoded into the preplanned route. If there were an object or uneven ground in the path it had intended to take, the Humvee was programmed to veer left or right to avoid hitting it.[15]

The eye was a combination of a laser and a light sensor, together called *lidar*, which is short for light detection and ranging. Lidar is like sonar or radar, except that it bounces light off objects instead of bouncing sound or radio waves off them. (I'll use the term *laser scanners* from this point when I refer to the technology). The giant eye also had a pair of cameras mounted on a gimbal that could be pointed by the robot in different directions.[16] (A gimbal is a fixture that enables an object to rotate along different axes, like that of a globe of the earth.)

But the Humvee's giant eye was also very rudimentary. The Humvee wasn't programmed to adjust its route in any material way in response to what its eye saw. It merely followed its preplanned path, veering left or right according to simple rules to avoid troublesome ground.

And this rudimentary eye was also what eventually gave the Humvee trouble, just before it skidded onto the shoulder of the road and crashed into a rock.

THE WINNER OF THE GRAND CHALLENGE

The Humvee hit the rock close to the place where we left it a few pages ago, just after passing its seven-mile mark in the desert. It had been following a switchback as it curved to the left, but the Humvee's turn was too sharp, and its left wheels went over an embankment at the edge of the road.

Its belly ground in the dirt as it slid forward until it hit the rock. A full minute on the race timer passed, followed by another, as the Humvee spun its wheels in the dust. A couple of race officials who had followed the Humvee to monitor its progress watched as the Humvee struggled in the morning light.

The Humvee's tires spun for nearly *seven* minutes before finally catching fire. The nearby officials slammed a remote e-kill switch to stop the robot and jumped out to extinguish the flames. The Humvee's wheels had been spinning so fast that both of its half-shafts split when they hit the kill switch.[17] Chris's team was officially out of the race.

A branch of the US Defense Department known as the Defense Advanced Research Projects Agency, or DARPA, organized this robot car race. Out of the 106 applicants to what became known as the DARPA Grand Challenge, 15 competed on the day of the race, including the robot Humvee designed by Chris and his team.

Exactly zero of these self-driving cars won the $1 million prize. To an onlooker, the competing cars might have looked like a rather pathetic bunch: one contestant, a large truck, slowly backed away from bushes, as another car, afraid of a shadow, drove off the road.[18] The self-driving motorcycle's creator, amid the excitement and cheering before the race, had forgotten to switch the motorcycle over to self-drive mode. It fell over at the starting line.[19]

The Humvee had driven 7.4 miles before grinding to a halt on the edge of the road. Although it was the race's best performer, it had traveled a mere 5 percent of the route.

The Red Team studied their race logs and published a lengthy report outlining the strengths and weaknesses of their Humvee. In their report, they enumerated some problems during its 25-minute run. It reads like the script of a Blues Brothers movie:

Impact with fence post #1

Impact with fence post #2

Momentary pause

Impact with fence post #3

Impact with boulder

High centering in the hairpin [i.e., the final accident][20]

These impacts were described as "off-nominal behavior" in the Red Team's report, but an insurance company might have more aptly called them "accidents."

DARPA had announced to contestants that the race could be completed with a stock four-wheel-drive pickup truck,[21] but the Red Team selected a Humvee because they didn't want hardware to be a bottleneck. This did help in some cases. For example, fence post #3 was reinforced, which meant that the Humvee—which was more reinforced, as it was a Humvee—pushed against it for nearly two minutes before finally pushing it over and continuing on its way. Chris even called their Humvee a "battering ram of a car ... at 22mph a Beast on a roll."[22] But a tough truck wasn't enough to win.

The problem was that the Humvee could barely see where it was going. Its gigantic eye was too primitive, its vision too poor. Except for its ability to navigate over long distances, most of the Humvee's intelligent behavior involved reacting to its sensors using simple rules. The Red Team, aware of these limitations, programmed the Humvee to ignore data from its camera and laser scanners when that data was likely to be unreliable, and then to follow its GPS coordinates, driving blind along its preplanned route. This is what happened right before the Humvee's fatal crash. Its eye, and any software to support that eye, would have to be improved.

A FAILED RACE

To an outside observer, the Grand Challenge might have looked like a failure. CNN summarized it with the headline "Robots Fail to Complete Grand Challenge."[28] *Popular Science* called it "DARPA's Debacle in the Desert."[23] On the bright side, as one spectator pointed out, it was "a good day for the tow-truck drivers."[24]

But many of the competitors were genuinely happy with the results. Contestants and organizers partied that night at Buffalo Bill's Casino at the finish line, where they were surrounded by fellow geeks with a passion for building robot cars. Soon they would be able to read in detail about how a robot Humvee had managed to travel 7.4 miles—7.4 miles!—in rough desert terrain. They could also finally catch up on sleep after having worked nights and weekends for months.[25]

DARPA officials were also excited, congratulating each other about the race. For the past eight years, the field of self-driving cars had been hibernating in virtual winter ever since Ernst Dickmanns, one of its leaders, had proclaimed that the field would need to wait until computers were more powerful. Now that computers were 25 times faster, DARPA's Grand Prize had quickly begun to thaw the self-driving landscape so that researchers could make progress again.[26]

DARPA was also a step closer to achieving its mandate from Congress—to make a third of military vehicles self-driving by 2015 (a mandate, to my knowledge, that they didn't achieve). Like the contestants, DARPA had documentation from the world's experts on how to make cars that could autonomously drive miles in the desert. "It didn't matter to us if anybody completed the course," DARPA director Anthony Tether explained. "We wanted to spark the interest in science and engineering in this area."[27]

Seen from that perspective, the race was a resounding success. It had attracted more than a hundred applicants and saw reporting from more than 450 television news segments and 58 newspapers within just a few months.[28] Top magazines like *Wired* and *Popular Science* featured the event in multipage spreads.[29] Although they didn't know it at the time, it would also precede at least a decade and a half of heavy industry investment in self-driving car technology.

Eager to continue the progress, DARPA officials announced that they would hold another race in just over a year. They sweetened the prize, doubling the payout to $2 million. Gary Carr, one of the sleep-deprived contestants in the weeks leading up to the first challenge, was among those who could hardly wait. "We will be here. Our vehicle will be different, but we will be here."[30] He wasn't the only one excited about the next race. Chris and the rest of the Red Team now had another shot.

3 KEEPING WITHIN THE LANES: PERCEPTION IN SELF-DRIVING CARS

Treat autonomous navigation as a software problem.
—Stanford Racing Team design philosophy, 2005

THE SECOND GRAND CHALLENGE

The second Grand Challenge took place a year and a half later, also in the Mojave Desert. One robot car would be released from the starting line every five minutes so the cars couldn't interfere with one another on the route.[1]

The Red Team's strategy was again to focus primarily on mapping and navigation. This time, over the course of a month, the team sent three drivers to scan 2,000 miles of desert to find potential routes the race might take. As before, a human team preprocessed the route for two hours before the race to help a computer plan a path that was then uploaded to the Humvee.[2] They also encoded a rule into the Humvee intended to prevent it from getting stuck behind another rock. If it got stuck—that is, if its wheels were turning but its GPS sensor said it wasn't moving anywhere— it was programmed to back up 10 meters, clear its estimates of obstacles, and try again.[3]

The most challenging part of the race for these cars was Beer Bottle Pass, a 1.5-mile stretch of dirt road with sheer rock on one side and a 100-foot drop-off on the other.[4] Competitors crowded around a live video feed of the pass to see whether their robot cars would make it.[5] The Red Team's Humvee made it through mostly fine, although it scraped itself a bit along the way. In fact, the Humvee successfully drove all 132 miles of the race, almost twenty times the distance it had traveled in the first race.[6] But it didn't win.

The winner of the race was Stanley, a car built by the Stanford Racing Team, newcomers to the race that year. Stanley drove so fast that it had to be paused twice to give the car in front of it more time.[7] Eventually race organizers paused the car ahead of Stanley to let it pass. In the end, Stanley finished over ten minutes faster than the Red Team's Humvee.[8]

The Stanford Racing Team was led by Sebastian Thrun, the head of Stanford's artificial intelligence laboratory and the youngest person ever to hold that role. Sebastian had also come from Carnegie Mellon, where he was a junior faculty member in the robotics lab just a few years earlier. Although he had never built a self-driving car before, he was inspired during the first Grand Challenge. Knowing the results of that challenge—the Debacle in the Desert—he asked himself: *Could we do better?*[9] With help offered by Volkswagen—two Volkswagen Touaregs and support from the company's Electronics Research Laboratory—he could turn this inspiration into action.[10]

As Sebastian wrote in a personal account of the race, he assembled the manpower to build Stanley by first organizing a seminar class to build a prototype.[11] This wasn't a normal class: it had no textbooks, no syllabus, and no lectures.[12] The 20 students in the course read just two papers for the class, so that they wouldn't be biased toward any particular approach.[13] Within eight short weeks, they had built a prototype that could travel farther along the desert route (albeit more slowly) than the Humvee.[14]

What made Stanley so successful in the race? The teams in the previous year had relied too little on things like obstacle detection.[15] The Stanford Racing Team had the insight that placing so much emphasis on mapping and navigation at the expense of sensing the environment was a mistake. Although their competitors, the Red Team, had scouted those 2,000 miles of desert roads in advance of the second Grand Challenge, the area amounted to a mere 2 percent of the actual race route.[16]

So the Stanford Racing Team—knowing that even a massive Humvee could be stopped by rocks, and reminded by DARPA that a stock pickup truck could traverse the route—converged on a different design philosophy: *treat autonomous navigation as a software problem.*[17] After the class in which students designed the initial robot, Sebastian and a smaller team (comprising just a handful of those students and some other researchers) threw out most of their code and began to rewrite the software for Stanley more carefully, setting a high bar for software to be included in the car.[18] But they didn't just plan to rely on any software: more specifically, they planned to use machine learning to solve driving.

MACHINE LEARNING IN SELF-DRIVING CARS

The Stanford Team wasn't the first research group to use machine learning to design self-driving cars: machine learning had been researched in the context of self-driving cars since at least the 1980s.[19] But they were one of the first modern self-driving car teams to take such a full bet on machine learning, embracing its role in self-driving cars nearly a decade before it became a buzzword in the mainstream media. As Sebastian's team wrote in a description of their car after the race:

> The pervasive use of machine learning, both ahead [of] and during the race, made Stanley robust and precise. We believe that those techniques, along with the extensive testing that took place, contributed significantly to Stanley's success in this race.[20]

When Sebastian and his team first embarked on building Stanley, they had an immense task ahead of them. They needed to design a way for their automaton to both perceive the world and react: Stanley couldn't wait for seconds at a time as it searched for a new path; it needed to make seamless decisions as its model of the world changed. The team thought about this task just as a team of architects would think about designing a new building. They needed to find an *architecture* for Stanley.

STANLEY'S ARCHITECTURE

The architecture they converged on was organized into three separate parts, as shown in figure 3.1. The leftmost part of the architecture was a hardware layer containing both sensors to collect data and actuators to control the steering, brakes, and engine speed. This layer didn't do anything smart; its purpose was solely to fetch data from the sensors (the cameras, laser scanners, and the GPS system) and to use commands from the planning layer (like engine speed and wheel angle) to control the hardware of the car. Except for the Kalman filters that might be embedded in the hardware, this

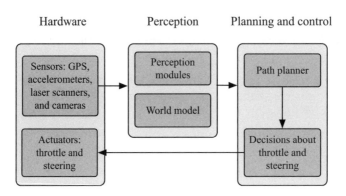

Figure 3.1
A simplified summary of the software and hardware organization of
Stanley, the Stanford Racing Team's 2005 Grand Challenge winner.

layer did very little that would typically fall into the realm of AI or machine
learning.[21]

At the opposite extreme, on the far right, was the "thinking" layer: it
performed high-level planning for the car. (There wasn't much high-level
thinking in Stanley—we'll see much more of it in a self-driving car in the
next chapter—but what little existed in Stanley existed here.) This layer
figured out, given obstacles in its path, how the car should swerve to avoid
them. This layer was in charge of making decisions about how the car
should actually drive. It sent orders to the leftmost layer, often to the three-
rule controllers we saw in the last chapter. If the planning layer wanted
the engine to target a specific speed, such as 25 miles per hour, it just
needed to send that command to the hardware controllers.

The middle layer in figure 3.1 intermediated between the sensing/
control layer on the left and the thinking layer on the right. It turned raw
sensor readings into interpretable models so the thinking layer could do its
job. Some of these models simply summarized the high-level route that
Stanley needed to follow, a route that Stanley had planned at the beginning
of the race. Other models crunched numbers to tell Stanley what its sensors were seeing. A variety of machine learning modules—including several road-detection systems that we'll take a closer look at in a moment—ran
continuously in the middle layer, interpreting a disorganized mess of sensor
readings and turning them into more meaningful interpretations of the
world for the planning layer.

These sensor readings came into the middle layer as just clouds of points. By interpreting them for the planning layer on the right, the middle layer made it easier for the planning layer to focus solely on its higher-level reasoning. And although the modules that ran in this central layer were often cleverly engineered and used complex machine learning algorithms, they weren't really "smart." They only appeared to be smart when working in combination with the planning layer. Let's take a closer look now at the perception modules from this middle layer.

AVOIDING OBSTACLES

Just as the Red Team had done, the Stanford Racing Team also outfitted their car with laser scanners to "see" the terrain around it. They programmed Stanley to imagine a grid around itself, a bit like the one in figure 3.2 (except that the size of each cell in their map was much smaller):

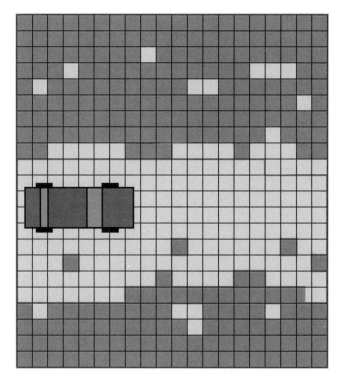

Figure 3.2

Stanley used data from its laser scanner to estimate which cells in this grid were "occupied" by some object (the occupied ones in figure 3.2 are the dark ones). Stanley's planning algorithms then allowed it to drive over cells that were *not* occupied while swerving to avoid any cells that *were* occupied.

But how could they tell whether a cell was occupied? Sebastian and his team programmed Stanley to do this by measuring characteristics about each cell, like the heights of different points in the cell—which was information they could get from the laser scanner—and how long it had been since the last good measurement of those points had taken place. They then used these measurements to estimate the probability that the cell contained two points that were of different heights. If the cell *did* contain two points that were likely to be very different in height, then Stanley could mark that cell in its map as occupied.[22]

Sebastian and his team had the right idea with this approach, but they also found that their algorithm for marking these cells wasn't very good. For one thing, their sensors tended to drift over time. If Stanley's laser scanner was tilted just a fraction of a degree, Stanley would think that there were obstacles in front of it, which led its planning algorithm in the rightmost layer to order Stanley to swerve off the road. The Stanford Racing Team could have invested hundreds of thousands of dollars in an expensive pose-estimation system designed by topnotch research scientists, but the team already had such scientists onboard; so they just built a model on their own that would be robust to these sorts of measurement errors. Their resulting model was correct, at least in spirit, but it also had many parameters to tune.[23]

Joshua Davis, a reporter for *Wired*, noted that Sebastian was well aware of these limitations. One day, a few months before the race, while Sebastian was out in the desert with Stanley, he kicked some dirt at the side of the road in frustration over the car's tendency to veer off the right path.[24] Stanley had nearly crashed into a ditch, and Sebastian saw that the car had the same problem as the entries in the first challenge that were afraid of shadows and bushes. So Sebastian thought carefully, trying to figure out which algorithms could enable the car to use data from its sensors better.[25]

Enter machine learning. Sebastian's solution was to have a person drive Stanley around while its laser scanners measured the world around the car (by one account Sebastian himself drove Stanley to collect these measurements), saving these measurements to use later. The idea was that whoever was driving Stanley would only drive Stanley on ground that was safe, and that some of the ground that Stanley didn't drive on was not safe. They could use their sensor measurements to tune the many parameters in their obstacle-detection model. By doing this, they would in effect be "training" their algorithm with data.

The method Sebastian's team used to predict which ground was safe to drive on was known as supervised classification.[26] We'll take a closer look at this approach beginning in a couple of chapters, but for now all you need to know is that a classifier like the one the Stanford Racing Team used provides a way for a computer to automatically predict which of two categories an item belongs to. The idea is that you combine your measurements using a simple mathematical function that produces a prediction. That mathematical function might have many knobs to tune, but—and here's where the machine learning comes in—since these knobs can be tuned with data, the predictions can become very accurate.

The Stanford Racing Team's data-driven tuning improved their terrain-detection algorithm by orders of magnitude. Before they used it, they mistook safe ground for unsafe ground—the type of mistake that could throw Stanley off the road—12.6 percent of the time. After fitting their classifier with data, they cut this rate down by a factor of 6,000.[27] This was their first major step in improving on the giant eye used by the Red Team.

FINDING THE ROAD'S EDGES

But was Stanley now able to drive safely down the road? Not quite. This classifier told Stanley what ground in its field of vision was drivable, but it didn't say anything about roads, and it didn't compel Stanley to actually stay *on* the road. With the classifier above, Stanley would have happily driven off the road as long as the off-road path was drivable.

Perhaps that was okay, though. After all, the race didn't technically require Stanley to stay on the road, and as long as the classifier said the terrain was drivable, then it was safe to drive on *by definition*, right? But the Stanford Racing Team recognized that leaving the road could be risky business. As they wrote after the race, "Obstacles—such as rocks, brush, and fence posts—exist most often along the sides of the road. By simply driving down the middle of the road, most obstacles on desert roads can be avoided without ever detecting them!"[28] It's perhaps no accident that some of the items they listed were those hit by the Red Team's Humvee. Still, their point was clear. And so they developed another algorithm for Stanley's vision system, this one to help Stanley find the edges of the road.

The Stanford Racing Team reasoned that the road's edges should typically be parallel to their preplanned path. So they fitted Stanley with extra laser scanners to scan the ground in the car's proximity for these road edges, in lines parallel to its planned path, as shown in figure 3.3:

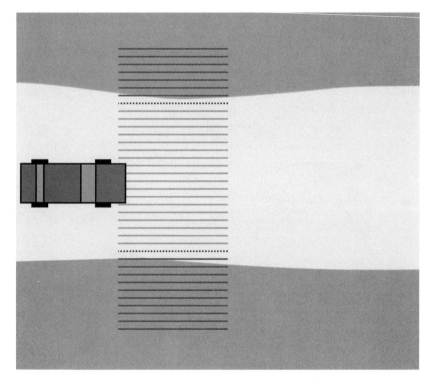

Figure 3.3

This road-edge–detecting module then heuristically checked whether the lines scanned by the laser were free of obstacles. The outermost line on either side without a detected obstacle was considered an "observation" of where the road boundary was located, so as Stanley drove along, the module collected many of these observations. In raw form these looked like a sequence of points—just lateral offsets on either side of the car. But once

Stanley passed them through another Kalman filter, it had a smooth and accurate estimate of the road's edges.[29] And once Stanley had an estimate of the road's edges, it could also keep an ongoing estimate of where the middle of the road was. Stanley's path-planning algorithm, which we'll see in a moment, was then programmed to drift toward the middle of the road if there weren't any other obstacles in its path (the route was blocked to outside traffic for the robot race, so there were no oncoming cars).

SEEING THE ROAD

But problems still remained with Stanley's vision system. Even though these modules could keep Stanley on the road, its laser scanners could only "see" about 30 meters ahead. This wasn't far enough for Stanley to safely drive any faster than about 25 miles per hour, because these desert roads often had switchbacks, like the one that stopped the Humvee in the first race.[30] Sebastian and his team calculated that 25 miles per hour would be too slow for them to be competitive, so they looked for another way for Stanley to see past the range of the laser scanner.

Their solution was to attach a color camera to the front of their robot. The camera could see farther than the laser scanners, so if they could determine that the road stretched out far ahead of Stanley, then Stanley could assume that the stretch could be driven on safely—and it could increase its speed from just 25 miles per hour to 45 miles per hour.[31]

When we humans look at a picture of a road, it's immediately clear which part of the picture is the road, which part is the side of the road, and which part is the sky. None of these details are obvious at first to a computer program. Again, Stanley needed a step-by-step recipe to find the road in its images from the camera. To do this, Stanley applied another technique from machine learning, called *clustering*, to group together pixels with similar colors. By doing this, Stanley would be better able to tell whether a pixel belonged to part of the road—or to a part of the ground on the side of the road.

To understand how Stanley did this, imagine you're a vampire who has just done a load of laundry. Since you're a vampire, your favorite colors are red and black, and your socks are various shades of red and various shades of gray. After coming home from the laundromat, you begin to sort through these socks, spreading them out on the bed so that similarly colored socks are near each other. Over time there will be a pile of red socks and a pile of gray socks, and they might overlap where the darker shades of red meet the darker shades of gray.

But then imagine that you find a bright green sock in your laundry. This sock clearly doesn't belong in either of these piles, so you conclude that it must have gotten mixed up with your clothes at the laundromat. You reject it.

This is exactly how Stanley reasoned about the pixels in the image from the camera. It created clusters of road pixels by looking at the pixels representing the ground just in front of the car. In the desert, you can imagine that these road-color pixels might be a mix of gray and brown, which would have caused Stanley to end up with a cluster of gray-ish pixels and a cluster of brownish pixels.[32] Stanley then tested whether the rest of the pixels in the image matched these clusters.[33] If they matched the clusters, they were part of the road; otherwise, Stanley rejected them, just as you rejected the green sock: they weren't part of the road. Once Stanley figured out which pixels "belonged" to the road, it could estimate how far ahead the road stretched by using simple geometry. If the road stretched out in front of Stanley for a long distance, then Stanley could speed up. This road-seeing module ran constantly in Stanley, repeating itself on a regular basis, continually adjusting its estimate of the road color.

Could Stanley be sure that it was actually picking the right pixels to build up its estimate of the road's color? Wasn't it possible that Stanley might accidentally select pixels from the side of the road to build up its clusters, instead of selecting pixels from the road? It was certainly possible for the algorithm to be wrong in identifying which pixels were road—just as it was possible for *any* of its algorithms to be wrong—but this was mitigated in part because Stanley had other modules, like the one to detect drivable terrain, and because the algorithm was only used to control speed, not steering. Even if Stanley went off the road for a bit, it was still resistant to crashing. And once Stanley was back on the road, its road-seeing module could quickly readjust to the correct road color.

PATH PLANNING

Stanley's modules for detecting the road and its obstacles were located in the middle of the architecture shown in figure 3.1, in the perception layer. The software that selected Stanley's speed was over on the far right of its architecture, in the planning layer. The rightmost layer didn't need to look at raw sensor data; it just used information from the perception layer to make its decision. Another algorithm in Stanley's planning layer was its software to plan paths around obstacles. But before Stanley could meaningfully avoid obstacles, it needed to have an overall route to follow.

Just as the Red Team had done for their Humvee, Stanley preplanned its overall route at the beginning of the race. Stanley's route didn't incorporate external information about terrain like the Red Team's did; as we'll see, the Stanford Racing Team's perception algorithms were good enough that Stanley could just detect and avoid obstacles on the fly. Instead, the primary goal of Stanley's route-planning algorithm was simply to provide a route that was close to the GPS coordinates they were given by the race organizers, and which smoothed out the zigs and zags that would have been in the route if they had simply drawn straight lines between the GPS coordinates. This algorithm took Stanley only 20 seconds to run at the very beginning of the race.[34]

Once Stanley had this smooth route planned out, all it needed to do was follow that route, avoiding obstacles it detected along the way with its perception algorithms. As we saw earlier, Stanley kept track of obstacles by finding which terrain around it was drivable; the obstacles were the square cells tagged as not drivable. To navigate around these obstacles, Stanley continuously recalculated the best path from its current position—wherever it was at a given moment—to a goal just a little further, say 10 seconds, along its preplanned route—wherever that might be. When Stanley planned this path, it just needed to find a way to get from its current position to its goal position without hitting any objects. As long as Stanley could continue to plan and execute these paths, the car would succeed in moving further along the route without hitting any objects.

Remember that the Humvee's path-search algorithm from the last chapter used a cost function that incorporated how long it would take the Humvee to drive over each small square in the map. Stanley needed a similar cost function to avoid its own obstacles. One idea might be to incorporate some penalty for each cell in the grid based on that cell's distance to the nearest obstacle; Stanley could use such a cost function to find a path that would keep it as far away from obstacles along its path as possible. In fact, this is exactly what the Stanford Racing Team originally tried. This algorithm kept Stanley away from obstacles, but it also made Stanley

swerve around erratically to avoid them. The team dubbed this algorithm the "drunken squirrel."[35]

To fix this, they programmed Stanley to follow a virtual corridor that
was parallel to the smooth route Stanley had calculated before the race.
Their goal was for Stanley to drive as fast as it could along this corridor,
only swerving left or right within the corridor to avoid obstacles. It was
as if Stanley were playing a classic arcade driving game in which the only
controls were to speed up or to brake, and to slide left or right along that
fixed route. Absent obstacles, Stanley was also programmed to drift toward
the middle of the road it detected with its road-edge detector. To figure out
whether to move left or right, and how quickly it needed to move—that
is, whether it needed a small nudge or a quick swerve—Stanley still used
a search algorithm, but it only considered smooth paths between where it
was and where it could be in a few moments. Its cost function penalized
several things, including driving far from the preplanned path, driving over
obstacles, and Stanley's distance from the center of the road. The path-planning algorithm then considered many of these paths and selected the best
one it found. The algorithm ran continuously as the car zipped along its
route, repeating itself about 10 times per second—fast enough that Stanley could notice and avoid objects about 15 to 25 meters ahead of it.[36]

HOW PARTS OF STANLEY'S BRAIN TALKED TO EACH OTHER

When they were designing Stanley, the Stanford Racing Team needed to
figure out how all of these algorithms should communicate with each
other. They knew how to connect them, but that wasn't enough: they also
needed to figure out the protocol these algorithms would follow when
talking to each other. Should there be a centralized "master process" direct-
ing everything? Should it be organized as some sort of hierarchy? The
team chose to do the exact opposite: they combined these different software modules together by simply letting them run independently, in parallel. There would be no "master" process telling everything what to do.[37]

You can think of these modules as workers in a grocery store who each
have a separate job. The "stockers" at the grocery store unload goods from
the delivery trucks parked in the back and put these goods onto the correct shelves in the store. The "cashiers" check out customers, and the "managers" periodically move cash from the registers to the bank and order

more groceries for the store. Each worker does his or her job continuously and mostly independently of the others.

Because the shelves are continuously stocked and the cashiers are always at their registers ringing people up, customers can expect to be in and out of the store very quickly. We would say that the service at the store has low latency. The service is fast because the cashiers have exactly one job to do—ringing up the customers—not making deposits at the bank or stocking the shelves.

Stanley could react quickly to events for the same reason: each of its modules—particularly those that needed to react to the environment—could do so quickly because each module had only one job to do. Stanley's modules could react quickly to the environment because they never held full conversations with one another. Doing so would have run the risk of getting locked in a conversation, a problem known as *deadlock*. If two components become deadlocked, the whole system could screech to a halt, unable to recover until one or more of the components were restarted.

This doesn't mean that the modules didn't communicate. They communicated all the time, by posting one-way, time-stamped messages to each other. This is akin to having a public announcement system at the grocery store, where managers, for example, can warn cashiers that the store is running low on $1 bills, and suggest using them only when necessary. Cashiers can serve customers more reliably if the cashiers are never stuck in long conversations with their managers.

In the self-driving car, the GPS and accelerometers estimated the car's position and orientation, "published" them with the current timestamp, and continued to take and publish updated position information for the rest of the race: that was their only job. The pixel-clustering, road-finding module fetched camera and laser scanner data, found roads, and then published this information so the speed controller and path planner could use them at their convenience. Meanwhile, the path-finding module estimated the best path for the robot given its current position and obstacles, repeating itself ten times per second—and so on, for a total of about 30 modules.

These modules won the Stanford Racing Team $2 million and a place in robot history. The team deserved their win, but Stanley was still very primitive by modern self-driving car standards. None of the five cars that completed the second Grand Challenge could drive on city streets, for example. They couldn't operate in oncoming traffic, and they couldn't reason about parking spots, changing lanes, or traffic stops.

This wasn't a design shortcoming: these cars were intended to drive only the race they entered, which didn't require them to do any of those things. But DARPA's next competition, the DARPA Urban Challenge—which would require robot cars to obey California traffic laws while navigating city streets with oncoming traffic—would change all of this. It would also give Chris and his team at CMU—the team that built the Humvee—one more shot at winning first place, provided that they could build a car to do all of these things.

At this point the question naturally arises: Why do so many independently designed architectures turn out to have such a similar structure? Are three components necessary and/or sufficient, or is three just an aesthetically pleasing number or a coincidence?

—Erann Gatt[1]

THE URBAN CHALLENGE

Chris Urmson's team spent the next two years preparing for the Urban Challenge. By this time Chris had become a professor at CMU. He was also the person in full charge of its racing team, now dubbed "Tartan Racing." Not only had Chris's team seen considerable turnover; it had also retired their Humvee, choosing instead a 2007 Chevrolet Tahoe they named "Boss." Boss would incorporate the best of their previous design and much of what they had learned from the Stanford Racing Team the previous year.[2]

This challenge would be much more difficult than the previous ones. In the previous Grand Challenges, all the robot cars had driven solo, released one by one and monitored so they couldn't interfere with one another. But the Urban Challenge was different. These self-driving cars would drive around an old military base with each other and with human drivers—a total of about 50 cars on the road at the same time—on city streets, at intersections, and in parking lots. And there would be no off-road driving allowed here: these cars could lose points or even be disqualified for disobeying California traffic laws.[3]

DARPA held several qualifying rounds before the November 2007 race. One called the Gauntlet required cars to carefully stay within their lanes while avoiding parked cars and other obstacles. Another qualifying round

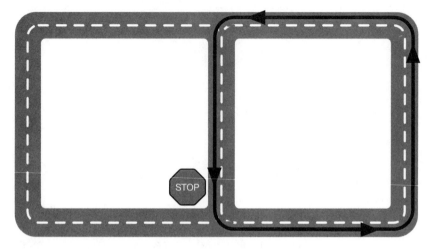

Figure 4.1
Area A in the DARPA Urban Challenge. Professional human drivers circled in the outer loop as self-driving cars circulated on the right half. The primary challenge here for autonomous cars was to merge into a lane of moving traffic at the stop sign. Self-driving cars were allowed to circulate as many times as they could within their time limit.

tested the cars' higher-level thinking: they needed to stop at four-way intersections, wait, and proceed when it was their turn, and they needed to be capable of deciding when a route was blocked—and of finding an alternate route when it was.

Another qualification round, known as "Area A," tested the cars' ability to detect and avoid moving objects. This round required self-driving cars to drive in a loop, making left-hand turns in front of oncoming traffic, as shown in figure 4.1. Self-driving cars needed to follow the black arrows on the right half of the loop while professional human drivers drove around on the outside of the loop.

PERCEPTUAL ABSTRACTION

To understand how Boss maneuvered through these environments, let's take a closer look at how Chris's team developed the car's brain. Like Stanley (the Stanford Racing Team's car in the second Grand Challenge), they designated a layer in Boss's brain to synthesize the data coming in from its eighteen sensors. They called this middle layer (shown in figure 4.2) the

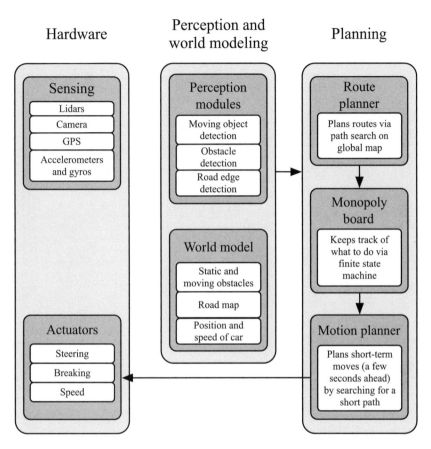

Figure 4.2
Boss's architecture, simplified: the hardware, the perception (and world-modeling), and the reasoning (planning) modules, organized in increasing levels of reasoning abstraction from left to right. Its highest-level reasoning layer (planning, far right) was organized into its own three-layer architecture: the controller (route planner module), the sequencer (Monopoly board module), and the deliberator (motion planner module). The motion planner could have arguably been placed with the sequencer.

perception and world-modeling layer. Like Stanley's perception layer, Boss's perception layer didn't do any complex reasoning because its sole purpose was to interpret the data coming from its sensors—its laser scanners, radar, camera, GPS, and accelerometers—and to generate higher-level models of the world from that data. The data abstractions generated by this layer would then be used by modules that reasoned at a higher level to perform more complex tasks.[4]

The perception and world-modeling layer performed some of the tasks we saw in earlier races: estimating where the edges of the road were, finding obstacles, and keeping track of where the car was, given its GPS data and its accelerometers. But for driving in urban environments, the perception layer needed to do more. Boss's environment could change, as other cars came and went. So this layer represented static objects like trees and buildings with a grid on a map, filling in those grid cells or clearing them as sensors detected the presence or absence of objects. It also kept track of a road map provided by DARPA and a description of the missions to be completed, adjusting the map when it detected that paths on the map were blocked or unblocked.[5]

Boss's perception and world-modeling layer also needed to detect and model the physics of *moving* objects. The module to detect moving objects had a rule that every observation made by its sensors should be associated with either a fixed or moving object in its object database. Boss calculated a quality measurement for that association; if the match between that measurement and an object was good, then that measurement would be incorporated into Boss's model for that object, so that, in Boss's mind, the object would move a little bit. But if Boss couldn't find a high-quality match between the measurement and an existing object, then the module *proposed the existence of a new object* to explain that observation. Occasionally the proposal took a static object and converted it into a moving object. This might happen, for example, if Boss encountered a car that was parked but then began pulling out from its parking spot.

Once Boss detected a moving object, it could track the object with a traditional tracking algorithm. Boss used—yet again—a Kalman filter to track its moving objects.[6] Boss also assumed that objects moved either like bikes—where they could move forward or backward and had an orientation—or like drifting points—where they could move in any direction but lacked an orientation; Boss based this decision on whichever model fit the data best. The assumptions for these models were then integrated directly into the Kalman filter: Kalman filters are very general, and they can be used to track not just objects' positions, but also their velocities and accelerations.

Boss then imagined these objects as rectangles and other polygons moving around in its virtual world.[7] Of course, Boss didn't "see" them as part of a scene but rather as coordinates on a grid. As far as Boss was concerned, each rectangle should be given enough clearance, whether Boss was following the rectangle in a traffic lane or bearing toward it from the opposite lane.

THE RACE

After many months of testing and anticipation, the day of the Urban Challenge arrived. During the race, Boss and other cars would need to complete several "missions," driving from one checkpoint on the base to another, all the while navigating through moving traffic along urban streets and amid other autonomous cars and human drivers. DARPA had provided a map of the compound to the competitors a couple of days before the race, and they provided mission descriptions to the teams just five minutes before the race. These missions required the cars to drive through the streets of the compound, park in parking lots, and navigate busy intersections fully autonomously.

DARPA officials wrote after the race that they had pared the applicant pool from eighty-nine to eleven for the final race by carefully reviewing the entrants' applications and putting them through the qualifying rounds, which meant that the cars on the road during the final event had been carefully vetted.[8] But this didn't mean the human drivers were completely safe: the humans on the route—all of whom were professional drivers—drove with safety cages, race seats, and fire systems, and each autonomous car had a chase vehicle whose human drivers had a remote e-kill switch. The robot cars, while vetted, still had the very real potential to kill them.[9]

Fortunately, there were no major accidents on the day of the race. One car malfunctioned in a parking lot and tried to drive into an old building before DARPA officials hit its e-kill switch. There was also a low-speed collision between another couple of self-driving cars. By the middle of the morning, almost half of the contestants had been removed from the course.[10]

Yet several cars managed to finish the race successfully, including Boss. Within three years, self-driving cars had gone from being unable to drive more than eight miles in the desert to successfully maneuvering busy intersections while spending hours on the road. In addition to *seeing* with its perception and world-modeling layer, Boss and the other cars needed a way to *reason* about their environment. None of the cars we saw in the past two chapters could have come close to doing these things: So how did Boss do them?

BOSS'S HIGHER-LEVEL REASONING LAYER

Were improvements in hardware a factor? Hardware had been improving, of course, but in the three years since the first DARPA Grand Challenge there hadn't been a notable revolution in the hardware of self-driving cars beyond what Moore's law had predicted (Moore's law predicted at the time that popular processors roughly doubled in performance doubled every 18 to 24 months). The real answer to this question—and the cause of hallucinations Boss would have during the race—lay in advances to these cars' software architectures.

At the core of Boss's brain were three components with decreasing levels of "reasoning abstraction." You can see this in the rightmost panel of the architecture in figure 4.2. At the top of this panel is the *route planner* module, which searched for a low-cost path from Boss's current position to the next checkpoint on its mission. This was a lot like the module in Stanley that planned that vehicle's smooth path at the beginning of the second Grand Challenge. Instead of planning a single path at the beginning of the race, Boss's route planner planned its path continuously, re-estimating the best path from its current position to its destination again and again. To estimate the path, the route planner used a combination of time and risk in its cost function, trusting that the perception layer always presented it with an up-to-date map. So all it needed to do was plan its path and tell the component *below* it—located in the middle of the rightmost panel of figure 4.2—what it needed to do next.[11]

We'll call this next lower layer of abstraction the Monopoly board layer, for reasons that will become clear very soon.[12] This layer was arguably the most complex because it needed to keep track of what Boss was doing and what it needed to do next. It was implemented with something called a *finite state machine.*[13]

A finite state machine provides a way for a computer program to reason about the world by limiting the things it needs to worry about. It works a lot like the game Monopoly: you have a piece that can move around on a board, and at any given time, your piece can be in exactly one "state" (that is, position) on the board. This position determines what you're allowed to do now and where you're allowed to move next. If you land on Park Place when you're playing Monopoly and nobody owns it, you're allowed to buy it. If you wind up in jail, your options for getting out are to roll the dice and hope to get doubles, pay $50, or produce a get-out-of-jail-free card. The rules of the game—and the position of your playing piece on the board—simplify the world for you as a Monopoly player so you aren't overwhelmed with possibilities. By implication, anything you're not expressly allowed to do when you're on a square, you're not allowed to do at all. If you land on Park Place, you can't buy Boardwalk or collect $200; you can't do anything except buy Park Place (as long as no one else owns it and provided you want it).

Your current state (again, your position) on the Monopoly board also determines which set of moves you can make next: sometimes you can move forward up to 12 squares, depending on a dice roll, and buy a property, and sometimes you might go directly to jail. But you can't jump to an arbitrary position on the board.

When Tartan Racing designed Boss, they created a variety of finite state machines for the Monopoly board module: one for each type of environment Boss might find itself in. As Boss drove along, its Monopoly board module moved a virtual Monopoly piece around its finite state machine in order to keep track of what the car was doing and what it needed to do to achieve its next goal.

Depending on Boss's current situation, its Monopoly board used one of three finite state machines: one to drive down the road, keeping track of whether it needed to change lanes, for example; one to handle intersections; and one to maneuver itself into a specific position, such as a parking spot or the other side of a crowded intersection. Each of these finite state machines outlined a set of simple rules the module should follow to achieve its goal. Wherever it was, Boss's Monopoly board module kept track of the world and its goals with its virtual piece on the board.

I show a simplification of Boss's *handle intersection* finite state machine in figure 4.3.[14] You can follow Boss's line of reasoning about crossing

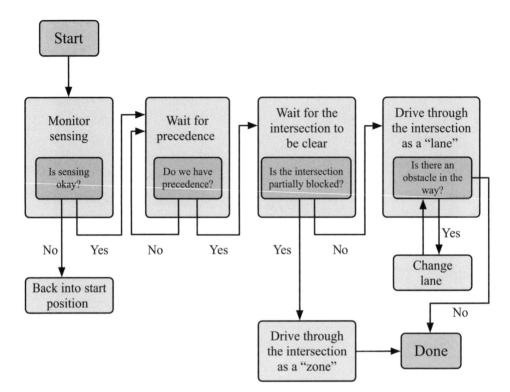

Figure 4.3
The *handle intersection* finite state machine. The Monopoly board module steps
through the diagram, from "start" to "done." The state machine waits for precedence
and then attempts to enter the intersection. If the intersection is partially blocked,
it is handled as a "zone," which is a complex area like a parking lot, instead of being
handled as a "lane"; otherwise the state machine creates a "virtual lane" through the
intersection and drives in that lane. This is a simplified version of the state machine
described in Urmson et al. (see note 7).

an intersection in this state machine. When it was Boss's turn to enter
the intersection, Boss waited until the intersection was clear *and* would
remain clear long enough for Boss to pass through it. It did this by using
another, smaller finite state machine called a *precedence estimator*, which
determined whether Boss had precedence to enter the intersection based
on common driving etiquette. How did Boss know these rules about
driving etiquette? A programmer simply encoded them into a set of states
and transitions for the finite state machine, the same way Monopoly's creator, Elizabeth Magie, originally created the rules to its precursor, the

Landlord's Game. This wasn't just the case for the precedence estimator; humans encoded the rules for *all* of the state machines.

The Monopoly board performed much of the "human" reasoning you might associate with driving, but Boss didn't need to be smart to use its Monopoly board module. A human playing Monopoly may make careful, deliberate calculations about which actions to take. But the Monopoly board module didn't actually *play* monopoly, and it didn't have any concept of success or winning, so it didn't make any careful, strategic decisions about what it should do or where it should go next. It was more like the rulebook for Monopoly. At each state, the Monopoly board module simply followed a set of dead-simple rules, and then it moved to the next state based on the results of another simple test. Boss did perform careful, deliberative planning, but that happened in its route planner—the module we saw a few pages ago, which searched for paths.

The functional responsibility of the Monopoly board module, then, was to take its assignment from the route planner, keep track of how far along it was in completing that assignment, and to delegate actions in the meantime to the next lower level—the motion planner—until its assignment was complete.

The responsibility of the motion planner, the module represented in the bottom-right of figure 4.2, was to find and execute a trajectory for the car that would bring it safely from its current position toward a goal state assigned by the Monopoly board. For example, the Monopoly board might order the motion planner to perform one of these actions:

- Plan and execute a way to park in that empty spot over there (giving the motion planner a position).

- Continue driving straight in this lane.

- Switch to the left lane.

- Drive through this intersection.

Once the Monopoly board gave the motion planner an order, the motion planner would find a path from its current position to its goal position. The motion planner was a bit like the route planner in this respect, except that the motion planner's goal was to plan out actions on a much shorter timescale. While the route planner planned movement at the scale of minutes and miles, the motion planner planned movement at the scale of seconds and feet: at its largest, it might have planned in areas up to about a third of a mile, or a half kilometer.[15]

The Monopoly board assumed that the motion planner would try to achieve its goal safely, although the motion planner was allowed to tell the Monopoly board that it had failed—for example, because the parking spot turned out to be occupied by a motorcycle that it hadn't seen until it tried to park—in which case the Monopoly board would find a contingency plan.[16]

Another difference between the route planner and the motion planner was that the route planner only needed to account for the car's position on a map when searching for a path, while the motion planner needed to search for a path while keeping track of the car's position, velocity, and orientation, all while making sure that Boss didn't violate any laws of physics. Cars can only move in the direction their wheels are pointing: they don't slide sideways unless something's going wrong, and the motion planner needed to account for this (roboticists would call this the car's *kinematic* constraints). The motion planner also made sure the car didn't accelerate, turn, or stop too quickly: it shouldn't brake or accelerate aggressively, and it shouldn't turn so quickly that it flips over. The Red Team's Humvee *had* flipped during testing, a mistake that devastated its sensors just weeks before the first Grand Challenge, as "a quarter million dollars' worth of electronics was crushed in an instant."[17] The Humvee's sensors were never the same again, and this likely had at least some impact on its performance during that race.

The path-finding algorithm for Boss's motion planner was a bit more complicated than its algorithm for route planning because it needed to keep track of Boss's position, velocity, and orientation (we can call these three things together its "state"). The motion planner couldn't search for a path in a simple grid because a grid alone can't keep track of all of these things. In parking lots, the motion planner searched for a best path from its current state to its goal state by searching for ways to combine very small path segments to make one large path, where each path segment ensured that Boss's velocity and position followed the laws of physics. For example, if the beginning of one path segment indicates that Boss would be at its current position, facing forward, and moving at five feet per second with no acceleration, then the end of that path segment needs to be consistent with the beginning: it must assert that Boss is five feet ahead of its current position, facing forward, moving at five feet per second.[18] I show an example of this process in the four diagrams of figure 4.4. This planning could take time, so Boss used a second motion planner to plan its subsequent path simultaneously so it didn't need to pause between motions.

For driving down the road, Boss's motion planner also used a search algorithm that was more like Stanley's steering algorithm. First, it generated a set of possible trajectories for the car. These began at the car's current position and speed and ended farther down the road but varied in lateral offset and curvature. Then the motion planner scored these paths based on factors like their smoothness, how close they were to the center

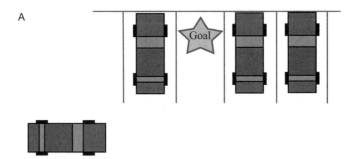

Figure 4.4a
The motion planner of a self-driving car has been instructed by the Monopoly board to park in the designated parking spot.

Figure 4.4b
The car has an internal map represented as a grid in which obstacles fill up cells in that grid. The motion planner also uses a cost function when picking its path (shaded gray). The cost function incorporates the distance to obstacles (in this case, other cars).

(continued)

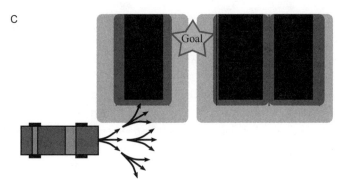

Figure 4.4c
The motion planner searches for a path to its goal. The path will comprise many small path segments that encode velocity, position, and orientation. Unlike this picture, the search is performed from the end state to the start state.

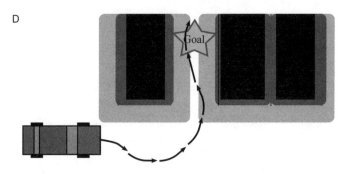

Figure 4.4d
A candidate path to the goal.

of the road, and how close they were to obstacles.[19] Boss then ran this motion planner constantly, continuously searching for the best path *from its current state*. This meant that it would continuously adjust its path, gracefully correcting its little errors as they occurred.

GETTING PAST TRAFFIC JAMS

The three layers of high-level reasoning in the rightmost panel of figure 4.2—Boss's route planner, its Monopoly board, and its motion planner—enabled Boss to travel through the old military base on the day of the race. However, none of the systems I've described so far would have saved Boss when it started to hallucinate during the race.

Boss had demonstrated in the qualifying rounds that it was among the best prepared of the contestants. But during the Urban Challenge, as it was racing down the road to complete one of its missions, it found the lane in front of it blocked by another car. Boss slowed, came to a stop, and waited. It made a couple of attempts to move forward, but there was no way through: the road was completely blocked by traffic.[20] So Boss waited, the seconds ticking by on the race timer.

The problem was, this traffic jam didn't exist. There was nothing in front of Boss at all; what it thought was a blocked lane was just a hallucination. And this wasn't the first time Boss had imagined things on the day of the race.[21]

Boss's hallucination was caused by a problem in one of its perception algorithms. When it saw a car in front of it, and that car moved away, it didn't always clear its estimate of the car's location, so it would occasionally think there was still something there. It's possible that improved perception algorithms would have prevented this specific hallucination, but Chris and his team were experienced enough in building complex software to know that all software has bugs. Fortunately they had the foresight to make Boss robust to problems like this.

This problem Boss faced was similar to the problem the Humvee faced in the first Grand Challenge, when it got stuck behind a rock. Chris's team fixed this in the second race by programming the Humvee to simply back up 10 meters if it was stuck, clear its estimate of obstacles, and try again. But that was a short-term hack: it was a brittle solution—a Band-Aid—and by no means robust, and it might not work at a crowded intersection. Chris's team needed a system that could handle bugs or unexpected situations, and they needed a system that would never give up. Tartan Racing formalized this idea in Boss by adding a more general "error recovery" system to the Monopoly board layer; it had three key principles, reminiscent of Isaac Asimov's three robot laws:[22]

- Until the error is resolved, the car should be willing to take greater and greater risks, and its attempts to recover should not repeat.
- The recovery behavior should be appropriate to the driving context. For example, Boss should have different recovery behavior in traffic lanes than in parking lots.

- The error recovery should be kept as simple as possible to reduce the likelihood of introducing more software bugs or undesirable behaviors.

As a last-ditch effort, if Boss didn't move more than a meter within five minutes, its error-recovery system simply selected a random nearby goal position in an algorithm called *wiggle*. The idea was that Boss should be able to dislodge itself from whatever predicament it had found itself in, and then it could clear its memory and try again.[23]

When Boss faced the (imagined) blocked lane during the Urban Challenge, five levels of error recovery kicked in. First, it tried to get to a spot a *little past* the traffic jam; second, it tried to get to a spot *farther* past the jam; third, it tried to get to a spot *even farther* past the traffic jam; fourth, it *backed up* and tried to get to a spot past the jam again. Finally, it assumed the road in front of it was completely blocked *and made a U-turn*. When it assumed the road was completely blocked, it actually marked the road as impassable in the route map in its perception and world-modeling layer, causing the route planner to find an alternative path.[24]

Boss hallucinated twice during the race, and the result was that the car drove an extra two miles that day, a minor inconvenience for a race that took about four hours. Despite these inconveniences, Boss went on to finish the race 19 minutes ahead of Stanford's car.[25] A redundant error-handling system—in which higher-level planning could resolve problems with lower-level planning or perception—was one of the most important parts of Boss's architecture, handing Chris and his team the prize he had focused on for so long.

THREE-LAYER ARCHITECTURES

What enabled Boss—and Stanley from chapter 3—to work so spectacularly? As we saw, it had a lot to do with their reasoning architectures. One key design principle in both Boss and Stanley was their organization into hardware, perception, and planning (reasoning) layers, the three layers from left to right in figure 4.2. As we've seen, the perception layer enabled the reasoning components on the right side of the figure to focus on higher-level tasks. They weren't burdened with the challenge of dealing with low-level sensor data, because that was the responsibility of the perception modules. The perception modules, in turn, were largely implemented with machine learning models that turned raw sensor data into actionable information, but they didn't focus on any high-level planning or decision-making. As we saw in the last chapter, each perception module had one job to do, which meant that each module could do its job quickly.

But Boss demonstrated some other, more important qualities of a self-driving car: the ability to carry out complex behaviors such as driving miles in an urban environment, parking in parking spots, and interacting with other moving cars, while still gracefully reacting to unanticipated situations.

While one of the self-driving cars from Alphabet, Google's parent company, was driving around Mountain View, California, it came upon a rather singular situation. Chris Urmson explained the scene during his TED2015 talk, gesturing to a video of the scene as he spoke:

> This is a woman in an electric wheelchair chasing a duck in circles on the road. Now it turns out, there is nowhere in the DMV [driving] handbook that tells you how to deal with that. But our vehicles were able to encounter that, slow down, and drive safely.[26]

If all unexpected contingencies occurred as infrequently as you encounter a woman in an electric wheelchair chasing a duck in the middle of the street, it might not be a problem for self-driving cars. But the curse of these rare contingencies is that, taken together, they happen frequently, and they're always a bit different. They could be caused by missing signs in construction zones, chain-installation blockades on snowy mountain roads, or even police guiding traffic through intersections. Each situation will have its own particular quirks, and a self-driving car must be able to handle all of them. What was it about Boss that enabled it to handle these situations?

We can answer this question by looking at the second important decision Chris's team made in designing Boss: the organization of its higher-level-reasoning components into three layers of increasing abstraction, represented by the three boxes shown in the rightmost panel of figure 4.2. This way of organizing an agent is sometimes called a *three-layer architecture* in the field of robotics, and it enabled self-driving cars like Stanley and Boss to react quickly in real-time environments. To emphasize, when I refer to a three-layer architecture, I'm talking specifically about the three boxes on the right of figure 4.2, *not* the left-to-right organization of Boss's brain.

The top layer in a three-layer architecture performs *deliberative* behaviors, which typically involves slow, careful planning. In the case of Boss, this slow, deliberative step was precisely its route planner, which searched for paths through the city environment. This is where Boss planned its highest-level goals—possibly its most "intelligent" behavior. Formulating these goals was possible because this planning layer didn't need to worry about perception (the perception layer handled that) *and* because it didn't need to worry about unanticipated contingencies (the Monopoly board handled that). The route planner just needed to plan missions and paths.

The bottom layer of a three-layer architecture is called the *controller*. In the case of Boss, the controller layer was its motion planner and its steering and speed controllers.[27] This layer performed relatively low-level actions, such as "park in that spot over there." The motion planner was tied to the actuators, which directly controlled the steering wheel, brake, and gas pedals. This layer also included the three-rule controllers we saw in the first chapter. Traditionally the controller layer doesn't do anything very smart: its purpose is to perform simple actions and react to simple sensor readings. A typical reaction to the environment might be to increase motor torque or apply brakes to bring the car's speed to the target speed.

In between the deliberator and the control layer is the *sequencer*. The goal of the sequencer is to carry out assignments from the top-level, deliberative layer by giving the controller below it a sequence of commands. Boss's sequencer was its Monopoly board. The sequencer can't just give the controller a fixed sequence of commands, because the state of the world may change before the full sequence is carried out. To see how things could go wrong in a robot that couldn't respond to a changing world, imagine that I've designed a robot butler to serve you a glass of wine. This robot might carry a bottle of wine out of the kitchen, roll over to you, and reach out its robot hand with the bottle to pour you some wine. You might helpfully lift your glass from the table toward the robot to make it easier for the robot. But the robot butler had been planning to pour the wine directly into the glass on the table, and thus would have ignored your gesture, pouring a glass worth of wine directly onto the table.

This wouldn't be acceptable for a robot butler, let alone a self-driving car. A real-time AI system needs to react to changes in the environment. For Boss, a finite state machine was its way of keeping track of which actions the controller had successfully completed and which it should try next. If the world changes before the controller is able to carry out its job, then the sequencer can come up with a contingency plan and send updated instructions to the controller.

Erann Gat was a researcher at Cal Tech's Jet Propulsion Lab when he and several other research teams simultaneously discovered this three-layer architecture—the deliberator, sequencer, and controller—while they were designing robots. He summarized the role of the sequencer based on their shared research:

> The fundamental design principle underlying the sequencer is the notion of cognizant failure. A cognizant failure is a failure which the system can detect somehow. Rather than design algorithms which never fail, we instead use algorithms which (almost) never fail to detect a failure.[28]

Why bother designing algorithms that could sometimes fail instead of designing ones that never fail? Gat continues:

> First, it is much easier to design navigation algorithms which fail cognizantly than ones which never fail. Second, if a failure is detected then corrective action can be taken to recover from that failure. Thus, algorithms with high failure rates can be combined into an algorithm whose overall failure rate is quite low provided that the failures are cognizant failures.[29]

The three-layer architecture may seem obvious now that you're reading about it, but it wasn't so obvious at first. To understand why, it's worth looking at some versions that preceded three-layer architectures. As Erann Gat recalled, one such architecture was *sense-plan-act*, which was widely used in robots until 1985.[30] This architecture lives up to its name: the robot senses the world around it, plans its next step, and executes that step. Information flows in a single direction, from sensors to the planner to the controller. The shortcoming of this architecture, of course, is that it is not *reactive*. If your robot butler used the sense-plan-act architecture, I would advise you to ask it to serve clear fluids only.

What followed sense-plan-act, Erann Gat observed, was a profusion of *subsumption* architectures. These look like sense-plan-act, with the flow of information from the environment to the planner to the controller; but they differ because their modules can react to the environment by "overriding" actions from lower layers. Robots designed with the subsumption architecture could zip around the research lab more impressively than their sense-plan-act predecessors, but roboticists found that their architectures grew complex very quickly. The connections between layers became confusing, and the modules interacted in unpredictable ways. A small change to the low-level layers might require a redesign of the whole system. Design of these systems became a mess. The three-layer architecture, on the other hand, enables robots to react quickly while still providing a clean separation between the different parts of the architecture so we can still reason about it.[31]

The motion planner in Boss, rather complicated for a controller, is almost a three-layer architecture by itself, without a sequencer. This complexity suggests another possibility: What if we nest three-layer architectures, with one serving as another one's controller? We might even imagine that cities will one day use AI to improve traffic congestion. At the top level of planning, some module might search for optimal traffic flows to decrease congestion during rush hour, telling individual self-driving cars in the controller which routes they *can't* take. The cities' sequencers might react to accidents and other contingencies.

Self-driving cars, treated by the city as controllers, might themselves be implemented with three-layer architectures; and given the constraints imposed by the city's sequencer, along with their own goals, would then plan their missions accordingly.

CLASSIFYING THE OBJECTS SEEN BY SELF-DRIVING CARS

Machine learning's role in self-driving cars has received a lot of attention, to the extent that many people confound the algorithms that perform perception with those that perform high-level planning. This is probably in part because Alphabet's self-driving cars were on the road and picking up media attention around the time other major breakthroughs in machine learning (many also by Alphabet companies like Google) were being reported in the news. Although clever machine learning algorithms can exist in the top-level planning layer of self-driving cars, much of the high-level reasoning layer comes from ideas that have been around in AI for decades—ideas like search algorithms and finite state machines—that wouldn't traditionally be considered machine learning (remember, machine learning deals primarily with teaching machines using data, while AI doesn't necessarily need data).

Instead, much of the machine learning used in self-driving cars lies comfortably within their perception and world-modeling layer.

One of the important perception tasks of a self-driving car is classifying objects seen by its sensors into categories. Boss didn't attempt to classify objects into fine categories; its urban environment was artificial, so the *only* moving objects in its environment were cars. In the wild, self-driving cars encounter many different types of objects, so they must classify these objects into different categories to react appropriately. By understanding whether an object is a car, a bicycle, a pedestrian, or a woman in an electric wheelchair chasing a duck, the car can better model it and predict its path.

How could a self-driving car categorize the objects it sees with its sensors? A certain class of machine vision algorithms showed significant advances in the years surrounding 2012. This class of algorithms, from a field known as *deep learning*, enable computers to classify the content of photographs as accurately as many humans. These algorithms advanced rapidly in the ensuing few years, to the extent that custom hardware was developed by companies like NVidia for express use in self-driving cars' vision systems. Later in this book we'll take a closer look at how these algorithms work.

SELF-DRIVING CARS ARE COMPLICATED SYSTEMS

There are a lot of important aspects to building self-driving cars that we haven't covered yet. Let's take a brief look at a few of these now.

Among other things, a huge amount of software must be written for a self-driving car. Writing this software requires a huge amount of human investment. The winning teams were large, on the scale of roughly 40 to 60 people, including researchers, engineers, and undergraduate students. Such large-scale efforts require careful management between people and parties to ensure that contributors are happy and productive. But even happy, productive workers can write bugs.

As we saw, one way to handle bugs was via graceful error-recovery systems. The successful teams in the Grand Challenges also put a lot of effort into testing and simulation. One *Wired* magazine reporter saw Chris Urmson bring up a visualization that resembled a "mountainous *Tron* landscape." It was detailed enough to run simulations of how a self-driving car could handle the road, right down to its tires and shocks.[32] These teams, especially in later years, developed simulation environments that would allow them to replay past drives so they could improve their learning algorithms and exception handling.[33] This topic alone is enough to fill an entire book, but we have other topics to digest.

After nearly a decade of winter for self-driving cars in the 1990s, DARPA's Grand Challenges had helped to reignite the field. Despite the advances made during those races, it would be years before these cars could drive without humans on public roads due to both technical and legal challenges.[34] A decade after the Urban Challenge, the ability to handle unexpected situations remained among the biggest problems these cars continue to face. Uber was still struggling with this problem as of 2017. Their experimental self-driving cars, which have humans behind the wheel at all times, could only drive about 0.8 miles on average before a disengagement—that is, before a human needed to intervene.[35] Waymo, Alphabet's self-driving car company, which has logged a great deal more miles on the road than Uber, logged just 0.2 disengagements per 1,000 miles at the time.[36] And beyond this, the teams behind these cars must build and maintain highly detailed maps.[37]

Many of the rivals in the DARPA Grand Challenges ended up working together to build self-driving cars in the years following the races. Sebastian Thrun, leading Alphabet's self-driving car project, eventually hired Chris Urmson and Andrew Levandowski, a creator of the self-balancing motorcycle, along with other leaders in the field. Chris himself eventually became Alphabet's self-driving car project lead in 2013.[38] The project—possible because of a field kick-started by a well-organized DARPA competition in 2004—would log over 1.2 million miles on the road by the time he left in 2016.[39]

5 NETFLIX AND THE RECOMMENDATION-ENGINE CHALLENGE

The Netflix prize contest will be looked at for years by people studying how to do predictive modeling.

—Chris Volinsky, senior scientist at AT&T Labs and member of Team BellKor[1]

A MILLION-DOLLAR GRAND PRIZE

As robotics departments were busy in 2006 preparing their cars for the DARPA Urban Challenge the following year, Netflix made an announcement to the budding data science community about their own Grand Prize: they were looking for teams that could create movie recommendation engines, and they were willing to pay $1 million to the best team.

When Netflix made their announcement, their streaming video business didn't yet exist; the company operated as a physical DVD rental service.[2] Customers could request DVDs from Netflix, and Netflix would send these DVDs to them by mail. But customers needed to give up one of their current DVDs to receive the next one, and the new DVD might take days to reach them. A bad selection could ruin days of quality movie-watching time, so customers tended to be careful about how they made their requests. This is where Netflix's desire to recommend movies came in.

As part of their service, Netflix allowed their customers to rate individual movies on an integer scale of 1 star (worst) to 5 stars (best). Netflix hoped to use these ratings to help customers decide which movies they should rent. After announcing the competition, Netflix released a dataset consisting of 100 million of these star-ratings, collected from 1998 to 2005, to the research community.[3] The first team to create a recommendation algorithm that improved on Netflix's own algorithm by 10 percent would win the grand prize.[4]

This dataset was a godsend to full-time and casual data scientists, and they approached the problem with gusto.[5] Within the first week some teams beat Netflix's own recommendation engine by 1 percent.[6] Within the first year, 20,000 teams had registered, some 2,000 of which submitted entries to the competition.[7]

THE CONTENDERS

The contenders for the prize were a ragtag group, but one three-person team maintained a strong position on the leaderboard. This team was BellKor, made up of three research scientists from AT&T Labs (one of them moved to Yahoo! in the course of the competition), whose expertise in the field of networks and recommendation systems equipped them with excellent skills for the project.[8] Another team, ML@UToronto, consisted of a group of well-known neural network researchers from the University of Toronto.[9] The members included Geoffrey Hinton, widely seen as one of the fathers of neural networks.

Not everyone in the competition had a PhD. One of the underdog teams with only three undergraduate members—two computer-science students and one of their roommates, a math student—came from Princeton University. The two computer science students were soon headed to top PhD programs to study machine learning, although one of them would stick around to work in Princeton's psychology department for a year. The math student was on his way to trade interest rate derivatives at JP Morgan. The young, overachieving trio named their team after the first movie listed in their dataset: *Dinosaur Planet*.[10] In spirit, they were similar to a couple of Hungarian graduate students who named their team *Gravity*.

The competition also included a variety of even less-credentialed contestants. Eventually a two-person team named Pragmatic Theory popped up. This French-Canadian duo had been working on the project in their spare time. One of them had set up shop in his kitchen, working from 9 p.m. to midnight while his kids were asleep. Having had no experience in the field of collaborative filtering, they were modest in their self-assessment: "Two guys, absolutely no clue."

The list of contestants went on, thousands upon thousands long, including dabblers from seemingly disparate fields like psychology. And although these teams were competing with each other, they would find themselves collaborating during the competition. In fact, as we'll see, it would have been virtually impossible for a team unwilling to learn from and collaborate with other teams to have succeeded in the competition. In the next two chapters, we'll follow the journeys of several of these teams in their quest for the $1 million prize.

HOW TO TRAIN A CLASSIFIER

You may be wondering why I've included chapters about movie recommendations in this book. Are movie-recommendation engines really a major AI breakthrough?

Imagine the reception to Vaucanson's Flute Player had it been able to accurately recommend books or songs to members of the audience based solely on what else they liked. The public would have been equally as floored. Indeed, a recommendation engine is an algorithm that aims to capture the preferences that make us human. As we'll see in this chapter, recommendation engines can model human preferences so well that they can rival lawmakers at their most important job: voting on legislation. It certainly wouldn't stretch credulity to suggest that they've already had a far bigger impact on our economy than self-driving cars and chess-playing computer programs, as they power online commerce.

There's also another, more important reason I've included the Netflix Prize in this book. Some of what happened during the competition, including how the contestants approached the problem and with what tools, will directly inform how we look at other breakthroughs in this book. As we'll see, the ideas poured into the competition touched on just about every theme we'll see later.

In that vein, let's look back for a moment at one of the building blocks of Stanley, the self-driving car from Stanford that we discussed a couple of chapters ago. Stanley depended heavily on machine learning, which enabled it to stay on the road and to perceive the world around it. As we saw, Sebastian Thrun and his team drove Stanley around while its sensors collected data from the surrounding environment. They then used that data to train a classifier to detect whether different types of ground were safe for the car to drive on. We glossed over some of the details about how Stanley's drivable-ground classifier worked, but knowing how classifiers work is important if we're going to understand how movie recommendations—and the neural networks we'll see in later chapters—work. These classifiers operate on a principle as simple as that of a physical gear or lever, except that, instead of transforming *energy* to produce a useful result, they transform data to produce a useful result. Let's go over those details now.

Imagine that you're editing a cookbook called *The World's Best Recipes for Kids*. For this cookbook, you'll collect recipes that appear on the website Bettycrocker.com. You have a simple decision to make for each recipe: is it, or is it not, a recipe you should include in the kids' cookbook?

One way to answer this question would be to prepare each recipe you found on the website, feed it to your kids, and ask them for their opinion. But if there were 15,000 recipes on this website, then even at a healthy clip of 9 new recipes per day, you'd be cooking for over four years. How could you determine which recipes are good for kids without a huge investment of time and energy?

A machine-learning student would eagerly tell you how to solve the problem: you could train a classifier! In the field of machine learning, a classifier provides a way to automatically figure out whether an item (like a recipe) belongs to a certain category—like "recipes that are appropriate for kids," as opposed to "recipes that are inappropriate for kids."

To use a classifier for this task, you first need to decide which characteristics of a recipe are likely to distinguish between the ones that are good for kids and the ones that are bad for kids. You can use your creativity and judgment here, but some things might stand out as particularly helpful in making that distinction. Users on the Betty Crocker website can provide star ratings of the recipes, and these are probably correlated with the recipes kids like, so you can use those ratings as one of these distinguishing characteristics. You also want to prefer recipes that are easy to prepare and easy to understand, for example, because they require a small number of steps or only a few ingredients. You may also want to consider the number of grams of sugar (kids like sugar) and the number of grams of vegetables (kids don't like vegetables).

In machine learning, we call these distinguishing characteristics *features*. The magic happens when we combine these features into a single "recipe score" that describes how good a recipe is. The simplest way to combine them—and the way you can assume they're always combined in other classifiers in this book—is by taking a weighted average, where we use weights that summarize how important we think each feature is in

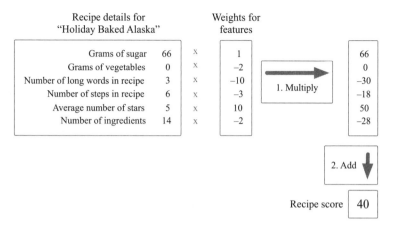

Recipe details for "Holiday Baked Alaska"		Weights for features		
Grams of sugar	66	X	1	66
Grams of vegetables	0	X	−2	0
Number of long words in recipe	3	X	−10	−30
Number of steps in recipe	6	X	−3	−18
Average number of stars	5	X	10	50
Number of ingredients	14	X	−2	−28

1. Multiply

2. Add

Recipe score   40

Figure 5.1
By applying a classifier to the recipe "Holiday Baked Alaska" we can see whether it would be good for kids. The weights stay fixed, and the details (and hence the recipe score) change for each recipe. "Holiday Baked Alaska" details are from the Betty Crocker website (see notes).

the final score. Take a moment to look at how I've applied this to the recipe "Holiday Baked Alaska" in figure 5.1.[11]

Why combine the features with a weighted average? It might seem arbitrary, and you've probably guessed (correctly) that machine-learning researchers have figured out a million other ways we could combine these features into a score. But this way of doing it is simple, straightforward, and easy to reason about. It's by far the most important "statistical gear" that makes up all of the automata in this book. And remember that this is just a building block: we want it to be simple, since we'll be combining it with other building blocks, and since we'll want to be able to understand what we've built.

To get a classifier from the weighted average, we just need to pick a threshold—let's just say "0" to be concrete—and call everything with a score above that threshold a good recipe and everything below it a bad recipe. According to the classifier in figure 5.1, Holiday Baked Alaska would be a very good recipe to add to the kids' cookbook, even though it's a bit complicated, because its other benefits—lots of sugar and no vegetables—make up for that.

If you're using machine learning to fit the classifier, you'd use data to figure out the weights for each feature and possibly to pick the threshold. You might collect this data by asking your kids to prepare some recipes and keeping track of how much they liked each one. Then you'd use a standard formula from statistics to estimate these weights from this data. You've probably already seen this formula (and promptly forgotten it) in high school, where you learned it as fitting the best line through a bunch of points (x, y) on a piece of paper. Here you use the same formula, except that you have more than one x-coordinate for each y-coordinate.

Once you've fit this classifier's weights using a handful of recipes—say, 100 recipes instead of 15,000—then you can have a computer run this classifier over the remaining 14,900 recipes to predict whether each one is good or bad. You could pick the top 200 recipes out of those 15,000 for your book according to this classifier, try them to make sure they're good, keep the best ones, and then you'd be all set.

With the skill of fitting a classifier in hand, now, let's turn back to the Netflix Prize to see how we can use it to recommend movies.

THE GOALS OF THE COMPETITION

What criteria should Netflix use to recommend movies to its viewers? What should its goals in recommending movies be? Clive Thompson pondered these questions in an article he wrote for the *New York Times Magazine* back in 2008, as the competition was underway.[12] Should Netflix's movie-recommendation service aim to recommend "safe bets" that you're very likely to enjoy, he asked, even if it doesn't push you out of your comfort zone? Or should it fill the role of that quirky movie-store clerk, taking bets to suggest movies that you may absolutely love, while running a risk of suggesting a movie that you'll think is a dud?[13]

At traditional video stores at the time, new and popular movies accounted for the majority of rentals; these stores could lean on this limited selection to make it easier to recommend movies. Netflix was different: 70 percent of their rentals were independent or older "backlist" titles. With such a large collection, and with a long delay between rentals, Netflix depended on Cinematch, its own movie-recommendation system, for its ability to recommend movies to its users. Improving Cinematch was important to the company's bottom line, because they risked losing customers who watched too *few* Netflix movies or who disliked a movie they had waited a few days to see: those viewers were the most at risk of canceling their subscriptions.[14]

So Netflix's own engineers worked and worked to improve their Cinematch recommendation algorithm. When they couldn't improve Cinematch any more, they decided to host the Netflix Prize, offering the $1 million to the first team that could beat their own algorithm by 10 percent. As Netflix CEO Reed Hastings pointed out, paying out the grand prize wasn't really a risk for them: the financial benefits in having better movie recommendations could far exceed the cost of the prize.[15] Even a small improvement in their recommendations could lead to big wins overall, because it was multiplied across the hundreds of millions of recommendations they made per day.[16] And in case none of the teams ever reached the 10 percent target, Netflix would also offer Progress Prizes: if the contestants made enough progress each year, the best team would be offered $50,000. Netflix attached just one condition to these prizes: *the winner needed to publish the details of their recommendation algorithm.*

Netflix made the task simple for their contestants by offering them a clear, objective target. The contestants needed to predict how many stars certain customers assigned to specific movies on specific dates. Netflix would evaluate the performance of each team by computing the average squared difference between their predicted ratings and the actual ratings the customers gave on a secret dataset that the contestants would never see.[17]

Whenever a team submitted some predictions to Netflix, Netflix measured the team's performance on the secret dataset and updated their scores on a public leaderboard that was closely followed by other teams and journalists.[18] It was technically possible for a team to still "peek" at these ratings by submitting a lot of predictions to be evaluated on this dataset, but Netflix was clever enough to have also stashed away yet *another* secret dataset that would never be revealed to the contestants. This double-secret dataset would only be used at the very end of the competition to evaluate the top candidates.

A GIANT RATINGS MATRIX

Given that the Netflix competition focused exclusively on customers' movie ratings, it's helpful to reason about the Netflix Prize by looking at the problem as a gigantic matrix of ratings. I show a small sample from this matrix (with made-up numbers) in figure 5.2.

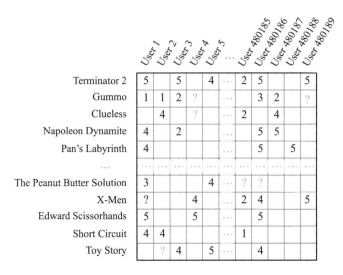

	User 1	User 2	User 3	User 4	User 5	...	User 480185	User 480186	User 480187	User 480188	User 480189
Terminator 2	5		5	4		···	2	5			5
Gummo	1	1	2	?		···	3	2			?
Clueless		4		?		···	2		4		
Napoleon Dynamite	4		2			···		5	5		
Pan's Labyrinth	4					···		5		5	
...	...	...	...	...	...	...	...	...	...	...	...
The Peanut Butter Solution	3				4	···	?	?			
X-Men	?			4		···	2	4			5
Edward Scissorhands	5			5		···		5			
Short Circuit	4	4				···	1				
Toy Story		?	4		5	···		4			

Figure 5.2
Some examples of star ratings that Netflix customers might have made on various movies. Netflix provided some of the ratings in the matrix (shown as numbers). Competitors needed to predict some of the missing recommendations (shown as question marks).

This matrix was immense: it provided ratings for 17,770 separate movies and 480,189 separate users.[19] Netflix provided some customers' ratings on some movies, and it asked contestants to predict some of the missing ratings (these are the question marks in the grid). Despite its size, only 1 percent of the matrix had any numbers at all: naturally most Netflix customers never rated most movies.

So where should the contestants begin?

Early into the competition, most of the top competitors converged on very similar approaches to analyze these ratings. The members of team BellKor—the team with researchers from AT&T and Yahoo!—noted the importance of starting with a simple "baseline" model to explain away the most basic trends in the ratings matrix. BellKor's baseline model began with two components. The first applied just to movies; we might call it the "*E. T.* effect."[20] The *E. T.* effect measured the popularity of a movie regardless of who was rating it. In the Netflix dataset, for example, the least popular movie was *Avia Vampire Hunter*, a low-budget movie about a woman who hunts poorly costumed vampires. *Avia* had 132 ratings on Netflix, with an average rating of just 1.3 out of 5 stars. One of two reviews on Amazon .com said the following about the movie:

> I should be paid for watching this trash. It was made in someones [sic] back-yard with a hand held camera. Don't order it. It is the worst movie, if you can call it that, that I have ever seen!!! If I knew before hand, you couldn't give it to me free of charge.

At the other extreme, the most popular movie was the extended edition of the fantasy *Lord of the Rings: The Return of the King*, which had 73,000 ratings in the Netflix dataset, with a respectable average of 4.7 out of 5 stars. Its Amazon.com reviews were also overwhelmingly positive; here is one review on Amazon.com for this movie:

> SOOOO GOOOOD! If you have never seen The Lord of the Rings Trilogy, I HIGHLY recommend it. It is an excellent trilogy. I especially love the extended editions ...

Although this review is more about the trilogy than the movie, it's clear that people like it. And the movie's negative reviews on Amazon.com tended to be more about the format of the video or the seller of the video, not the movie itself.

Another part of BellKor's baseline model, which we might call the "Scrooge effect," aimed to capture whether Netflix users rated movies with a glass-half-empty mentality or a glass-half-full mentality. Some users assigned 1-star ratings to all the movies they rated; but most were some-where in-between. Whether these viewers were trying to be objective wasn't relevant, but the fact that such trends existed in the data meant that teams like BellKor needed to capture them.

With the two effects BellKor outlined—the *E. T.* effect and the Scrooge effect—we can begin piecing together a rudimentary recommendation engine. BellKor combined the *E. T.* effect, the Scrooge effect, and an over-all bias term—which described the average movie rating across all movies and customers—into a single model using a classifier like the one we cre-ated for our *World's Best Recipes for Kids* book. In this simple model, they learned a weight for each movie, a weight for each user, and the intercept. With such a "recommendation engine," BellKor could recommend the best movies to Netflix's users—a decent start in the absence of any other information.

The problem with this recommendation engine is that it would always recommend the same exact shows to all users—specifically, *The Lord of the Rings* and other popular DVDs, like the first season of *Lost* and the sixth season of *The Simpsons*. It couldn't produce *personalized* recommendations. If Netflix used this approach to recommend movies to each user, then it would never satisfy Netflix users who only like foreign films, cult classics, or kids' movies. It would be decent for everybody but great for nobody.

And it really is the case that most people aren't well served by a one-size-fits-all system. The US Air Force discovered this when they were trying to understand what was causing so many airplane crashes in the 1950s. Cockpits had been built since the 1920s to match the average measurements of American men, but Lt. Gilbert Daniels, a scientist who studied the problem, discovered that *most men aren't average*. As Todd Rose explains in his book *The End of Average*:

> Out of 4,063 pilots, not a single airman fit within the average range on all 10 dimensions. One pilot might have a longer-than-average arm length, but a shorter-than-average leg length. Another pilot might have a big chest but small hips. Even more astonishing, Daniels discovered that if you picked out just three of the ten dimensions of size—say, neck circumference, thigh circumference and wrist circumference—less than 3.5 percent of pilots would be average sized on all three dimensions. Daniels's findings were clear and incontrovertible. There was no such thing as an average pilot. If you've designed a cockpit to fit the average pilot, you've actually designed it to fit no one.[21]

Based upon these findings, Daniels recommended that the cockpits be adjusted so that they could be personalized to the pilots, a recommendation the Air Force adopted:

> By discarding the average as their reference standard, the air force initiated a quantum leap in its design philosophy, centred on a new guiding principle: individual fit. Rather than fitting the individual to the system, the military began fitting the system to the individual. In short order, the air force demanded that all cockpits needed to fit pilots whose measurements fell within the 5-percent to 95-percent range on each dimension.
>
> They designed adjustable seats, technology now standard in all automobiles. They created adjustable foot pedals. They developed adjustable helmet straps and flight suits.
>
> Once these and other design solutions were put into place, pilot performance soared, and the US Air Force became the most dominant air force on

the planet. Soon, every branch of the American military published guides decreeing that equipment should fit a wide range of body sizes, instead of standardized around the average.[22]

We need to determine the equivalent of adjustable seats for the Netflix recommendation engine so that it can be customized for each user. We need something that can capture the *Terminator* effect: the fact that some Netflix users—but not all of them—like science-fiction and action movies, and that other users like kids' movies, that some users like both, and that some like neither. To capture the *Terminator* effect, most teams converged on a method known as *matrix factorization*.

MATRIX FACTORIZATION

Matrix factorization relies on the fact that the giant ratings matrix in figure 5.2 has a lot of redundant information. People who liked *Futurama* tend to like *The Simpsons*, and people who liked *Shrek* tend to like its spinoff, *Puss in Boots*. That there would be redundant information in this matrix isn't such a crazy idea—after all, the very premise that we can offer personalized recommendations assumes that there are predictable patterns in peoples' ratings.

To see the key insight behind matrix factorization, let's assume for the moment that we can summarize movies and users with just a handful of numbers apiece. For each movie, those numbers might just represent its possible genres: Is it an action movie, a comedy, a thriller, or some combination of these? We could represent each movie as a short, ordered list of numbers: 1 where it fits a certain genre and 0 where it doesn't.

We could also do the same thing for Netflix user preferences: 1 if the user likes the genre, −1 if the user doesn't like it, and 0 if the user doesn't care about it. If the user really likes or dislikes a genre, we might use more extreme numbers, like 1.5 or −2.2. Don't worry for the moment about where we get this information about our movies and users. For now, just assume that we can find which movies belong to which genres from public sources like Wikipedia and the Internet Movie Database (IMDb), and that we can simply use a survey to ask people which genres they like.

Once we've described each movie and person in our database with these descriptive numbers, we'd like to use them to predict whether any one person likes a given movie. Let's try to predict whether the director

Steven Spielberg likes *Jurassic Park*. That movie is mostly science fiction and adventure, so let's say it has a 1 for those two genres and 0 for everything else. And let's say that Steven Spielberg really likes science fiction (1.2), sort-of likes adventure and comedy movies (0.6 and 0.5), and dislikes horror movies (−1.2). How should we combine these numbers to predict whether he likes *Jurassic Park*?

One simple way is to take the numbers describing whether *Jurassic Park* falls into each genre, multiply those by how much Steven Spielberg likes those genres, and then add these products up to get a score that describes how much he likes *Jurassic Park* (see figure 5.3). I'm making no promises that this is the "best" way to combine these numbers, but if you're willing to suspend your disbelief for a moment, you'll probably agree that this should at least point us in the right direction.

In a nutshell, this is matrix factorization. This is the most important algorithm we'll see for making personalized recommendations, and here's the

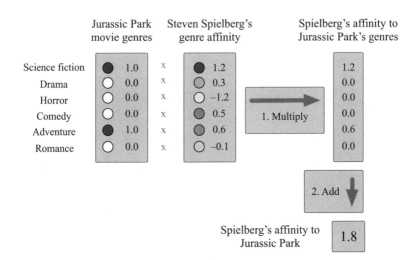

Figure 5.3
A test to determine whether Steven Spielberg would like the movie *Jurassic Park*. Here, we can assume *Jurassic Park* falls into two genres: science fiction and adventure. Steven Spielberg tends to like science fiction movies, comedies, and adventures, and tends not to like horror movies, as indicated by his genre affinities. We combine these into a score by multiplying together the genre scores, which are 0 or 1, with Spielberg's affinities for those genres, and adding the results together. The result is a fairly high "affinity" score describing how much Spielberg likes *Jurassic Park*.

key intuition I want you to internalize about it: this algorithm assumes that we've summarized each movie with a few numbers and each user with a few numbers, and it provides a way—precisely the way I showed you in figure 5.3—to combine these sets of numbers into a score to describe how much any user will like any movie. This is called matrix factorization because, the way the math works out, it's equivalent to approximating the original, gigantic ratings matrix in figure 5.2 as the matrix product of two or more much smaller matrices—its factors—which encode exactly the numbers we've used to describe the movies and users.[23]

If you compare figure 5.3 with figure 5.1, you'll notice that we've created a classifier in both. In figure 5.1 the features are recipes and the weights are kids' preferences; in figure 5.3 the features are movies' genres and the weights are Mr. Spielberg's movie preferences. This hand-built classifier gives us personalized recommendations for Steven Spielberg.

As you might imagine, we can do better if we learn these weights from data. If Mr. Spielberg has rated movies on Netflix, we could use those ratings and the genres of the movies he's rated to learn his movie preferences automatically. This is exactly the same thing we did when we trained the classifier to find good recipes for kids, except that now we're training a classifier to make movie recommendations for Steven Spielberg. This classifier will only work for Steven Spielberg, but it's trivial to repeat this process for each Netflix user. Using each user's past movie ratings, we could automatically create a classifier for everyone, without needing to directly ask them which genres they like.

It turns out that we can improve these predictions even more. To see how, look again at figure 5.3. Notice that *Jurassic Park's* genres are fixed to either 0 or 1. I chose these numbers by looking at IMDb, but we can improve our predictions by learning about movies' genres from data. Instead of requiring that *Jurassic Park* be described by either 0 or 1, we could represent it with numbers that we've learned from users' ratings of the movie, applying the exact same approach we used to learn Steven Spielberg's preferences for different genres.

Why bother learning movies' genres from data when we already know the actual genres for each movie? We do this because we have no reason to believe that the genre labels selected by humans are the best way to summarize movies for the task of making movie recommendations. Fixed genres are too coarse a way to describe movies; and in fact, we have plenty of evidence that movie genres are fluid. Movies like *Jurassic Park* illustrate this perfectly: *Jurassic Park* was both a science-fiction film and an adventure film, but it also had some elements of comedy and some elements of horror. So it should have at least a little weight for these latter genres. And some genres are too coarse: comedy movies might be dry, slapstick, or raunchy; and each type of comedy might draw vastly different audiences. Genres are a useful way for movie store clerks and other people to describe movies, but they don't tend to be very useful for predicting how much people will like them, at least compared to what we can learn from the data.[24] We can actually predict movie ratings much better if we ignore "real" movie genres altogether and just use the artificial ones we've machine-learned from the ratings matrix.[25]

In fact, as Chris Volinsky of BellKor pointed out, *none* of the data that came from outside the ratings matrix during his team's experiments seemed to be very useful in predicting ratings. They tried a bunch of things—movie genre, which actors were in the movie, what the movie's release date was, and so on—but nothing seemed to help. Chris's intuition was that the dataset of movie ratings was so large and so rich that peoples' ratings told you all you really needed to know about who would like a movie. Knowing how thousands of different people voted on a movie could tell you more about that movie than any amount of external knowledge ever could. The ratings for a movie are like its digital fingerprint, and matrix factorization provides a compact but excellent summary of that fingerprint.

If we repeatedly alternate between these two steps—that is, learning movies' genres while holding users' affinities for those genres fixed, and then estimating users' affinities for those genres while holding the genres fixed, then our recommendations will get better and better until eventually the genres stop changing. At that point, we'll have learned a set of weights for each user and another set of weights for each movie that we can multiply together and sum up to provide rich, personalized recommendations for each user-movie pair. This is what most data scientists mean when they refer to matrix factorization, and this alternating process of relearning the genres and genre affinities from data is how they often compute the matrix factorization.

As we learn these artificial genres with this alternating method, they'll diverge from the original genres we started with. By the time we're done, they might not look like the original genres at all, but they'll still often be interpretable.

The way I've described matrix factorization just now probably isn't the way you'd hear about matrix factorization in a college class. Often when researchers talk about matrix factorization to other people, they draw up an image of the movies in the ratings matrix forming a point cloud, where movies with similar ratings are near one another and movies with very different ratings tend to be farther apart. In fact, it's easy to create such a cloud from the matrix, although it's difficult to visualize, because each movie-point has 480,189 coordinates: one for each of the 480,189 users' ratings for the movie.

But just like the matrix, this cloud has a lot of redundant information. Matrix factorization takes the high-dimensional cloud of movies and collapses it down into a lower-dimensional cloud that still captures the trends we care about—namely, that similar movies cluster near one another, while different movies tend to settle farther apart from one another. In the new space, each movie might be described with only half a dozen or a hundred numbers apiece—exactly the numbers we'd find with the alternating method above.

Matrix factorization and its brethren are often the first approach researchers try when they're working with any data that can be put into a large matrix.[26] For example, political scientists use matrix factorization to understand how lawmakers vote on legislation. If we place US lawmakers' votes on different bills into a giant matrix and apply matrix factorization to it, we can summarize each lawmaker and each piece of legislation very well with just one or two numbers apiece.[27] In one two-year period, for example, it was possible to explain 98 percent of the votes coming out of the House of Representatives by using just a single number to describe each lawmaker, and this number turns out to explain their political party. If you use this number to place lawmakers along the real line, Democrats and Republicans are usually perfectly separated. Matrix factorization tells us that US congresspersons' voting is, quite literally, one-dimensional.

THE FIRST YEAR ENDS

Armed with tools like matrix factorization to capture the *Terminator* effect, and combining them with models that captured the Scrooge effect and the *E. T.* effect, the top teams made considerable progress toward the Netflix

Prize. By the end of the first year, the top teams were around 8 percent better than Netflix's own Cinematch algorithm. This wasn't enough for them to win the grand prize, but it was more than enough to guarantee that some team would be eligible for the $50,000 Progress Prize. The Progress Prize was to be awarded annually, which meant that the contestants faced a fast-approaching deadline.

Among the top teams as the deadline approached was BellKor, whose members were the researchers from AT&T Labs and Yahoo!, and who had held the lead throughout most of the first year. But earlier in the game, the top of the leaderboard had changed frequently. The neural network researchers from the University of Toronto were near the top for a bit, and they produced an influential paper with a model that was used by other teams, including BellKor. But the three Princeton students making up Dinosaur Planet, free for the summer, had been working aggressively to challenge BellKor.[28] And another team of young upstarts—the two Hungarian graduate students from the team Gravity—was challenging the Princeton students for second place.

Then, on October 21, 2007, one day before the first year's deadline, the ground shifted. The two teams that had been hanging around second and third place—Dinosaur Planet and Gravity—formed an alliance. They combined their models, submitting the average of their models' scores to the leaderboard, and suddenly they were in first place. BellKor had just one day to try to regain its position to claim the Progress Prize. Although they didn't realize it yet, this was also the beginning of a phenomenon that would shape the rest of the competition.

6   ENSEMBLES OF TEAMS: THE NETFLIX
PRIZE WINNERS

Pragmatic (adjective)—Dealing with things sensibly and realistically in a way that is based on practical rather than theoretical considerations.

Chaos (noun)—The property of a complex system whose behaviour is so unpredictable as to appear random, owing to great sensitivity to small changes in conditions.
—*Oxford English Dictionary*, 2017

CLOSING THE GAP BETWEEN CONTENDERS

The first year of the Netflix Prize had been a whirlwind of ideas and a blur of progress. Before BellKor rose to the top of the leaderboard, a handful of other teams came in and out of the top spot, while a flurry of discussion and exchange of ideas taking place in the community helped to close the gap between the remaining contenders. Some of this discussion took place at academic conferences and workshops focused on data mining. Another venue was the Netflix Prize Forum, an online community Netflix had set up for the contestants.

The Netflix Prize Forum offered a place for contestants to share their results and insights informally. Soon after the competition began, the forum was humming with activity. As one of the competition's organizers observed:

> In addition to active submissions, there has been substantial engagement between contestants on the Netflix Prize Forum, including sharing of code and coding ideas, additional data, insights on the patterns found in the data, even pooling of submissions (and hence teams) themselves to achieve increased accuracy ("blending").[1]

Before the teams had published much of their research, Netflix also studied comments in the forum to find which methods performed well. On this forum, within less than a year after the competition began, Netflix noticed two of the key ideas that became ubiquitous among the top teams' submissions: an influential description of matrix factorization as well as an approach known as model blending.[2]

Newspapers and magazines had also begun to chronicle the real-life stories of casual and part-time data scientists working nights and weekends from their home offices. One contestant, a 48-year-old management consultant with a degree in psychology, was considering whether to get a PhD in machine learning. He went by the name "Just a guy in a Garage" in the competition, although technically he worked out of his bedroom.[3] Soon after that, the *New York Times* chronicled a 32-year-old father of four who worked at his dining room table, along with a 51-year old "semi-retired" computer scientist who brainstormed with his 12- and 13-year-old kids about which new ideas to try. They suggested looking carefully at movie sequels to get a leg up on the competition.[4]

THE END OF THE FIRST YEAR

In the final weeks of the first year of the competition, Team BellKor—the AT&T and Yahoo! researchers—held first place. But near the end of the first year they found themselves challenged by the second- and third-place contenders, teams consisting of young and ambitious recent graduates from two teams, Gravity and Dinosaur Planet.

A day before that first year ended, these second- and third-place teams literally merged. The combined team, which called itself "When Gravity and Dinosaurs Unite," averaged their predictions and submitted this average of their two models to Netflix, and the newly minted team was suddenly in first place.[5] Over the next day, BellKor and the new team raced against the clock, furiously coding and debugging. Technically they could only submit one model to Netflix per day, so their final submission needed to count. In the end, BellKor managed to submit an entry that barely beat When Gravity and Dinosaurs Unite, coming in at 8.43 percent above Cinematch—and just 0.05 percent above their competitors. BellKor won the first year's $50,000 Progress Prize, but not by much.[6]

To claim the reward, BellKor needed to publish a report about their algorithms. After they did this, their secrets were out in the open for everyone to see, and the moat around them continued to fill with other contestants.[7] To make matters worse, BellKor found that it was becoming more and more difficult to beat their own results. Having averaged an improvement of 0.16 percent per week toward the Prize goal of 10 percent in the first year, BellKor averaged just 0.02 percent per week the second year. Their progress had ground to a near-halt.

They had already picked most of the low-hanging fruit in the first year, when the teams established the most successful components of their models. This included the baseline model—the Scrooge effect (to describe users' tendency to rate high or low) and the *E. T.* effect (to explain whether movies were good or bad regardless of who was rating them)—along with models like matrix factorization to handle the *Terminator* effect, which summarized users' unique preferences.

In the second year, these teams were facing what we might call the *Napoleon Dynamite* problem. Teams competing for the Netflix Prize found it famously difficult to predict the effect the 2004 cult classic *Napoleon Dynamite* would have on different viewers.[8] Clive Thompson explained the reason the film posed such a challenge in the *New York Times Magazine*, citing one of the contestants:

> The reason, [the contestant] says, is that *Napoleon Dynamite* is very weird and very polarizing. It contains a lot of arch, ironic humor, including a famously kooky dance performed by the titular teenage character to help his hapless friend win a student-council election. It's the type of quirky entertainment that tends to be either loved or despised. The movie has been rated more than two million times in the Netflix database, and the ratings are disproportionately one or five stars.[9]

The difficulty in predicting whether a Netflix customer will like *Napoleon Dynamite* gets at both the core strength and the core weakness of any recommendation system: *personalized recommendations can only work if there is some redundancy in users' preferences*. If a movie existed that was completely un-redundant with other movies, then neither matrix factorization nor other methods would be useful for making personalized recommendations about that movie.[10] This doesn't mean that *Napoleon Dynamite* wasn't redundant, but with many of the methods people tried, they couldn't find where that redundancy was hidden.

It felt like the ratings matrix was a wet towel that they had been trying to squeeze dry for a while, collecting the precious water from the towel in a bucket. They had squeezed it as long as they could in a certain way, so it was time to unfold the towel to try squeezing it in a different way. And so these teams tried some different approaches to capture the *Terminator* effect, turning the towel this way and that.

One model that became popular, even in the first year, was an artificial neural network developed by the researchers in the team ML@UToronto. This neural network was mathematically very similar to matrix factorization, but it dealt with missing ratings differently, and it treated ratings as discrete categories 1, 2, 3, 4, or 5 instead of real numbers in the range 1.0 to 5.0. In other words, it twisted the towel a bit differently than matrix factorization.

Another method the teams used searched for movies that were similar to one another. If you like a certain movie—say, *Cinderella*—and this movie is very similar to another one that you've never rated—say, *Sleeping Beauty*—then these methods should be able to recommend the latter movie to you. The teams also tried to find which users were similar. If you were similar to a fellow over in Wyoming in the way you've rated movies, and this fellow has given a high rating to a movie you've never seen—say, *Back to the Future*—then these methods should recommend that movie to you, too. The trick with getting these methods to work, of course, was in how they decided what made one user "similar to" another user. There's no single, correct way to do this, but the teams did their best, writing out mathematical functions in their programs to encode their intuitions.

Another trick to solving the *Napoleon Dynamite* problem was by looking not just at which star ratings users gave to different movies, but also at which movies they had rated. For example, regardless of whether you like the movie *Star Trek IV*—the one in which they go back to present-day Earth to find whales—the fact that you have even rated a *Star Trek* movie gives a lot of information about which types of movies you tend to like.[11] The teams found that by incorporating this "implicit" information—that is, information about *which* movies you've watched, not just *how you rate them*—they could decrease their relative error by roughly 10 percent. This was a small but welcome improvement, given how difficult it was to squeeze water out of their towel by this point.[12]

PREDICTIONS OVER TIME

The second year of the competition, these teams also turned their attention to a different part of the data: *when* users rated movies.[13] But contestants faced a problem because Netflix ratings reflect a changing world: the popularity of movies changes over time, and people themselves change their preferences over time. If you asked a viewer to rate a movie one month and have her rate the movie again a month later, her rating would change by an average of 0.4 stars.[14] And to make things even more difficult, she'd tend to assign different scores to movies on Mondays than she will on Fridays.[15]

The researchers behind BellKor addressed this problem by letting parts of their model be flexible enough to reflect their observations about how ratings changed over time. They revisited the movie-popularity offset in their baseline model. Instead of measuring a movie's popularity once over the entire period, they measured it more often, grouping the ratings into 10-week "bins."[16]

Figure 6.1 shows what the average popularity looked like for *The Matrix*, which came out in 1999, if we break it up into 10-week intervals. Over the two years following its release in 1999, *The Matrix* gradually decreased in popularity. Its sequel, *Matrix Reloaded*, was released in May 2003, which might have explained the spike in popularity of the original *Matrix* in early 2003.

A bigger challenge in how time impacted movie ratings rested in the viewers themselves. Sometimes a user rated many movies at a time, and

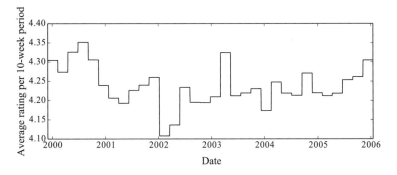

Figure 6.1
Popularity of the movie *The Matrix* over time.

those "bursts" might occur when she was in a particularly good or bad mood. Other times the primary Netflix user in a household changed—for example, as a teenager began watching more Netflix than her parents. BellKor addressed this by assuming that customers' preferences might drift gradually over time in a fixed direction, while also assuming that their ratings on a given day might be a bit higher or lower than this gradual drift suggested.[17]

The data was wildly distorted in other ways, too. BellKor noticed that Netflix customers' rating scales could moderate over time, as if they were becoming more or less apathetic in rating movies. It wasn't that their ratings became higher or lower on average (although this happened too). It was that they also became more or less extreme over time. As before, BellKor captured this effect by assuming that users rated movies in bursts on a given day, when they were particularly moderate or extreme in the ratings they assigned.[18]

Sometimes these trends were harder to explain. The members of Pragmatic Theory—the "two guys without a clue" we briefly met in the last chapter—noticed that the *number* of ratings made by a customer on a given day was a useful predictor of whether the movie was good or not.

The team's observation was confusing because it wasn't just due to anomalies in the users who made the bulk ratings: that part was old news. This was a peculiarity about the *movies* being rated. Some movies tended to receive more stars than expected when included in a bulk rating, while other movies tended to receive fewer stars than expected when included in a bulk rating. When team BellKor eventually learned about this result from the guys in Pragmatic Theory, they hypothesized that *users remember movies asymmetrically*. Some movies are memorably good or memorably bad, while others are just not very memorable. When users rates movies in bulk, they tend to include movies they saw a long time ago—particularly those movies that were memorably good or bad. Those who loved or hated a memorably good or bad movie will remember it long afterward and likely rate it during a bulk rating, while those who didn't feel strongly about it will simply forget about it by the next time they bulk-rate movies.[19]

The Netflix Prize dataset was chock-full of data-mining gems like this. Here's another one: a team named BigChaos noticed that the number of letters in a title was predictive of whether users liked it (the effect wasn't large, but it was present). As the competition wore on, the different teams mined these gems, bit by precious bit.

OVERFITTING

Since Netflix gave its contestants so much data, the teams could just about "assume" parts of their model into existence by adding parameters to their model in a way that matched their intuitions. If a team had a hunch that movies' popularities were predictive of customers' ratings (they are), they simply needed to add a new parameter to their model for each movie that could "absorb" that information.[20] If the team had a hunch that customers might be somewhat biased in their ratings (they are), then they simply needed to add a new parameter to their model for each customer to absorb *that* information. These two parameters made up their baseline model. And when a team wanted to also assume that movies' popularities change over time, and that customers' biases vary over time, they did so by adding parameters to their model for each of those things.

The main risk the teams faced with these parameters was whether they were adding more flexibility to their models than justified by the amount of data they had. If they added too many parameters, they ran a risk of "overfitting" to their dataset. Overfitting means that their apparently good performance in predicting ratings might be a mirage. They might think that they're predicting ratings well because the error in their predictions looks low, when it's instead because they have so many parameters to work with—basically, so many knobs to tune—that they end up making their model look better than it really is. If they were overfitting, then their apparently good predictions might not carry over to the secret dataset that Netflix used to evaluate the contestants. For example, BellKor could have added a parameter to their model for every customer-movie pair in their dataset. This could explain the ratings in their movies dataset with perfect accuracy.[21] But it would be useless in predicting ratings for any user-movie pairs they hadn't seen before. Fortunately it was easy for the contestants to keep an eye on whether they were overfitting, because they could keep aside a fraction of their own dataset (Netflix provided them with a sample for this very purpose) and test against it to make sure they weren't overfitting. We'll see a couple more ways to deal with overfitting when we look at neural networks in a few chapters.

MODEL BLENDING

The progress toward the Netflix Prize and its conclusion in the first year had transfixed the contestants. After BellKor published their work for the community, their peers pored over their report carefully, reading about their baseline model, their matrix factorization model, and the neural network BellKor used. They also read about how BellKor had blended a whole bunch of different versions of these models together. It wasn't a surprise to the other contestants that BellKor had been blending models— it hadn't exactly been a secret, and blended models had already been discussed in the online forum. But it was now undeniable from BellKor's paper that blended models worked. Besides, when Gravity and Dinosaur Planet combined, they had implicitly used model blending when they averaged predictions from their two separate models.

When BellKor was researching how to predict ratings, they needed to make a lot of decisions about what should go into their model. When they fit a matrix factorization model, they needed to answer questions such as: *How many "genres" should we use to summarize each movie? Should we include the implicit ratings information?* When they fit a nearest-neighbor model for movies, they needed to decide what it meant for two movies to be similar. They could try a bunch of educated guesses and validate their guesses with data, but they had a lot of different decisions to make. If they tried to tune all of their parameters to find the perfect setting for all of them, there was a good chance they might overfit.

Instead, BellKor created many models with somewhat different parameter settings, and then they averaged them. To win their first Progress Prize, they averaged 107 different models. Did BellKor need to combine so many separate models? Probably not: they noted that they used so many models in part for convenience. They already had those models from earlier experiments, and it didn't hurt to keep them in the final blend, so why not? But they found that they could get results that were comparably as good or better with only about fifty models.[22]

Why does model blending work? When a contestant asked BellKor on the Netflix Prize Forum which of their 107 models was best, Yehuda Koren, one of the members of the team, listed some of its benefits:

> It allows concentrating on relatively simple models, which are fast to code and to run. The result is also more robust against programming bugs and overfitting. ...

I will not recommend just one of the predictors. You want at least to explain the data at multiple scales (local+regional).[23]

In other words, blending models is good for both practical and modeling reasons. It's practical to use the average of many simple models, because simple models are easy to program and less prone to bugs. And if you use many different models, you can capture the uncertainty in your dataset at many different "granularities." For example, if you're debating between using 10 genres and 100 genres in your matrix factorization model, you can simply use both. The 10-genre model can capture the high-level "gist" of each user's movie preferences, while the 100-genre model can capture the fine nuance of her preferences.

This idea of model averaging is also supported by a rich set of theoretical results, and the intuition is easy to get at. Let's say that you're investing in the stock market, and you are deciding whether to put all of your money into stock A, which returns, on average, 12 percent per year; or into a hundred different stocks which each return, on average, 12 percent per year. If you have the same uncertainty about the outcome of all of these stocks, then you're better off splitting your money equally among the hundred stocks.[24] Why? Because you can still expect to get an average of 12 percent per year, but you'll have lower uncertainty about your outcome: some of the stocks that return less than 12 percent will be offset by the stocks that return more than that.[25] Each of BellKor's 107 models was "trained" to make a different prediction of users' movie-ratings; so by blending these 107 models, BellKor's new predictor still predicted the same thing, but with less uncertainty.

But wait, you might say. We saw that with the financial crisis of 2008 and 2009, the entire stock market went down. Having a portfolio of 100 stocks wouldn't have offered much protection against this, so this "less uncertainty" argument is bogus. This is correct, and it gets at the core of when model blending works and when it doesn't work. Most stocks are correlated to one another, and model blending works well when the models are uncorrelated. If one model predicts too high a Netflix rating, the other models should help to mitigate this, not to reinforce it. This can happen more easily when they are uncorrelated.

We can get some further intuition for how model blending helps by looking at *boosting*, one of the methods the top teams used to blend their models as their submissions improved. The intuition behind boosting is that by combining many "weak" models—each one of which might not be very good, but each of which is at least a little good—we can end up with a much more powerful model than any of the original ones.[26]

To apply boosting to a problem like the Netflix challenge, we would begin by training a very simple model to predict movie ratings. Its predictions won't be perfect, so we take the ratings that the model got wrong and magnify them—that is, we give them more weight than the other ratings, because we want the classifier to care about them more the next time around—and then we fit a second model with these adjusted weights. Then we repeat the process again and again, magnifying the incorrect ratings and refitting a new model each time. By the time we're done, we'll have easily trained tens, hundreds, or even thousands of models. If we average these models with the right weights, the result will be a single, blended monster of a model that works better than any single one.

THE SECOND YEAR

As the second year wore on, several other teams began threatening BellKor on the leaderboard. The team When Gravity and Dinosaurs Unite was never very far behind, but after the first summer, the three Princeton undergrads from the Dinosaur Planet part of the team found themselves busy with grad school and work.[27] As the end of the second year of the competition grew near, another team called BigChaos began to threaten BellKor.

BigChaos was experimenting a lot with the way they blended their models. In the first year, they combined models by simply using a weighted average of them. During the second year they found a neural network to be especially useful when combining their models. The neural network could learn a more sophisticated way to combine the simple models than by taking a simple average.[28]

But as the second year continued, all of the top teams struggled to make more progress. The prize organizers were starting to wonder whether contestants would make enough progress to win the prize at all.[29] As the deadline for the second Progress Prize approached, the situation grew more intense. For any team to win the second $50,000 Progress Prize, they needed to exceed the previous year's 8.43 percent improvement by an entire 1 percent. BellKor and BigChaos were the top two teams, but at the rate they were progressing, it could take them over a month to reach the 9.43 percent goal.[30]

In the end, BellKor and BigChaos caused another upset: they combined into a single team. The merged team, which they decided to call BellKor in BigChaos, exceeded Cinematch by 9.44 percent. This was precariously close to the threshold they needed for the second Progress Prize, and it was still far from their 10 percent target, but it was enough for the new team to win their $50,000.

The five members of BellKor in BigChaos could pause to make a collective sigh of relief, but they couldn't rest long. If no team hit that 10 percent goal in the coming year, nobody would qualify for the Progress Prize either. Would that be the end of the competition? There was also palpable speculation in the air about another topic: *Which teams would merge next?* The competition had entered a new phase, and the teams' attention began to shift from predicting ratings in the ratings matrix to finding the best strategy for teams to merge.

THE FINAL YEAR

As the final year progressed, BellKor in BigChaos continued to top the leaderboard, with When Gravity and Dinosaurs Unite never far behind. But by then, another team had begun to show up on the leaderboards: Pragmatic Theory, the Canadian duo we've seen a couple of times already, the two guys without a clue. Despite their initial unfamiliarity with the field, they found the Netflix community to be extremely collegial, and they carefully studied the methods of the other contestants. When BellKor in BigChaos published their results, the members of Pragmatic Theory immediately downloaded and carefully studied their papers. Over time, and working nonstop, Pragmatic Theory continued to move up the official leaderboard.[31]

If BellKor's emphasis was on the theory of collaborative filtering, and BigChaos's emphasis was on blending algorithms, then Pragmatic Theory's emphasis was the sheer quantity of effort they invested and results they obtained. In one paper they published about their methods, I counted 707 separate models that went into their blend. Although this would have been impractical for the production system that Netflix would need to implement, Pragmatic Theory didn't care about that. They cared about predicting the ratings as accurately as possible. They outlined this philosophy in one of their papers (emphasis added):

> The solution presented in this document was exclusively aimed at building a system that would predict subscriber ratings with the highest possible accuracy. ... The solution is based on a huge amount of models and predictors which would not be practical as part of a commercial recommender system. However, this result is a direct consequence of the nature and goal of the competition: *obtain the highest possible accuracy at any cost, disregarding completely the complexity of the solution and the execution performance.*[32]

In other words, Pragmatic Theory developed a solution that would have been impractical to implement precisely because they were being *pragmatic*. BellKor in BigChaos saw another trait in them. Chris Volinsky, of the original team BellKor, explained that he and his colleagues converged on the adjective *fearless* to describe Pragmatic Theory. But Pragmatic Theory was also alarming to BellKor in BigChaos for another reason.

This late in the competition, the focus of the community had moved somewhat away from optimizing and blending their models and toward optimizing their teams. Since each team was facing the same difficulties in eking out improvements in their models, the tone of the competition was beginning to suggest that these teams would continue to merge to reach the 10 percent target.

BellKor in BigChaos noticed that Pragmatic Theory—the fearless Canadian duo—was a prime "merge target" by another team. If another team picked them up, that team could become a serious threat. Should BellKor in BigChaos try to merge with Pragmatic Theory? Maybe, but BellKor in BigChaos were also in secret discussions with other teams, and there might be a better team to merge with, such as When Gravity and Dinosaurs Unite—the recent grads from Princeton who went off to industry and grad school, who had combined with the Hungarian graduate students.

BellKor in BigChaos needed to act, and they needed to do so quickly. Around this time, When Gravity and Dinosaurs Unite formed a new team called Grand Prize Team. This new team invited anyone to join, offering a fraction of the $1 million prize proportional to how much closer the newcomers brought them to winning. This frightened BellKor in

BigChaos, as it could quickly spell the end of them if a team like Pragmatic Theory joined Grand Prize Team.

In the end, BellKor in BigChaos decided to merge with Pragmatic Theory to form the new team BellKor's Pragmatic Chaos (you can keep track of how the leading teams merged in figure 6.2). BellKor in BigChaos had been in secret discussions with Pragmatic Theory and other teams for some time before their merger. When BellKor's Pragmatic Chaos submitted their combined model, they beat Cinematch by 10.05 percent, putting them past the 10 percent threshold.

But this wasn't quite the end of the competition. Netflix's rules dictated that, once the first team breached the 10 percent barrier, a 30-day "last call" period would begin. At the end of *that* period, the winner would be decided, based on whoever had the lowest prediction error on that double-secret dataset that Netflix had set aside at the very beginning of the competition. Scores on that double-secret dataset would be rounded to four decimal points, and ties would be broken by submission time.

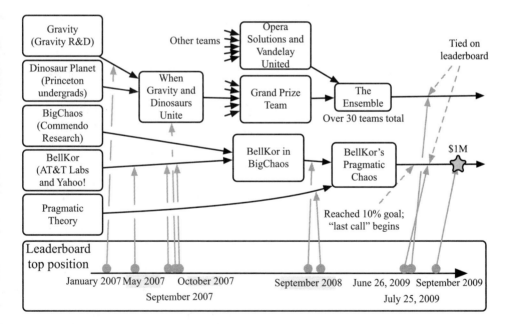

Figure 6.2
The chart shows team progress toward the Netflix Prize. The final team to win the competition was BellKor's Pragmatic Chaos.

The remaining teams had a month to catch up. The bubbling phenom-enon of team merging spilled over into a desperate froth. The other lead-ing teams, including Grand Prize Team, brokered a deal to form a massive consortium called "The Ensemble," which contained over thirty teams (an "ensemble" in machine learning is another name for a blend of different models).[33]

Internally, the members of The Ensemble debated about their strategy in the final month: Should they wait until the last minute, and then sub-mit their combined model? Or should they make submissions early and often? Submitting late could keep their existence a secret and catch BellKor's Pragmatic Chaos by surprise. But submitting early could enable them to avoid any last-minute catastrophes. Ultimately they voted to keep the existence of The Ensemble a closely held secret and to make their first submission as a team one day before the deadline; when that day arrived, they submitted their model as The Ensemble, coming in at 10.09 percent, just barely beating BellKor's Pragmatic Chaos, who had gotten up to 10.08 percent by then. Twenty-four minutes before the final deadline, BellKor's Pragmatic Chaos submitted again, and also came in with a score of 10.09 percent. And then, four minutes before the final deadline, The Ensemble submitted a model that reached 10.10 percent on the leaderboard. The competition was over, and Netflix needed to evalu-ate the models on their double-secret dataset.

On the double-secret dataset, BellKor's Pragmatic Chaos and The Ensemble tied up to four decimal places, which, according to Netflix's rules, put them at a tie; and ties were to be broken based on the time of submission. BellKor's Pragmatic Chaos had made their submission 20 min-utes earlier than The Ensemble, and so the three-year competition came to an end. BellKor's Pragmatic Chaos claimed the $1 million prize.[34]

AFTER THE COMPETITION

Despite the impressive performance of the final teams, Netflix never imple-mented the final suite of models submitted by either BellKor's Pragmatic Chaos or The Ensemble. A few people, apparently upset about this, even called the Netflix Prize a failure. And although Netflix tried to anonymize their dataset, one group of researchers pointed out some ways the dataset theoretically exposed its customers' privacy, claims which were widely misinterpreted in the media. As a result, Netflix withdrew their dataset from the public and attempted to scrub all traces of it, a move one contestant called a "damned shame."

This aside, the competition was a success by a number of metrics. First, Netflix had incorporated some of the ideas from the competition. They found that two of the methods described by teams in their first year—matrix factorization and the neural network developed by the Toronto team—offered significant improvements over Netflix's own algorithm; these two alone netted them a 7.6 percent improvement over Cinematch. For paying out two Progress Prizes of $50,000 and the grand prize of $1 million, they received in return many thousands of hours of cutting-edge research by world experts along with exposure to this talent in a tight labor market.[35]

They also received—possibly most importantly of all—strong evidence that they shouldn't invest significant effort beyond a certain point. They had seen from the contestants where they should start to expect diminishing returns. In the meantime, they had also seen their business moving much more in the direction of online, streaming video, and away from DVD rental. While their recommendation engine would still be an important feature of their new product, they also had other things to think about.[36]

The Netflix Prize was a success for the research community as well. While the DARPA Grand Challenges received hundreds of submissions, the Netflix Prize had tens of thousands.[37] On the technical side, the competition empirically established matrix factorization and model averaging as some of the best methods for recommendation systems. While these ideas had been around for a long time, the competition helped to publicize them by offering objective and public evidence of their performance.

Why don't we have robots that can tidy the house or clean up after the kids? It's not because we're not mechanically capable—there are robots that could do that. But the problem is that every house, every kitchen, is different. You couldn't pre-program individual machines, so it has to learn in the environment it finds itself in.

—Demis Hassabis, founder of DeepMind[1]

DEEPMIND PLAYS ATARI

In early 2014, as Google's self-driving car project was humming along, the company was on an acquisition spree, gobbling up a variety of artificial intelligence and robotics companies. During this spree they acquired a small and mysterious company named DeepMind for over $500 million. At the time, DeepMind had only about 50 employees. Its website appeared to consist of a single webpage listing its founders and two email addresses.

Google holds an all-hands meeting at the end of every week called TGIF. The founders and other leaders of the company use the meeting to make announcements and to share details on projects within its various organizations. A number of months after Google acquired DeepMind, word spread around the company that DeepMind would be presenting at TGIF. Everyone at Google could finally learn what the secretive unit had been working on this whole time.

DeepMind explained at the meeting that they had figured out how to let a computer program teach itself how to play a wide variety of Atari games, including classic games like *Space Invaders* and *Breakout*. After Deep-Mind allowed their program to play millions of games, it often became far better than human players.

DeepMind then gave a demonstration to the audience, showing them a video of its program playing *Space Invaders*, a game in which the player must move a spaceship around the bottom of the screen to shoot aliens before the aliens make their way down to the bottom (you might recognize screenshots of this game and of *Breakout* in figures 7.1a and 7.1b).

As the audience looked on intently, the program played the game impeccably. Every shot it fired hit a target. As the game's round neared its end, a single alien remained. The computer fired one stray shot, as the alien was moving step by step away from the missile and toward the right side of the screen. The humans in the room relaxed slightly: maybe this AI wasn't a threat to their existence after all.

And then, as the audience continued to look on, the alien bounced off the side of the screen and began moving back toward the screen's center.

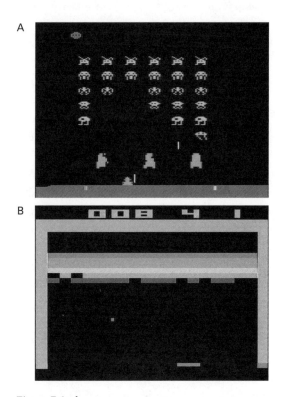

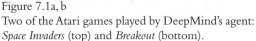

Figure 7.1a, b
Two of the Atari games played by DeepMind's agent:
Space Invaders (top) and *Breakout* (bottom).

The program's strategy became clear. The alien moved directly into the trajectory of the stray missile and was destroyed. The computer had won a flawless game. The room erupted in cheers.

Why was the audience of Googlers so excited? Hadn't IBM created Deep Blue to defeat the Garry Kasparov, the world's best chess player nearly two decades earlier, in 1997? Hadn't Watson defeated the *Jeopardy!* champion Ken Jennings in 2011? Didn't Google's engineers already know about its self-driving cars, which had traveled nearly 700,000 autonomous miles on the road? If self-driving cars were possible, why was everyone impressed that a computer could beat a simple video game, when computers had been playing video games competitively for years?

The computer program was so impressive because it had learned how to play the game without any human guidance. Earlier breakthroughs had involved a high degree of human judgment and tweaking for the algorithms to work. With the self-driving car, a human needed to carefully develop the features for detecting drivable terrain and then tell the car that it could drive on that terrain. A human needed to manually create the finite state machines in the self-driving car's Monopoly board module. Self-driving cars had not learned how to drive on their own by trial and error.

In contrast, the DeepMind program was never told by a programmer that tapping the joystick left would make the spaceship move left, or that hitting the button would shoot a missile, or even that shooting a missile at an alien would destroy the alien and earn it points. The only inputs to the Atari-playing agent were the raw pixels on the screen—their red, green, and blue colors—and the current score.[2] Even more impressively, DeepMind used the same program to learn how to play all of 49 Atari games—the majority of which it learned to play well—with no hand-tuning whatsoever. All that the program needed was the time to practice each game. DeepMind did this with an idea called *reinforcement learning*, a field of artificial intelligence devoted to giving computer programs the ability to learn from experience.

REINFORCEMENT LEARNING

In this chapter and the next I'll explain the key intuition behind how DeepMind used reinforcement learning to master these Atari games.[3] Computer programs that use this technique learn to do things when they receive occasional rewards or punishments; so to train them, we just need to program them to seek these incentives—and then we need to give them these incentives when they've done something we want them to do (or not do) again. Just as your dog will learn to follow your commands when you give him a treat, a program that learns by reinforcement learning—the lingo for such a program in the AI community is *agent*—will also learn to follow your commands.

Reinforcement-learning agents may seem too smart to be automata, but, as we'll see in the next two chapters, they still follow deterministic programs. Once the Atari-playing agent had been trained, for example, the agent just needed to look at the four most-recent screenshots from an Atari game (see figure 7.2). After looking at these screen shots, it evaluated a mathematical function to select a joystick action: left, right, or press the "fire" button, for example. It then repeated this process, over and over again, looking at the recent screenshots of the game and selecting an action based on what it saw, until the game was over. As you might guess, though, the magic wasn't in how it played the game: as I just explained, that part was simple. The real magic was in how it *learned* to play the game—and in how it *perceived* what was happening on the screen. In this chapter we'll begin with the first of those questions: How can an agent learn which actions to take given its past experience?

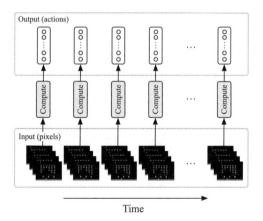

Time

Figure 7.2
DeepMind's Atari-playing agent ran continuously. At any given moment, it would receive the last four screenshots' worth of pixels as an input, and then it would run an algorithm to decide on its next actions and output its action.

I'll use a virtual game of golf to illustrate how reinforcement learning works. With this game of golf, which we'll play on the course shown in figure 7.3a, the goal of the agent is to hit the golf ball into the hole in as few strokes as possible. We're interested in designing an agent that can "learn" in which direction it should swing to get it closer to the hole when it's in different parts of the golf course. Should it aim north, east, south, or west? To teach the agent, we will train it until it has enough experience to play golf on its own. At that point, it will be able to select on its own the direction in which it should to aim to make progress toward the hole, no matter where it is on the course.

Are we overcomplicating things? Do we really need to use reinforcement learning to tell the agent where to aim on the golf course? Couldn't we just program the agent to aim directly toward the hole? As you'll see in the next section, that's not a viable option because there will be many obstacles in the way. Instead, the agent will need to make subtle adjustments to its swings depending on where it is on the course. Reinforcement learning won't just be *a* tool for the job; it will be *the* tool for the job.

INSTRUCTIONS TO THE AGENT

You, the agent, will play golf on the course shown in figure 7.3a. You can aim your swing in any of the cardinal directions (north, east, south, or west) or halfway between these (northeast, southeast, northwest, or southwest). If you succeed in hitting the ball, it will move one square in the direction you aimed, as in figure Figure 7.3b, and your hope is to use as few strokes as possible to get the ball into the hole. Note also that this is a humongous golf course, so it might take 150 strokes or so to play a full round.

Two more things will make this game of golf interesting. First, and most importantly, there are explosive mines all over the place, as shown in figure 7.3c. You know where these mines are as you play the game—and they stay fixed every time you play the game—but you must avoid stepping on them at all costs.

The mines wouldn't be a problem if you could aim perfectly, so I'm going to add a final rule to make this game more difficult: the ball will not always move in the direction you swing. Sometimes it will end up in a different cell adjacent to you, and sometimes it may not move at all. You could attribute this to whatever you want—maybe it's wind, or maybe it's

A

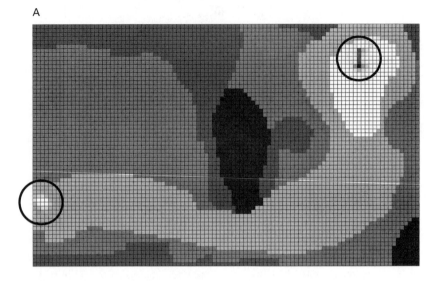

Figure 7.3a
The golf course used in the reinforcement-learning example. Terrain types, ranging
from light grey to dark black: the green (least difficult), fairway, rough, sand trap, and
water hazard (most difficult). The starting point is on the left, and the goal is in the
top-right corner.

B

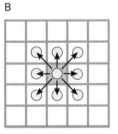

Figure 7.3b
Your goal is to hit the ball from the start position into the hole in as few swings as
possible; the ball moves only one square (or zero squares) per swing.

c

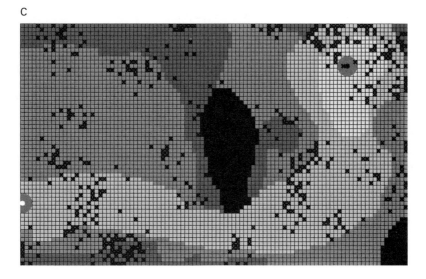

Figure 7.3c
The golf course also has explosive mines, each of which is marked with an *x*. You must avoid hitting these.

a bad swing. You don't know details of how it moves when you swing—there's some randomness involved—but you suspect that the ball is more difficult to hit on difficult terrain like *rough* than on easy terrain like *green*; these are all details you need to learn from experience. From easiest to most difficult, the types of terrain are *green*, *fairway*, *rough*, and *sand trap*. There is also a *water hazard*. If you hit the ball into the water hazard, you've wasted a stroke and need to retry from your last place on the course.

What should your strategy be to get the ball into the hole in as few strokes as possible? Should you aim directly for the hole no matter where you are, crossing the sand trap if need be? Should you try to stay on the fairway and the green so you can maintain control of the ball? And how far from the mines should you stay to remain safe?

PROGRAMMING THE AGENT

The answer to these questions will depend on a lot of factors, but even if the agent doesn't have this information, we can still teach it a good strategy if we let it play for a while and give it rewards at the right times. How

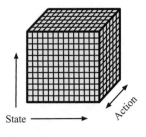

State ——————→   Action

Figure 7.4

do we train the agent? We will offer it an immediate reward of a chocolate bar (for a value of 1) whenever it has reached the end position—the
hole at the end of the golf course—at which time the game ends. If the
agent steps on a mine, we will punish it with an electric shock that is equal
to a reward of minus one-half a chocolate bar (value of −1/2). For stepping
onto any other square, we'll neither give it a reward nor punish it.

The more interesting and technically challenging question we need to
answer is: *How can we create an agent that can learn from these rewards?* We can't
just give the agent chocolate bars and expect it to do what we want. We
also need it to know that chocolate bars are worth seeking.

There are two observations that will help us to answer this question. The
first relates to how we let the agent store its model of the world. The model
must summarize the agent's experience in a way that it can use to make
future decisions. Let's have the agent store its model of the world in a giant
cube of numbers, like the one in figure 7.4.

Each cell of this cube will store a number that tells the agent the
expected "value"—that is, how much chocolate it should expect to
receive—for taking certain actions from different positions on the course.
Each time the agent needs to decide which action to take, it looks up all
eight actions for its current position—those actions form a "stack" of
values going straight through the cube—and then it selects whichever
action has the highest value. After taking this action, the agent will find
itself in another state—possibly a state it didn't expect to find itself in—
and it will repeat the same process. If the cube already has the correct
values filled in, this strategy seems like it could work, and it's simple
enough that we could encode it even with a physical device, to create a
mechanical automaton. But this still begs the question: How do we figure
out which values go into each cell of the cube?

To answer that question, we need to make another key observation, this time about what the values in the cube should represent. Note that if the agent moves to a state that's not the end goal, the agent receives no chocolate bar. This is problematic because a lack of rewards conveys little sense of progress to the agent. We might say that the "landscape" of rewards in the golf course is too flat. If the agent followed rewards blindly in this environment, it would struggle to make progress. This brings us to the final observation we need to design a reinforcement-learning agent: even when the agent receives no chocolate bar from some state, it still has the *opportunity* to eventually reach the chocolate bar from that state. The values in the cube should represent, at least intuitively, this opportunity.

One property we want in designing this idea of "opportunity" for the agent is that the agent should prefer to receive chocolate bars sooner rather than later. This makes intuitive sense: if your dog is across the room and you hold out your hand with a treat for your dog, he will immediately bound over to you. Provided that you've already trained your dog to do some tricks, he will sit and roll over, maybe even before you've given him the commands to do so. Your dog is behaving in a way that will earn him a treat as soon as possible. If the dog has a choice between doing something to get the treat now and doing the same thing to get the treat in thirty seconds, he will do what it takes to get it now. However we decide to define this idea of "opportunity," our hope is that this preference for chocolate bars sooner rather than later will fall out naturally from that definition.

We can formalize this idea of opportunity—again, the opportunity is the value we want represented by each cell of the cube—by defining it as the total of all future chocolate bars the agent can expect to receive, adjusted for how long it will take the agent to receive those bars. A chocolate bar far into the future should be worth less than a chocolate bar now. This time-adjustment works a lot like how you would value money. Let's say you could put a $10 bill into a change machine for $10 in quarters. If the machine had a delay of one day—that is, you put in your $10 today and get $10 in quarters tomorrow, you probably wouldn't think it's a good trade-off, because you've given up the ability to spend that money in the meantime and because there's some uncertainty that you'll be able to recover it tomorrow. So maybe you'd be willing to put just $8 into the machine today to get your $10 in quarters tomorrow. If the machine had a two-day delay, you'd be even less willing to put in money today—maybe you'd be willing to put, say, just $6.40 into the machine. The longer you need to wait to receive some reward, the lower the value you'll typically assign to that reward. Researchers call this idea *temporal discounting* (but I'll just call it *time adjustment* from now on).

To program an agent to seek out the opportunity to earn chocolate bars, then, we will need to develop a way to fill in each cell of the cube with an estimate of the total of all chocolate the agent should expect for taking an action, adjusted for how long it will take to receive each payout of chocolate in the future.[4] Actions with high values in the cube suggest more chocolate, earlier chocolate, more frequent chocolate, or some combination of these; while actions with low values suggest smaller, fewer, or later chocolate bars. An agent in a certain state faced with a choice between an action that offers a time-adjusted reward of 2.5 pounds of chocolate, and another action that offers a time-adjusted reward of 1.5 pounds of chocolate, should choose the first one.

This time adjustment gives the agent a chance at making progress toward the hole when the majority of the actions it takes lead to no chocolate bars. It turns the flat landscape faced by the agent into a hilly landscape, where the reward is at the peak of a mountain. The agent doesn't actually do any complex planning: at each step it simply needs to "follow the gradient" in an effort to reach the top of the mountain.

This time adjustment also gives us a knob to adjust for the agent. This knob controls the tradeoff between having the agent seek an immediate reward and having it take a path that might postpone the reward for an even bigger reward later. Usually the way we apply this time adjustment is by multiplying the reward by a fixed amount between 0 and 1 for every unit of time—every hour, second, or day, for example—the agent needs to wait to receive its reward. This multiplier changes the reward landscape the agent sees, and it controls how much willpower the agent has: if it's close to 0, the agent will tend to think very short-term, taking whatever chocolate it can get as soon as possible, even if that means giving up chocolate down the road. If this number is close to 1, the agent will be willing to give up short-term chocolate in favor of even more chocolate later.[5]

HOW THE AGENT SEES THE WORLD

One obvious difference between a dog and DeepMind's Atari-playing agent—aside from the fact that dogs aren't supposed to eat chocolate—is that the dog lives in the real world, while the Atari-playing agent lives in a simulated, virtual world. Instead of sitting or begging for treats, the Atari agent's actions are limited to whichever joystick actions it can play in the game. And instead of using its eyes, ears, and nose to perceive the world around it, the Atari agent must perceive its world by looking at the pixels on the screen and tasting the virtual treats we give it. When DeepMind designed the agent, they needed some way to link what was happening in the game with what the agent perceived. How could they do this in a simple, coherent way that made their agent easy to reason about?

Fortunately for DeepMind, researchers at the University of Alberta had created a platform called the Arcade Learning Environment, which enabled them to let the agent move around in its Atari universe. The environment was built on top of an Atari emulator—that is, a program that mimics the behavior of an Atari console—and the environment pulled information directly from these games' computer memory.[6] By using the Arcade Learning Environment, DeepMind could simply "look up" the inputs to its agent—the pixels and the current score—to present them as sensory input to their agent, and send the agent's commands to the environment to be interpreted as joystick actions. The Arcade Learning Environment then dealt with the messy details of simulating the Atari world correctly.

NUGGETS OF EXPERIENCE

From everything we've seen so far, we still don't have a concrete way to fill in the values of the action-value cube. We know that each value of the cube should represent the time-adjusted chocolate the agent will receive in the future, and we know that to create an agent to use these values, we need to program it to select the action with the highest value for whichever state it's in; but it's not clear how to compute the values that go into the cube in the first place.

If we had perfect information about the game—such as how likely we are to hit the ball in a certain direction on each area of the course—then we could use some mathematical formulas from the field of reinforcement learning to compute the values of the entire cube without ever having the agent play a game. But perfect information is a luxury we don't have. In the golf game, as with Atari games, we don't even know how likely we are to end up in different states after performing an action.

DeepMind resolved this problem by having their agent learn the values in the cube by trial and error. At first, their agent chose completely random actions so it could learn from experience which state-action pairs tended to be followed by rewards. Using a trick from the field of reinforcement learning called *off-policy learning*, the agent learned a good strategy for its games even though it stumbled around randomly. Then, as the agent gained experience, it began to prefer actions that weren't random.

Let's apply an off-policy learning algorithm to the golf game. First we let the agent play through a game, selecting random actions each time it needs to make a move. This will generate a sequence of state-action pairs, as in the left panel of figure 7.5. After the agent has played through the game, we need to update the values in the action-value cube using what the agent experienced during the game.

We can summarize the agent's experience by breaking it into chunks, each of which has several bits of information: what state it was in when it selected and performed an action, which action it chose (north, northeast, east, and so on), which state it ended up in after it made its action, and whether it earned or lost any chocolate when it reached the next state. You can see such a chunk outlined in the left side of figure 7.5. The agent will learn everything it needs to from these "nuggets" of experience.

We need some way to update the value of the action-value cube to incorporate each of these nuggets. If the agent ended up at its final destination—the hole—*after* experiencing some state-action pair, we nudge the value of that state-action pair in the cube a little bit toward the reward of 1. We don't set it to 1; we just nudge it a little bit toward 1. If a state-action pair led to a spot on the course with an explosive mine, we nudge the value of the state-action pair a bit toward −1/2. Otherwise, we nudge the value of the state-action pair closer to 0. When I use the word "nudge," I'm using the term casually, but reinforcement learning offers a mathematically precise way to adjust these values that agrees well enough with the intuitive meaning of the word.

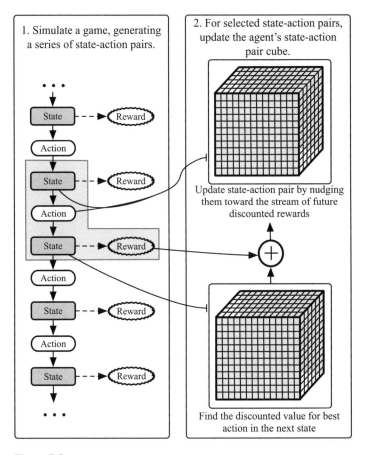

Figure 7.5
One way to train a reinforcement-learning agent is with simulation. First the agent plays through a game to generate a series of state–action pairs and rewards, as shown in the left panel. Next, as shown in the right panel, the agent's estimate of future rewards for taking different actions when it's on a given state is updated using the state–action pairs experienced by the agent. This particular method is sometimes called "temporal difference, or TD, learning."

This is enough to teach the agent about the rewards it will see immediately after its action. But remember: we want the action-value cube to represent the time-adjusted stream of *all* future chocolate, since we want the agent to pick actions that will move it toward chocolate even when it is far away. We need some way to estimate the stream of chocolate the agent will see after this action. And herein lies the secret to training the agent: since we already know from the experience-nugget the state in which the agent ended up after choosing some action, we can look this information up in the cube itself!

More specifically, since we already know that the agent's strategy is to select the *best* action for whichever state it's in, then we can figure out exactly which action a clever agent will take *after* the experience-nugget. Because we know—by definition—that the cube stores the amount of time-adjusted chocolate the agent will receive for that next action, we can use that information to update the current state-action pair.

Since that action (and its chocolate) are one step into the future, we time-adjust the chocolate the agent will receive for that future action, and then we nudge our original state-action pair toward the value of that time-adjusted chocolate. To train the agent, we repeat this process for the states the agent visited during its game, and then we repeat this process for many games.

This self-referential trick might set off some alarm bells in your head. When we first start training the agent, the numbers in the cube will be garbage. Combine this with the fact that the agent starts out by selecting random actions, and it's hard to believe it could possibly learn a good strategy. Doesn't garbage in equal garbage out? It's true that the values in the action-value cube will start out very bad at first, and the initial changes we make to the cube won't be very helpful. But the quality of learning will gradually improve over time.

There's an important assumption I've made about the world hidden in the way I've described how the agent populates and uses the action-value cube. Here is the assumption: in anticipating the agent's future, the only state that's relevant is its current state. This doesn't mean that its past states and actions don't matter: they might have been important in getting the agent to its current state. But once we know the agent's current state, we can forget about everything before that, because we assume its current state captures all of the history that's relevant in anticipating its future. This is often called a Markovian assumption. While simple, the Markovian assumption enables us to update the action-value cube with experience nuggets that link the past to the future, so that the values in the action-value cube themselves link the past to the future. This is how, with each game the agent plays, the cube's values will become a little more accurate. The cells of the cube will improve in a virtuous cycle, as they change from "bad" to "good" to "great."

In each game of golf, the sequence of states the agent visits form a "trajectory" on the golf course. You can see what some of these trajectories look like in figures 7.6a and 7.6b. At first, on the top, the agent moves around completely randomly, and it takes many strokes to reach the hole at the end. With a few games, the agent can bumble toward the hole at the end of the course. Once it has played through a few thousand games, however, it moves precisely around the mines. In the lower half of the figure, you can see that the agent is even able to anticipate and steer to avoid the mines far in advance of reaching them. Once the agent has learned a perfect strategy, it still bumbles a bit: there's no way for it to avoid the randomness it faces in each swing. But the agent has become optimal in a different way: it learns to anticipate the mines long in advance of reaching them.

PLAYING ATARI WITH REINFORCEMENT LEARNING

The method I describe in this chapter is one of the most common ways reinforcement learning is used in practice. In this method, the agent moves around from state to state by selecting different actions, and we give the agent rewards—chocolate—when it has done something we approve of. When it needs to perform an action, the agent references its action-value cube: it looks up which actions it can make, selects the one with the highest time-adjusted reward stream—and performs that action, moving to a different state and possibly receiving another reward as a result. When we want to train the agent, we let it play many games and then we use its "nuggets" of experience to update its action-value cube.

It's possible to play golf with this action-value cube because there were $60 \times 100 = 6,000$ states in the golf course and $6,000 \times 8 = 48,000$ cells in the action-value cube. That's a lot of cells, but it's not so many that we can't accurately estimate the values in this cube by telling the agent to bumble around randomly for a while.

Unfortunately the method I've just described wouldn't work if we wanted an agent that could play Atari. The problem is that the action-value

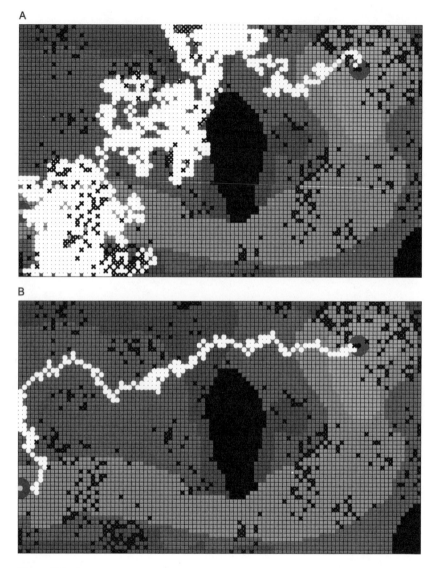

Figure 7.6a, b
Trajectories (white paths) made by the golf-playing agent. (a): a trajectory made by the agent after playing 10 games. (b): a trajectory made by the agent after playing 3,070 games.

cube needs to be many orders of magnitude larger for the Atari-playing agent than it is for our golf-playing agent.

As we saw at the beginning of the chapter, DeepMind considered the state in an Atari game to be the arrangement of the pixels on the screen for the past four screenshots.[7] For a game like *Space Invaders*, the action-value cube would need to keep track of many trillions of states.[8] The approach we used to estimate the values in the action-value cube when we played golf—learning by choosing actions randomly—wouldn't have worked, because we would need to play far too many games to fill up the action-value cube with reasonable values.

This may sound like just a technicality, but it's a very real limitation.[9] Even if we had enough time to fill up the cube, or even if we only needed to fill up a fraction of the cube, its size would also push up against the memory limits of computers. The cube for most Atari games would simply be too big.

DeepMind needed some other way to represent the information we put into the action-value cube. The tool they turned to was neural networks.

8 HOW TO BEAT ATARI GAMES BY USING NEURAL NETWORKS

NEURAL INFORMATION PROCESSING SYSTEMS

Even before Google acquired DeepMind in 2014, word about this new research company was spreading quietly. At a machine learning conference in late 2012, for instance, DeepMind had been competing aggressively with companies like Facebook and Google to recruit members of the machine learning community.[1] And conference attendees learned that the founder of this mysterious company was Demis Hassabis, a quiet, brilliant, and ambitious neuroscientist.

At the conference, known as Neural Information Processing Systems, artificial neural networks was one of the main topics for discussion. The excitement was unusually palpable: breakthroughs in the field had been occurring rapidly for the past few years. The convergence of better hardware, huge datasets, and new ways to train these networks was suddenly allowing researchers to create neural network architectures that could perform feats only dreamed of decades earlier. This year in particular, researchers from the University of Toronto had created a neural network that gave computers an uncanny ability to perceive objects in photographs.

APPROXIMATION, NOT PERFECTION

To create agents that play Atari games, we need some way to summarize which action the agent should take for each state it might find itself in. In chapter 7 we learned how a cube of state-action pairs keeps track of these values. If there aren't too many states or actions, this works swimmingly. But when we have a huge number of states—as with Atari games—the cube of state-action pairs grows unwieldy, and it's impossible to fill in the values for that cube in a reasonable amount of time.

Another way we can think about the action-value cube is by looking at these values as defining a mathematical function:

time-adjusted reward $= q$ (current state, joystick action).

Just as with the cube, this function tells the agent the time-adjusted stream of rewards it should expect for taking a certain action, assuming that the agent always chooses the best action after that. If the agent knows this function, it simply evaluates that function for each action it is considering and the state it's in, and then it chooses whichever action has the highest value. In reinforcement learning this function is called the action-value function or, simply, the q-function.

The problem with this q-function is that, if we want it to represent the action-value cube perfectly, then to encode that function on a computer, we would still need an enormous amount of disk space to store the program. We would run into the same problem we faced with the original cube.

The key to making this function tractable is the recognition that it doesn't need to be perfect. There is a lot of correlation in the values of the state-action cube, just as there was a lot of correlation in the Netflix ratings matrix. And as with matrix factorization, we can use that correlation to describe the function succinctly. If you're over on the left side of the golf course, for example, you need to generally head to the east, and if you're anywhere along the bottom of the course, you need to generally head north. Instead of trying to stuff the entire cube into the function, we can use a much simpler function—a function that uses characteristics about the state and actions— to *approximate* the value of the q-function. The idea is to create a classifier exactly like the one we used to create *The World's Best Recipes for Kids*; except that instead of classifying recipes, we'll be classifying state-action pairs.

For the children's cookbook, we chose features that were intuitive and easy to calculate. It's difficult to specify features that will be useful for an Atari-playing agent, since the features might vary from game to game. But at a high level, we want these features to simplify the original state space while still capturing the salient information that's useful for playing the game well.

For the q-function, we'll need something a little more complicated than a simple classifier. The form of the q-function needs to be flexible enough to approximate the true action-value cube well, which means that it should be able to represent a wide variety of functions. At the same time, we must be able to "train" the q-function with experience nuggets we collect from our simulations.

Neural networks have the properties we seek. Even better, they provide a way to automatically generate features so we don't need to worry about handcrafting them for 50 different games.

NEURAL NETWORKS AS MATHEMATICAL FUNCTIONS

A neural network is a biologically inspired mathematical function made up of artificial "neurons" that interact with one another. (I should point out that many neural network researchers believe that favoring a method because it's biologically inspired can be "fraught with danger.")

When researchers explain the structure of a neural network, they often draw a picture that looks something like the one in figure 8.1.

In that neural network diagram, each circle represents a neuron, and the arrows between neurons represent weights that describe the relationships between neurons. You can think of each neuron in the network as a little light bulb that is either on or off, depending on whether or not it is "activated." If it is activated, it can take a range of numerical values. It may glow very dimly, or it may be extraordinarily bright. If it is not activated, it will not glow at all. Whether each neuron is off or on—and, if it is on, how brightly it glows—depends on the brightness of the neurons that feed into it and the weights that connect those neurons to this one.

The greater the weight between a neuron pair, the greater the influence of the upstream neuron on the downstream one. If the weights between

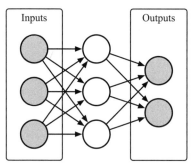

Figure 8.1
A simple neural network.

neurons are negative, a brightly glowing neuron will inhibit the brightness of the neuron it points to.

You can see how the value of a neuron depends on the values of upstream neurons in figure 8.2. You'll probably recognize immediately that this diagram is familiar: each neuron is just a simple weighted-average classifier with some function that squashes the output of the classifier in some way. In other words, the entire neural network is just a bunch of little classifiers wired together.

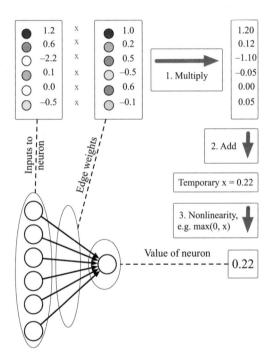

Figure 8.2
Propagation of values through a neural network. In neural networks, the value of a neuron is either specified by outside data—that is, it's an "input" neuron—or it is a function of other "upstream" neurons that act as inputs to it. When the value of the neuron is determined by other neurons, the values of the upstream neurons are weighted by the edges, summed, and passed through a nonlinear function such as max(x,0), tanh(x), or an S-shaped function, exp(x)/(exp(x) + 1).

To use a neural network, we typically set the input neurons to specific values—for example, to match the colors of pixels in an image—three numbers in the range 0 to 1 for each pixel—and then we "run" the network. When we run it, the brightness of the neurons in the first layer will determine the brightness of neurons in the next layer, which will determine the brightness of neurons in the following layer, and so on, the information flowing through the network until it reaches the output layer. By the time the output neurons are activated, their values will hopefully be useful for some purpose. In the case of an Atari-playing agent, these neurons will tell us which action the agent should take.

Despite the biological inspiration for neural networks, there's nothing mystical or mysterious about them. The brightness of the input neurons will determine precisely and unambiguously the brightness of the rest of the neurons in the network. Neural networks are just fancy calculators that evaluate a series of mathematical formulas; the connections between the neurons dictate, as in figure 8.2, what those formulas are. There's no uncertainty, randomness, or magic in figuring out whether different neurons in the network will glow, as long as we know the weights of all of the connections between the neurons along with how the input neurons were set. A neural network is a computer, and it is therefore a prime building block for an automaton.

The network above is called a *feedforward* neural network, because information flows through it in a single direction, from the inputs to the outputs. In general, a neural network could have a different number of neurons in each layer, or it may have a different number of layers, or it may not even be organized into layers; but this feedforward architecture is still very common, and it's what DeepMind used to play Atari games.

Let's step back for a moment, though. Why bother using a neural network at all? Are we overcomplicating things? Could we design a simpler approximation to the q-function, maybe with just a simple classifier?

If our goal were to design an agent that played a single, specific game, the answer is probably yes. We could carefully handcraft features for the game and combine them with a weighted-average classifier. But doing so wouldn't move us toward the goal of developing an automaton that can perform a wide variety of tasks, which was one of DeepMind's goals in designing the Atari-playing agent in the first place. Remember: DeepMind's agent could play about 50 different Atari games, many (but not all) of them very well, and DeepMind did no custom tuning for these games. It just let the agent play each game for a while. It *needed* a q-function that was flexible enough to play a wide variety of games.

It turns out that neural networks—even networks as simple as the one above—provide exactly the flexibility we need. An important theorem about neural networks, called the universal approximation theorem, states that if we were to use a network like the one above, with a single layer sandwiched between the input layer and the output layer, then we could approximate any function from the inputs to the outputs to any degree of accuracy.[2] This is a profound theorem. It tells us that *some* neural network will indicate the best possible moves to make in an Atari game, given the pixels on the screen—provided that we select the network's weights carefully. We just need to create the network to have the right shape and then find what those weights are, which brings us to the other major benefit of neural networks: their weights can easily be learned with data.

I show the universal approximation theorem in action in figure 8.3. First, look at the picture of the smiley face in figure 8.3a. This is a target we'd like to "predict" with a neural network. The remaining images in figure 8.3 show how well several neural networks with a single middle layer can approximate this target (the layers between the inputs and outputs are sometimes called "hidden" layers because we don't directly observe their values. The input layer to each of these networks is two neurons, which are set to the x and y coordinates of each pixel in the image. The output of each network is a single neuron, which describes how dark the pixel at those coordinates should be: 0 for black and 1 for white. As we add more neurons to the middle—that is, the hidden—layer of the network, it can approximate its smiley-face target better and better. Figure 8.3c, which has 200 hidden neurons, somewhat resembles the face, while figure 8.3d, which has 2,000 hidden neurons, very much resembles the face.

This network with a single hidden middle layer is the most "shallow" network we can use to still allow the network to represent arbitrary mappings from its input neurons to its output neurons. If we removed the middle layer and connected the input neurons directly to the output neurons, then the network wouldn't be nearly as expressive. Our approximation to the smiley face would just be a gray box that gradually ranges from light gray to dark gray in some direction. We wouldn't see eyes or a mouth. So we need at least one hidden layer between the inputs and the outputs.

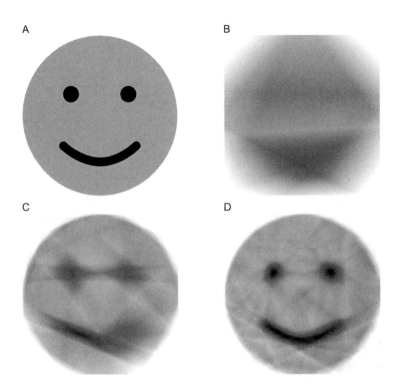

Figure 8.3
The performance of several neural networks (b)–(d) trained to represent a
target image (a). The networks take as their inputs the x and y coordinates
of each pixel in the image and predict the brightness of each pixel, in the
range 0 to 1.

The universal approximation theorem also doesn't say anything about
how big the middle layer of the network must be to approximate the smiley face as well as we'd like: we might need millions or billions of hidden
neurons to represent the face beyond the limits of human perception, just
as we might need millions of neurons in the hidden layer of a similar network to play Atari games. This observation is important to our goal of
building an Atari-playing agent, because such a network might be too large
to store on disk or too large to "train" with data, just as the original state-
action cube was. This is the price we pay for trying to stuff all of this information into a single hidden layer. But it doesn't mean that we can't design
a simpler network to play Atari in some other way—for example, by using
more layers with fewer neurons per layer.

Before we build a network for the Atari agent, then, we need answers for two questions: *What shape should we pick for the neural network? How do we select its weights?* In the rest of this chapter I'll answer these questions, and again we'll again use the golf game to build the network.

THE ARCHITECTURE OF AN ATARI-PLAYING NEURAL NETWORK

In figure 8.4 I show a neural network designed to play the golf game. It has an input layer that takes the agent's current position (x, y), an output layer that predicts in which of the eight directions the agent should aim, and a large hidden layer.

In this network, we will set the values of the input neurons so that they equal the coordinates of the current position of the ball using its position (x, y). When we run the network, the input neurons will activate the neurons in the middle hidden layer, and those neurons will then activate the output neurons. We want the output values of the network to approximate the values from the action-value cube we saw in the last chapter. Given the position of the ball, the output values of the network should be equal to the time-adjusted future rewards—that is, the amount of future chocolate—the agent should expect to receive for choosing that action.

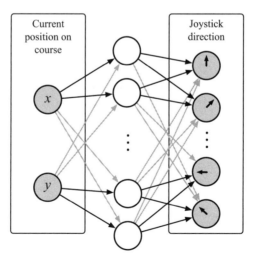

Figure 8.4

Once we've figured out this network's weights, the agent will be able to choose its moves by setting the input neurons of the network with its position on the course, evaluating the network to produce values for its eight actions, selecting the action with the highest weight, performing that action, and then repeating this process.

As before, we just need to let the agent bumble around for a while so we can use its nuggets of experience to give the agent chocolate or an electric shock at the right times. I'll explain in the next chapter how to "train" a neural network with data, but for now you just need to know that it's possible to do this. We know that this architecture will work because the universal approximation theorem tells us that it will: we've already seen this with the smiley faces in figure 8.3. Because we're starting with the coordinates (x, y), the network won't need to be too large; it just needs to store eight different maps of where the agent should go—one for each output direction.

But wait—doesn't the Atari-playing agent use raw pixel values instead of (x, y) coordinates as its input? I did kind-of cheat by letting our network take as its inputs the coordinates of the ball on the course instead of taking pixels representing the course. But it's easy to get around this: we can do so by adding more layers at the beginning of this network to convert raw pixels into the coordinates of the ball on the course. This will be the last leap that will enable us to create neural networks that can play Atari games.

I've done this in figure 8.5. The right two layers in this network perform the exact same function we saw above, transforming the current position (x, y) into output values predicting chocolate yield; so we just need to convince ourselves that the left two layers can turn an image into the (x, y) coordinates of the golf ball.

How could they do this? One way is to use a *convolutional layer* for the first hidden layer. A convolutional layer of a neural network contains classifiers that identify objects in the original input image, like the ball or the hole. Each classifier (we technically need only one in this case, to identify the ball's position) is applied over *every* 8 × 8 patch of pixels in the input image. The output of this layer contains one image for each classifier. Each pixel of each output image is the result of applying the classifier over the respective patches in the input layer: black if there was no match with the classifier and white if there was a match.

You can see how this works for a single classifier in figure 8.6, which shows a convolution that uses 3 × 3 patches instead of 8 × 8 patches. In the

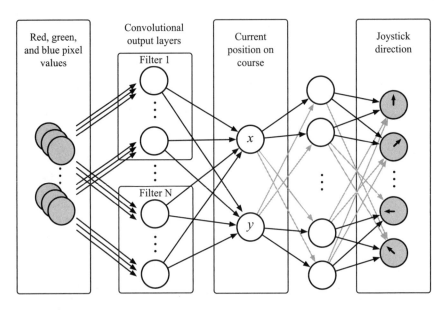

Figure 8.5
A neural network designed to play the game golf. The right two layers, from the "Current position on course" to the "Joystick direction," determine where the agent should aim, given the current position of the ball and the goal. The left two layers convert the pixels of the screen into the coordinates.

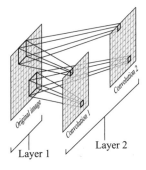

Figure 8.6
A convolutional layer with two filters. Each filter scans the image and produces a resulting image in which each "pixel" corresponds to a patch of the input image passed through that filter.

figure, a classifier predicts whether each patch in the original image matches a certain pattern. The convolutional layer produces an image that aligns with the input image and describes where that image matches whatever the filter is looking for.

How do these classifiers work? Each classifier is just a weighted-average classifier like the one we used for the kids' cookbook, possibly followed by a squashing function (more on this function in the next few pages). Remember: that's all a neuron in a neural network is. Each pixel in the output of the convolutional layer is a neuron, where the weights correspond to the classifier's weights.

To make things more concrete, let's just assume that the golf course is a grayscale image, and that we're using the original start-position of the ball and goal from the last chapter. The pictures in figures 8.7a and 8.7b show weights for classifiers that classify the flagpole and the ball from the original golf course in figure 7.2a. These filters will "activate"—that is, they will produce a value of 1—exactly when they are directly over the flagpole or the ball, respectively; otherwise they will produce a value of 0. If you squint a little, it's clear that the filter in figure 8.7a looks a bit like the flagpole. The filter in 8.7b (for the ball) is less intuitive. It looks for lightly colored pixels surrounded by darker pixels, which is the defining characteristic of the ball.

The output of these convolutional filters is *two* images, each the result of applying one of the two classifiers over the original image, as you can see in figure 8.8. The output images are mostly black, except for one neuron in each that is glowing where the filter has found its pattern in the input image.

To get from the second layer to the third layer, we simply need a mapping from each "pixel" in a black-and-white image to the coordinates (x, y) of the white pixel. The network has no idea that the pixel at one place in the image is adjacent to its neighbors: it just sees each image as big list of numbers. However, the network can learn the mapping from each pixel to its position by seeing enough data and encoding each neuron's coordinates into the weights themselves, as shown in figure 8.9.

Now it turns out that this last step—that is, converting the output of the convolutional layer into coordinates—is useful for interpreting what's happening in the network, but it's not a necessary step for the network to work. Because we didn't squash the neurons' values after converting the position of the ball to its coordinates, it's mathematically possible to fully

Figure 8.7a–b
Convolutional filters for the flagpole in the hole (left) and the ball (right).

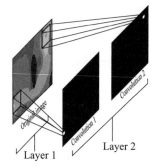

Figure 8.8
A convolutional layer with two filters. The filters are classifiers that scan the input image looking for certain patterns. The output of each filter is a set of neurons, organized as an image, which are "bright" wherever patches of pixels in the original image matched the filter.

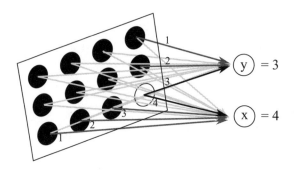

Figure 8.9
A layer that converts white pixels in a convolutional layer into coordinates. In this figure, the weight between a pixel and the neuron giving the x-coordinate is equal to the x-coordinate of that pixel, and the weight between a pixel and the neuron giving the y-coordinate is equal to the y-coordinate of the pixel. If the neuron at (4,3) in the left layer is glowing with a value of 1 and all other neurons are dark, then the values of the output of this layer will reflect this: they will be x=4 and y=3.

connect the output of the convolutional layer to the final hidden layer before the output, and setting the weights to account for this. That lets us skip the middle layer that stores the (x, y) coordinates of the ball entirely.

And with this, we've constructed a network that is similar in spirit to the one used by the Atari-playing neural network. The first layer is a convolutional layer that looks for objects on the screen, squashing the result into the range 0 to 1. This layer is then fully connected to a hidden layer with 32 units, followed by another squashing function, and the result is fully connected to the output layer, the values of which represent the time-adjusted stream of chocolate the agent can expect to receive for taking different actions.

There are a few differences between this network and the one used by the Atari-playing agent. We used only two filters for the golf game (and we only needed to use one), but the Atari-playing agent used 32 separate filters in its first convolutional layer. The output of this first layer was then placed into 32 separate images, where each image glowed wherever the original image matched the respective filter. Since it had 32 filters, it could search for a wide variety of objects, from the paddle in the game *Pong* to the aliens or spaceships in *Space Invaders*. You can see an example of how it might apply this with several filters in figure 8.10.

The Atari-playing network also had more convolutional layers than our golf network. The layers were stacked, so that the output of one layer was the input to the next layer. A later version of their network had three convolutional layers followed by the same two fully connected layers. By using three convolutional layers, their network could find more complex patterns of the input image. We'll get some more intuition for why this can be useful in the next chapter, when we look at how deep neural networks can accurately interpret the content of photographs.

The architecture of this agent is somewhat reminiscent of the architectures in Stanley and Boss. You can compare the architecture of the Atari agent in figure 8.11 with Boss's architecture, which was figure 4.2. An important part of those architectures was a separation of the components into a perception layer and a reasoning layer. The "perception" part of the Atari agent is the neural network, which takes the raw pixels on the screen and transforms them into useful features about the world. The "reasoning" part of the Atari agent is nothing more than a program that continuously looks at the output values of the neural network and selects the action with

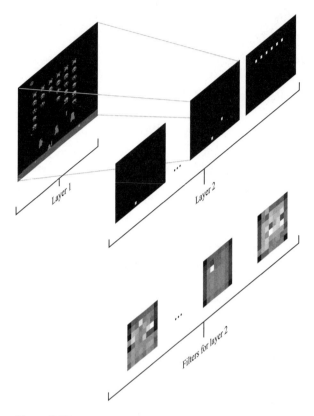

Figure 8.10
The convolutional layer of the Atari neural network. Layer 1
shows the input to the network: a screenshot of the game
(the Atari network actually used 4 recent screenshots). The
next layer is a convolutional layer that searches for 32 distinct
patterns of pixels in the first layer with 32 filters. The result of
applying each filter is 32 images, each of which is close to 0
everywhere except where the filter matches part of the input
screenshot.

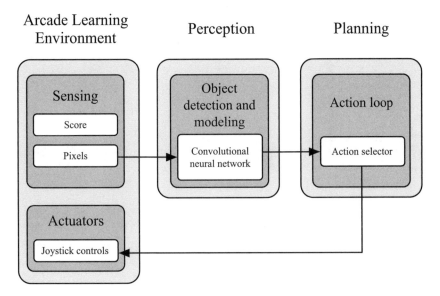

Figure 8.11
The architecture for an Atari-playing agent.

the highest value. You might even interpret this action-selection loop as a very simple type of "search" algorithm, whose goal is to search for the best among eight actions.

DIGGING DEEPER INTO NEURAL NETWORKS

Atari was in many ways a perfect testbed for DeepMind to demonstrate the strengths of neural networks. Atari games provided an explicit objective function for the agent—the number of points it had scored—while simultaneously offering a virtually unlimited amount of data for DeepMind to train its networks. Since the University of Alberta researchers had developed the Arcade Learning Environment, DeepMind could focus solely on the task of developing an agent that could play many games, exactly as the creators of the learning environment had intended. As we'll see in chapter 9, quantity of data is one of the most important factors allowing us to train complex neural networks.

We've seen, at least at a high level, what happens in the neural network as it plays an Atari game. But many questions remain unanswered. For example, when does the Atari-playing agent *not* perform well?

Although the agent used the same neural network architecture—that is, three convolutional layers followed by two fully connected layers—for each game, it learned different network weights for each game it played. After training, it played 29 of these games better than professional human players could play them.

The neural network performed best relative to humans on the Atari game *Video Pinball*. In pinball, the most important task of the agent is to react to a relatively small part of the game: where the pins hit the ball. The network simply needs to react, quickly and precisely, when the ball is near the bottom of the screen. The game also allows the player to "tilt" the pinball machine in either direction to nudge the ball to a better position. The agent could use this tilt operation to position the ball perfectly as it approaches the bottom of the screen. Since the network could learn about motion, and since it could react with machine precision, it earned about 20 times more points than professional human players at the game.[3]

The agent performed terribly on the game *Montezuma's Revenge*.[4] In *Montezuma's Revenge*, the player is expected to explore a labyrinthine underground Aztec pyramid (think of *Super Mario Brothers* with ladders). The player moves from room to room while avoiding enemies and searching for jewels. The second-most-difficult game for the agent was a game called *Private Eye*, in which the player must search for clues and items throughout a city.

Both of these games involve exploration, which requires the player to maintain context throughout the game. The player must keep track of what it has done and what it hasn't done, where it has gone and where it needs to go next. The Atari-playing agent couldn't do this because it had no memory. It had no way to keep track of which rooms it had visited and which it hadn't visited, of what it had done and what it hadn't done.

There was also another, related reason it couldn't play these games well. Remember that the agent initially trained itself by choosing completely random actions. By taking random actions, the agent couldn't make much progress in games that required exploration. In *Montezuma's Revenge*, the agent just stepped and bounced around the room, rarely if ever making it past the first room of the labyrinth. Because it couldn't make much progress in its exploration, it couldn't earn enough points to learn anything useful. Later we'll see some ways agents can keep track of game state, but I'll warn you now that we won't get all of the answers we need: this is still an open problem and an active area of research for reinforcement-learning researchers.

One of the more successful parts of the Atari agent was its ability to perceive its world with convolutional neural networks. While relatively new, deep convolutional networks have quickly matured in the past few years, to the extent that computers can now classify objects in photographs better than many humans. In the next few chapters, we'll take a look under the hood of some of these networks to see get a better sense for how they can do this.

9 ARTIFICIAL NEURAL NETWORKS' VIEW OF THE WORLD

THE MYSTIQUE OF ARTIFICIAL INTELLIGENCE

In 2016, a *Bloomberg News* reporter wrote that several startup companies had begun offering intelligent "chatbots" as personal assistants.[1] One of these chatbots, named Amy Ingram, was marketed by her company as "a personal assistant who schedules meetings for you." You simply needed to "cc" Amy to an email thread for her to do her magic. Users of the service liked Amy's "humanlike tone" and "eloquent manners." One user said she was "actually better than a human for this task." Some men even asked her out on dates.[2]

Before we get into the details of how Amy worked, let's go back in time a bit to see some trends in machine learning leading up to her debut. Beginning around 2006 and extending for the next decade, the ability of computers to recognize the contents of images and other media has improved dramatically because of a technology known as deep neural networks. These are like the networks we saw in the last chapter, but many layers deep. By some metrics, deep networks are now better than humans at recognizing objects in photographs, and they've become capable of artistic feats like rendering photographs as "paintings"—complete with brush strokes—and going the other way, creating photorealistic renderings of paintings. These breakthroughs have been the result of several factors, including more data, better hardware, better neural network architectures, and better ways to train these networks.

In the last chapter we learned to think about a neural network as a mapping that takes some input (pixels in an image) and produces some output (the value of performing joystick actions). Importantly—and consistent with the fact that neural networks can be the building blocks of automata—the mapping from inputs to outputs is fixed. There's nothing magical or unpredictable about neural networks. Rather, they're the exact opposite: perfectly predictable. Neural networks are just deterministic functions, compositions of the simple operations performed by their artificial neurons, which are just classifiers when we look at them closely enough.

We also learned that a network with just a single hidden layer can represent any function, from the network's inputs to its outputs, to any degree of accuracy—provided that that hidden layer is big enough.[3] Finding this function is just a matter of adjusting the weights of the network like knobs until it gives us the output we want, for whichever input we might give it. And as I mentioned in the last chapter, it's possible to fit these weights automatically, by training the neural network with data.

At this point we might pause to ask ourselves whether these two facts are sufficient to say we understand neural networks well enough to move on to other topics. We know that it's theoretically possible for a neural network with a single hidden layer to represent any function, and we know that it's possible to train the network by feeding it enough data. Is this enough?

I'll make the case below that the answer is an emphatic *no*. Knowing that it's possible to train a neural network to recognize whatever we want still doesn't shed light on important details, like what internal representation the neural network uses to understand the world, how a network could classify objects in photographs, and when a network won't work well. Knowing these details is important for us if we hope to understand the capabilities and limitations of neural networks and the automata made out of them. Let's turn briefly to a famous automaton for a more concrete lesson on why this is true.

THE AUTOMATON CHESS PLAYER, OR THE TURK

A mysterious mechanical device was built in the year 1770, a few decades after Vaucanson's Flute Player. Like the Flute Player, this device was an automaton, and it looked and moved like a human. It sat at a desk, surrounded by the haze of two nearby candelabra. This device could perform an impressive—albeit mechanical—feat on the chessboard called the knight's tour. Holding the chess piece with its gloved hand, which was attached to a wooden arm and torso, the device could move the knight from square to square with legal chess moves, visiting each square of the chessboard exactly once.

More impressively, this strange device could also play an expert game of chess, winning its games against the vast majority of human competitors.[4]

The public was even more enamored of the device than of the Flute Player; they came to know this one as the Automaton Chess Player, or sometimes, simply, as the Turk, given its headdress and the rest of its garb.[5] The device's owners took it around Europe and eventually to parts of the New World for public demonstrations, as growing crowds of spectators stared at it in awe, puzzling over its mechanical secrets. It even played legendary games against Napoleon and Benjamin Franklin in Paris.

But how did it work? Skeptics suspected that there was a child hidden inside, but the device's owners invariably showed spectators its innards before they gave presentations. The spectators had seen clear through the Turk's desk as the operator opened various drawers for them, one by one. They saw the mass of clock-like gears that powered the device. They even heard the whir of these gears, all devised by a mechanical genius who also had an inkling for building steam engines and devices to replicate human speech. When the operator lifted the robes of the human-like Turk to reveal its backside, the spectators saw that it was just wood and gears; the wooden figure was definitely not a person in a costume.[6] And to make matters even more confusing, the original owner presented a small, coffin-like box that he claimed was necessary for the device to run properly, which he peered into from time to time. People wondered whether it was somehow magical.

Speculation abounded, as books with titles like *Inanimate Reason* were published to make sense of the phenomenon. Unlike Vaucanson, who shared his device's workings with the French Academy of Sciences, the owners of the chess-playing automaton kept its workings a closely held secret.

The Turk was eventually destroyed in a fire some 84 years after it was built. Despite years of speculation, the secret of the automaton was never fully revealed during its lifetime. It had remained shrouded in mystery for two generations.

After it was destroyed, the son of the device's final owner recognized that there was little reason to keep the secret, so he described the machine in a series of articles. The Turk was operated by an expert human chess player who was hidden inside the desk.[7] It was nothing more than a giant puppet that used misdirection and some clever mechanics to trick viewers into thinking there was no human operator. The setup included magnets to transmit information through the chessboard to the hidden puppeteer and a sliding seat that enabled the chess player to move out of sight as the mechanic opened various drawers before the game. During the games, the puppeteer worked by candlelight within the dark confines of the desk. The smoke of his candle, in turn, was disguised by the haze of the candelabra. And the mysterious coffin-like box and clockwork served no useful purpose except to distract the audience. It was misdirection, a ruse to make it look as though the Turk was driven by other forces.

MISDIRECTION IN NEURAL NETWORKS

The Turk, with its "mysterious" mechanics, demonstrates that we should be unwilling to accept an answer such as "it works because it uses a neural network," because that's exactly the sort of thinking that allowed people to believe in the Turk. It leaves us open to getting caught up in some of the unfounded hype in AI, when that attention could be better focused on the more promising breakthroughs. Even worse, this careless thinking could leave us open to believing in hoaxes like the Turk—hoaxes that we still see every day. For example, Amy Ingram, the "artificially intelligent" chatbot I described at the beginning of this chapter, appeared to be such a hoax (although, if you looked at the fine print in her company's advertising, you might conclude that humans could step in from time to time, and you might call it "rosy marketing" instead of a hoax). Several of the companies offering these bots were powered by humans working behind the scenes around the clock. Amy, for example, was powered by a variety of people, including, sometimes, a 24-year-old dude named Willie Calvin.[8]

One way to be sure we aren't falling for hoaxes or for rosy marketing like this is to study these devices carefully, as we'll do in the next few chapters, and to insist on a clear exposition from their creators about how they work. It's unreasonable to expect everyone to understand these things in detail: people are busy, automata old and new are complicated, and the technology behind them continues to change rapidly. In those cases, however, we can still insist that these devices be scrutinized by scientific or engineering organizations, just as the French Academy of Sciences reviewed (and then accepted) the thesis that Vaucanson had presented to them. In the remaining cases—for example, when companies have a reasonable interest in protecting their intellectual property—you can hopefully be better prepared to make the judgment on your own.

For the reasons above, we'll spend the rest of this chapter emphatically digging more deeply into some of the details behind how artificial neural networks—particularly deep neural networks—work; and we'll start by creating a neural network that can recognize photos of dogs. Some of the details in the next few chapters will be involved, but they'll pay dividends, as they will offer us a better understanding not just for *what* neural networks can do, but also for *how* and *when* they can do certain things.

RECOGNIZING OBJECTS IN IMAGES

Let's imagine for the moment that you've already designed your neural network, and that you're ready to train it to recognize photos of dogs. The process for training a neural network is, just like reinforcement learning, reminiscent of the process for training a pet with treats. First, we pick a picture that we want the network to understand. This "training example" is just a photo—a picture with a dog or a picture without a dog—that we want the network to remember. For the network to understand this training example, we first need to encode the example numerically. We do this by describing the picture with numbers to represent the color of each of its pixels: since we need three colors (red, green, and blue) per pixel, a picture with 300×200 is be represented with $300 \times 200 \times 3 = 180,000$ numbers.

Once we've set the network's input neurons to these numbers, we can "run" the network, letting the neurons propagate their information through the network. They will activate (or not) layer by layer until they produce an output at the end.

Remember from the last chapter that we can think about neurons in the network as little light bulbs that turn off or on, shining more brightly when their activation level is higher. Once the network has run, some of the little neurons in the network will be dark, while others will glow. Some might glow very brightly.

Generally we care most about how brightly the neurons at the output layer of the network are glowing, because those neurons represent what we're trying to predict. Because we're training the network to identify pictures of dogs, let's assume that there's exactly one neuron in the output layer; we'll call this the "dog" neuron. If this neuron is brightly glowing, we'll say that the network thinks that there was a dog in the picture, whereas if it's dark, the network thinks there was not a dog. If it's somewhere in-between, glowing but not bright, the network thinks there may be a dog but isn't quite sure.

Once we've run the network to get a prediction of whether the training picture has a dog in it, we compare the brightness of the output neuron with the label of our training example, which tells us whether the photo actually had a dog or not. We would encode the label of this training example numerically: 1 if the picture has a dog in it and 0 if it doesn't. So if the neuron at the end was glowing brightly and the label was 1, or if the neuron was dark and the label was 0, then the network was correct; otherwise, it was incorrect. We then create a new message describing how much error there was in the network's prediction and propagate that message backward through the network, adjusting the weights between the neurons like little knobs so that the network will give a slightly better response the next time around. When the network is correct, or mostly correct, we will still send back a message and adjust the knobs, but we won't adjust them by much.

At first, the network will usually be incorrect. It will be guessing randomly. But over time, the network will become more and more accurate. After we've trained the network for a long time, we would also adjust its weights less and less, just as you would fine-tune the volume knob on a radio once you're close to the volume you want.

In a nutshell, this is the way many standard neural networks are trained. This method, while simple, wasn't discovered and well understood until the 1970s and the 1980s, even though neural networks had been around for decades before that.[9] It should also go without saying that "we" aren't doing much work here. The computer does all of the hard work for us, and we just need to feed the network as many training examples as we can find for it.[10] If we were fitting a network to classify images, we would repeat this process with image after image,[11] and we'd repeat the process until the network was no longer improving. As long as we have enough data and a big enough network, we could train the neural network to recognize just about anything we want it to recognize.

If you tried to train your neural network with a few pictures of your pet dog from around your house and a few pictures of your trip to Scotland, it wouldn't work very well. More likely, the network would learn a simple rule, such as that the colors of the inside of your house are predictive of there being a dog in a photo, and the presence of lots of green in the image is predictive of there not being a dog in the photo. That's because the operative phrase in the paragraph above, on which everything depends, was this one: *as long as we have enough data and a big enough network.*

OVERFITTING

One of the biggest challenges in fitting neural networks is that if the network is too flexible, or if we don't have enough data to train the model, then we might learn a model that explains the training examples well but doesn't generalize to other, unseen examples. We saw this same problem in chapter 6, about the Netflix Prize; this risk is called *overfitting*. What does overfitting look like in practice?

In figure 9.1a, I show a small sample of data. In this case, it's just pairs of points, *(input, output)*. Let's say we want a model for these points that, given an *input* value, produces an estimate of the *output* value. This is exactly what you're doing when you fit a neural network: you're just fitting a model to predict some output values from the input values. And just below this, in figure 9.1b, is a model I've fit to these points. The model is the curvy line that goes through or near many of the points. From this model—the curvy line—you can see what it would predict for each input value, both for the inputs we had seen during training (the black dots) and for many values we hadn't seen in training.

But there's a problem with this model: although it matches the training data well, it's unlikely to explain new data very well. It's too complex. It makes too many assumptions about the data, so it's got too many squiggles. Overfitting can become problematic because it might make assumptions about the data—assumptions like "lots of green in a photo means there isn't a dog in it"—when it's not justified in making these assumptions. We have no evidence yet that a much simpler model wouldn't be better, or that we have enough data to fit the complex model. We would be remiss if we didn't follow the principle of Occam's razor, which states that we should favor the most simple model for our data absent compelling

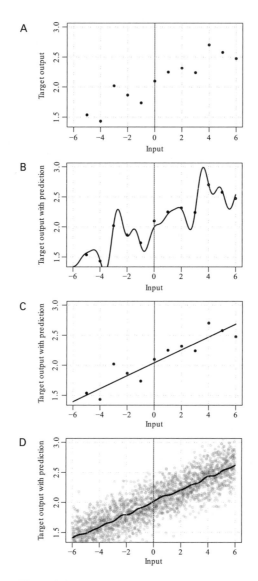

Figure 9.1
Plots to illustrate overfitting: (a) a sample of points (input, output) for which we hope to build a model; (b) a complex and overfit model of these points (the black curvy line); (c) a linear model of these points (the straight line); and (d) a complex but not overfit model of these points (the black, not-very-curvy line).

evidence for a more complex one. (A linguistics professor of mine once explained Occam's razor succinctly as, "Keep it simple, stupid.")

The two most common ways to avoid overfitting are either to use a simpler model—that is, a model with fewer knobs to tune (as I show in figure 9.1c) or to use more data with the complex model (figure 9.1d)—or some combination of these. As you can see, the model we find when there is a lot of data looks a lot more like a straight line, which confirms our hunch that we did indeed overfit the data with the first, curvy model.

Neural networks are especially prone to this problem of overfitting because they might have billions of connections between neurons—and, hence, billions of knobs to tune.[12] If you don't have lots of photos to train your network to find pictures of your dog, then you will very possibly overfit the neural network. Researchers typically address this with some combination of the solutions I mentioned above: by using a network that has fewer knobs to tune and by using as much data as possible. We'll explore both of those now, starting with having lots of data.

IMAGENET

One popular source of photos to train neural networks is the web, but unfortunately most photos on the web don't have explicit labels attached to them. It's possible to use data like this to train neural networks; but in general, explicitly labeled pictures are better.

Enter Li Fei-Fei. Fei-Fei is an energetic and intensely focused machine learning and computer vision professor at Stanford University (who has recently joined Google to lead its cloud AI efforts). Fei-Fei became famous in part for her work on producing large, well-labeled collections of images that can be used for training computers to understand images—and for evaluating their ability to do so. She began this work as she was developing an algorithm in her research. To train and evaluate that algorithm, she and her colleagues collected images by flipping through the pages of a dictionary, finding entries with illustrations. Once she and her colleagues found 101 different entries that could serve as object categories, they looked for as many images as possible from each category with Google Image Search. The result was a collection of about nine thousand images that researchers could use to train and evaluate their own algorithms.[13]

Recognizing how useful this data was, Fei-Fei and her students embarked on a more ambitious project over the next decade: ImageNet. She and her colleagues again collected images for a variety of categories using Google Image Search, adjusting their queries and issuing the queries in different languages to get a broader variety of images.[14] After doing this, she and her research teams had millions of images, but some didn't match the expected category very well. For example, if I search for "kayak" on Google Image Search, one of the results is the logo for the travel website Kayak.com, when what I probably want is the thing I'd use to travel down a river. To filter out these images, Fei-Fei and her team turned to Amazon Mechanical Turk.[15]

Amazon Mechanical Turk is a relatively recent milestone in the history of automata. It's a website provided by Amazon.com that allows any user to dispatch small, simple tasks to a "computer" that performs these tasks. The user must provide simple instructions to the website describing how these tasks should be accomplished and then pay a small fee for each task. Fei-Fei and her team gave the Amazon Mechanical Turk precise instructions asking the computer in effect to "tell us whether this image contains a kayak" or "tell us whether this image contains a Siamese cat."[16] Once tasks like this have been uploaded to Amazon.com, the website's computers then process the tasks as instructed.

Amazon Mechanical Turk takes its name because, like the chess-playing Turk, its "computers" aren't actually automata: they're people, often just sitting at home on their own personal computers. The website "abstracts away" the people behind the service, making it feel as if these tasks are being performed automatically by a computer. (The website doesn't keep it a secret that humans perform these tasks, and you can still interact in limited ways with the users who have worked on your tasks.)

The result of Fei-Fei's effort—downloading images from Google Image Search and cleaning up their tags with Amazon Mechanical Turk—is that ImageNet grew to over 14 million high-resolution images, labeled with over 22,000 categories.[17] Compared to other benchmark datasets at the time, ImageNet provided an order of magnitude more labeled images. While other datasets might have a category for *cat* or *dog*, ImageNet also had fine-grained labels for some categories. Among the 120 different labels it had for dogs, for example, were Dalmatian, Keeshond, and Miniature Schnauzer.[18]

In 2010, Fei-Fei organized a competition with 1.4 million images from 1,000 categories in this dataset: the ImageNet Large-Scale Visual Recognition Challenge. One part of the competition required researchers' algorithms to identify which of the objects across the 1,000 categories were in an image; these categories ranged broadly, from *great white shark* to *hen* to *hourglass.*[19]

The first two years of the competition saw measured improvement, as the error rate dropped from 28 percent in 2010 to 26 percent in 2011. Like the second year of the Netflix Prize, researchers in the field of computer vision had picked all of the low-hanging fruit over the years. Each year the field eked out small gains by adding more and more handcrafted features. But a paradigm shift happened in 2012, when an inelegant and underdog submission became the undisputed winner of the ImageNet Challenge. The submission was a deep neural network, and it came in with an error rate of 16 percent, far below the previous year's rate of 26 percent.[20]

CONVOLUTIONAL NEURAL NETWORKS

The paradigm-shifting 2012 network became known as AlexNet, named after the first author on the paper that made it famous. AlexNet worked better than its competitors for several reasons, two of which I mentioned above: it had been trained on a huge amount of data, and it was built in such a way that it didn't have too many weights to tune. The researchers had architected the network so that the number and locations of its knobs made efficient use of their data. (In fact, AlexNet wouldn't be called efficient or accurate by our "modern" standards of just six years later, but I'll come back to this point shortly.)

Let's return to our goal of building a neural network that can detect pictures of dogs and use the ideas from AlexNet. AlexNet was, like the Atari-playing network, a convolutional neural network using a sequence of convolutional layers followed by a sequence of fully connected layers (five of the former and three of the latter as shown in figure 9.2).[21]

This pattern—convolutional layers followed by fully connected layers—turns out to be very common in networks used for image recognition. What's so special about this architecture that makes it successful across a range of applications?

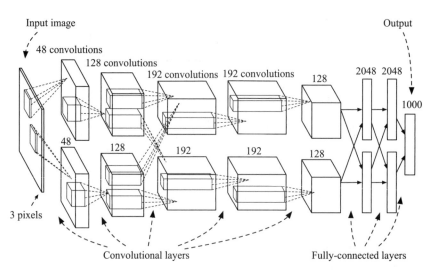

Figure 9.2

The architecture of AlexNet, the artificial network that won the 2012 ImageNet Challenge, set the stage for further improvements in image classification. AlexNet had five convolutional layers followed by three fully connected layers. Much of the network was trained on two different processors, so that some layers didn't process any inputs from the convolutional layers handled by the other processor. The input layer represented the red–green–blue values of an image, while the output layer had 1,000 neurons corresponding to each of the categories predicted by the network. Image adapted with permission from Russakovsky et al., "ImageNet Large Scale Visual Recognition Challenge."

Remember from the last chapter that convolutional layers transform the image by finding objects in it. Each convolutional layer has a set of filters that look for distinct patterns in the image (or images) in the previous layer. The convolutional layer slides each filter over patches of neurons in the previous layer. You can imagine this as looking for different items on a beach with a bunch of magical "thing detectors." The "thing detectors" are the filters. One filter might look for beautiful shells on the beach, while another might look for wristwatches left behind by beachgoers. The output of the convolutional layer is a collection of maps of the beach, one for each filter. If the shell filter doesn't find a shell in any patch of the image that matches its pattern, then the map for that filter will be dark everywhere; otherwise it will have a bright spot wherever it found a shell; the same applies to the watch detector. As we saw in the last chapter, a neuron in the output layer of the convolution will be very bright if there is a strong match for the filter at that position of the input to the convolution.

In the last chapter I discussed filters for aliens and paddles. But that was a bit idealistic and unrealistic for the filters in the first convolutional layer for a network that recognizes natural images (and, probably, for one that plays Atari games as well). It's unlikely that any single filter of a convolutional layer would recognize complex objects like this, in part because the filters in the first layer are usually fairly small. In AlexNet, for example, the filters in the first layer looked for patterns in 11 × 11 patches of pixels.

If these filters can't recognize aliens and spaceships from pixels, how can they identify pictures of dogs, let alone dogs of different breeds? Remember that AlexNet has five layers of convolutions. It's not until the final layers that the network is able to recognize complex objects like dogs and spaceships. Before we can understand how they do that, let's look back at the first layer. AlexNet used about a hundred filters in its first layer, which meant that it had a hundred magical "thing detectors."

I show a set of filters from a convolutional neural network just like AlexNet in figure 9.3a. Each square in this image shows a patch of pixels that will brightly light up one of the filters in the first convolutional layer. Although you can't see it in these black-and-white images, these filters also matched different colors; some tended to match blue and white, while others matched yellow and red, and so on. A lot of researchers interpret these filters as "edge detectors" because they match edges or other simple patterns in the input image. These patches of pixels may not look very meaningful, but they become meaningful when combined with other edge detectors by layers deeper in the network. In other words, they're the building blocks used by the layers further downstream in the network. And this is where the magic of convolutional neural networks really starts.

AlexNet's remaining four convolutional layers each have a few hundred more filters.[22] Each successive convolutional layer uses filters from its preceding layer as building blocks to compose them into more complex patterns. The second convolutional layer doesn't think in terms of pixels; it thinks in terms of filters from the first layer—that is, in terms of edges—and it builds up patterns of these edges to search for. You can see some of these patterns in figure 9.3b. Each square in this figure represents which pixels in the input image would brightly light up a filter in the output of the second

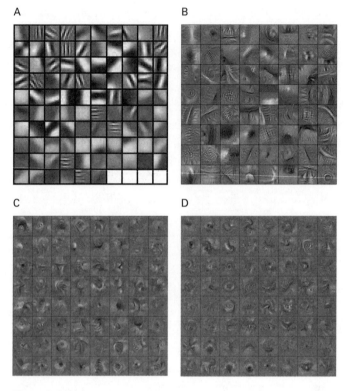

Figure 9.3
Patterns of pixels that activate filters in various layers of AlexNet in convolutional layers 1 (a), 2 (b), 3 (c), and 4 (d). These filters search for patterns of light and dark (they also search for certain colors, which you can't see in this picture). Images used with permission from Yosinski et al., "Understanding Neural Networks Through Deep Visualization."

layer. These patterns are still not full objects, but it's clear that they're starting to become more interesting: some of them look a bit like fur (which is useful for recognizing dogs), while some of them look like curvy segments (which is useful for recognizing snakes, lips, or other curvy objects).

As we continue to move deeper into the network, the compositions captured by the convolutional filters continue to become more and more complex. You can see the filters for the third and fourth convolutional layers in figure 9.3c and figure 9.3d. As before, each square represents a patch of pixels that would highly activate some filter in that layer. Here you can begin to make out coherent parts of objects: some patches appear to be animals' eyes, while others appear to be larger patches of fur. Others yet appear to be larger parts of animals. One even looks a bit like a face! This increasing abstraction continues as we go deeper into the convolutional layers in AlexNet.

Once we've moved past the fifth convolutional layer, we find three fully connected layers. The output of the network had a thousand different neurons, corresponding to each of the categories in the ImageNet Challenge. AlexNet was trained so that, when presented with an image containing one of these categories, the corresponding output neuron should light up. If presented with an image of a shark, then the shark neuron should light up. If presented with an image of an hourglass, the hourglass neuron should light up. Otherwise these neurons should stay dark.

You can see a sample of image patches that would light up some of the neurons in the final, output layer of this network in the four images shown in figure 9.4. Not surprisingly, image patches that light up the neuron for one of these categories tend to match our intuition: the image patch that lights up the great white shark neuron appears to have great white sharks in it, and the image patch that lights up the hourglass neuron appears to have an hourglass in it. Amazingly, the objects in these images didn't come from any single picture: these image patches were generated from the network itself, to reflect precisely what each neuron "looks" for.

The images in the ImageNet Challenge were biased toward animals, with 120 different categories for domestic dogs alone, out of its 1,000 total categories. This means that, to create our network to recognize your pet dog, we can probably just use the AlexNet network with only a small modification: we just remove (or ignore) all output neurons except for the ones that best match your dog. But in general, we might want to keep the other output neurons, since it can be helpful to know whether the image matches other things, such as a different type of dog or even a cat.

WHY "DEEP" NETWORKS?

What is it about deep neural networks—and AlexNet in particular—that enabled them to work so well in the ImageNet Challenges? Did the networks' architectures help? For example, did these networks need to be so deep? As we already know, neural networks with just a single hidden layer should be capable of representing arbitrarily complex functions, so it should

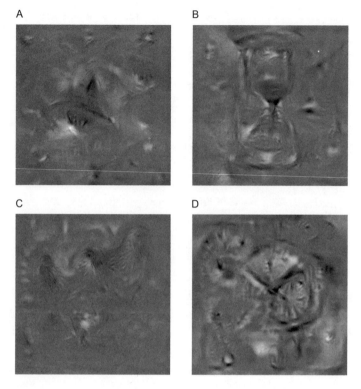

Figure 9.4
Image patches that activate the neurons in the output layer of our net-
work. Neurons correspond to categories in the ImageNet Challenge
(A: great white shark; B: hourglass; C: hen; D: wall clock). Images used
with permission from Yosinski et al., "Understanding Neural Networks
Through Deep Visualization."

be possible, at least in theory, for a network with just a single hidden layer
to beat the ImageNet Challenge.

The problem with a single hidden layer is that we have no guarantee
that the hidden layer won't need to become extraordinarily large to represent the function we want. If the hidden layer becomes too large—that
is, too wide—then we would need to learn too many weights, and we're
likely to overfit without an extraordinarily large amount of data. On the
other hand, there's theoretical evidence that suggests that by going
deeper instead of wider, we can represent complex functions much
more efficiently—that is, with far fewer neurons, and therefore with far
fewer weights to learn.[23]

What is it about going deeper instead of wider that makes a network more efficient? If you've ever used a Nintendo Wii, there's a good chance that you've created a Mii. A Mii is a cartoon character that represents you, as a player. It's your avatar for certain Nintendo Wii games. To create your Mii, you select eyes, nose, skin color, hair, and a variety of other facial and body features to make a character that looks like yourself. For each characteristic, you have a handful of options—we'll say about 5 to 10—from which to select. While the end result is often more cartoonish than photorealistic, it can still bear a striking (and humorous) resemblance to you, or to anyone else for whom you make a character. By using just a handful of building blocks—the eyes, nose, hair, mouth, and other features shared as building blocks for all Mii characters—you can create a wide variety of Mii characters that can faithfully represent just about anyone you might imagine.

Now let's think back to the benefit that convolutional layers provide. Neural net researchers have suggested that convolutional layers are powerful because they use a *distributed representation* to process an image. They let you reuse components among different neurons. If your neural network can recognize 120 different breeds of dogs, the first few layers can focus on recognizing the very basic characteristics we might use to describe dogs: the different types of fur they might have, different types of ears, and different patterns of coloration. Then the deeper layers can focus on combining these different "primitives" in various ways. Just as you can construct a Mii using a variety of well-defined and reusable facial and body features, higher-level convolutional layers can construct objects—like dogs—from the features found in earlier convolutional layers. And this can repeat at each level, giving an exponential increase in the things that can be represented with each layer. As you can imagine, in some layer beyond where the network can recognize dogs and people, you might have neurons that can explain entire scenes. You might have, for example, a neuron that recognizes recreational parks (by leveraging neurons earlier in the network that recognize dogs, people, and playground equipment); or you might have a neuron that recognizes urban environments (cars, streets, and commercial storefronts). In the next chapter we'll actually look at neural networks that can generate captions for scenes like this. The creators of AlexNet saw this benefit to using multiple layers empirically as well. If they removed any convolutional layer, then their network's performance degraded.[24] The

ImageNet Challenge contestants also noticed this in the years following AlexNet: as they continued to build deeper and deeper networks, their performance on the challenge continued to improve.

Many of the submissions to the ImageNet Challenge after 2012 followed AlexNet's lead and used deep neural networks. Although AlexNet won by a commanding lead in 2012, a number of other teams beat AlexNet in 2013, when all of the top teams used deep learning. In a research field otherwise used to eking out small gains each year, the error rate plummeted over the next few years, as researchers continued to improve their new favorite toy. In 2014, Google produced a network that by some metrics exceeded the accuracy of humans.

In 2018, as I write this book, the field of research is still extraordinarily active and fruitful, as researchers are discovering new ways to connect layers to one another. The top-performing networks in the ImageNet Challenge now have an error rate of 2.3 percent, a small fraction of AlexNet's 16 percent error rate.[25] As Dave Patterson, a computer architecture researcher at Google Brain and former professor at UC Berkeley, noted, it's shocking even to pioneers in the field that these methods in deep learning are working so well.

Noticing that network depth can be helpful, contestants in the ImageNet Challenge have made their networks deeper and deeper, to seemingly absurd levels. One 22-layer network designed by Google, for example, was called the Inception Network, a reference to the 2010 movie *Inception* and the internet meme, "We need to go deeper."[26] But adding more layers increases the number of parameters we need to tune; so how did Google's researchers manage to go so deep without overfitting? One way was by recognizing that the neurons in its convolutional layers might be too simple (they are, after all, just weighted-average classifiers). So they replaced them with miniature networks that could find more complicated patterns. Critically, however, they did this in such a way that they used *fewer* parameters per layer (for example: two 3×3 filters and one 1×1 filter, and three weights to combine them, require 22 parameters altogether, while a single, "dumb" 5×5 filter has 25 parameters). Depths like that of the Inception Network are no longer considered extreme; it's not uncommon now for a network to be 10 to 20 layers deep, with billions of weights to tune. Some networks have gone thousands of layers deep.[27]

Researchers have discovered ways to improve networks besides depth. They've discovered, for example, that networks can perform better when information is allowed to "bypass" certain layers, something made possible by adding connections between nonadjacent convolutional layers. They've also found ways for neurons to reinforce one another within a layer, a process called excitation. This is useful when, for example, one part of a convolutional layer recognizes cat fur: that should be a signal to other parts of the layer to be on the lookout for related items, like cat eyes and cat tongues.

DATA BOTTLENECKS

AlexNet's network architecture was important, but another factor in its success was the sheer scale of the data its researchers used to train it. They used 1.2 million images from the competition to train their network, but, observing that "object identity is invariant to changes in the intensity and color of the illumination," they augmented their training data by flipping their images horizontally, translating them, and adjusting their color balance.[28] As a result, they ended up with 2,000 times the amount of training data they started with, or about 2 billion images with which to train their network. If they hadn't augmented their training data like this, they would have needed to use a much smaller—and less expressive—network.[29]

With so many images for training, their bottleneck wasn't how many images they could feed into their network, but rather how fast they could feed them in. As the creators of AlexNet observed:

> In the end, the network's size is limited mainly by the amount of memory available on current [processors] and by the amount of training time that we are willing to tolerate. Our network takes between five and six days to train. ... All of our experiments suggest that our results can be improved simply by waiting for faster [processors] and bigger datasets to become available.[30]

Conveniently, the hardware most suited to train these networks has continued to improve since then. Training neural networks involves performing many matrix operations. Computer games must perform exactly the same types of operations to render high-quality graphics, and graphics cards have been optimized over the past few decades to support these operations. Deep learning researchers have begun using these cards because they can speed up the time it takes to train a network by a factor of anywhere from

10 to 50. The market for computer graphics cards that perform these operations had become large and competitive even before deep learning depended on them, which had forced the cards to become affordable, until demand for the cards picked back up in the past few years.[31] NVidia, one of the primary manufacturers of these cards, has been printing them like newspapers and selling them like hotcakes; the company has also begun producing even more specialized hardware for self-driving cars. These facts have not been lost on its investors, who are willing to pay $242 for a precious share of its stock in 2018 when they only paid $20 per share 2015. Google has meanwhile introduced specialized chips that appear to improve upon the speeds of the graphics chips by a similar order of magnitude.[32]

So far we've focused on the high-level details of how neural networks allow computers to perceive the contents of images. We've looked at the way their layers are organized and the way they're trained, and at how improvements at this high level have pushed the boundaries of what's possible with computer perception. But as researchers have been figuring out useful ways to architect these networks at a macroscopic level, they've also been looking at ways to improve these networks at the microscopic level—that is, at the level of individual neurons. Changing the way neurons in a network light up, given their inputs, can have surprising effects on these networks' ability to retain the information we use to train them. We'll take a closer look at why this is the case in the next chapter.

10 LOOKING UNDER THE HOOD OF DEEP NEURAL NETWORKS

COMPUTER-GENERATED IMAGES

On June 10, 2015, a strange and mysterious image showed up on the internet, posted anonymously on the website Imgur.com. At first glance, the picture looked like one or two squirrels relaxing on a ledge. But the resemblance ended there: as you looked more closely, you could make out bizarre detail—and objects—at every scale. The image on the internet was psychedelic, like a fractal, with a dog's snout on the squirrel's face, a mystical pagoda here, a human torso there, and a bird-giraffe creature over there, seamlessly embedded into the fine detail of the image. Uncanny eyes peered out from every nook and cranny. Looking at this image felt like looking for objects in clouds, except that it wasn't your imagination. Or was it? You had to look again to see.

It was clear that the image hadn't been created by a human. It was too bizarre to be a photograph, and its detail was too fine to be an illustration. The anonymous user who had posted the picture on Imgur.com described it only with this note:

> This image was generated by a computer on its own (from a friend working on AI).[1]

As the image began to spread and the denizens of the internet tried to make sense of it, engineers over at Google were generating more images just like this and sharing them with one another. A week later, they published a blog post explaining the phenomenon. The image had indeed been generated by AI—specifically an artificial neural network. The phenomenon became known as Deep Dream. With the arrival of these images, people began asking some uncomfortable questions that had been lurking beneath the surface. Are these really android dreams? Do we even understand what's going on in these networks? Have researchers gone too far in their efforts to recreate human thinking?

These concerns about intelligent machines had been further stirred up because the likes of modern industrialist Elon Musk were voicing their own worries. Musk, who had reportedly invested in DeepMind to keep an eye on the progress of AI, worried that his good friend Larry Page—one of Google's founders—might "produce something evil by accident," including, rather specifically, "a fleet of artificial intelligence–enhanced robots capable of destroying mankind."[2]

When these images came out, we already knew that neural networks could be useful in playing Atari games and in understanding the content of images. The images did stir up some uncomfortable questions, but as we'll see, the reasons neural networks can be good at playing Atari games and the reasons they're able to produce psychedelic dreamscapes are actually closely related. And even though these dreamscapes seemed at first to make deep neural networks *more* mysterious, it turns out that they can also make them *less* mysterious.

SQUASHING FUNCTIONS

In the history of neural networks, there was a period during which researchers eschewed deep architectures. They had the universal approximation theorem, which suggested that maybe they didn't need to go so deep, and they also knew in practice that deep networks were difficult to train. But these networks were difficult to train because researchers hadn't yet discovered the best way for neurons in their networks to light up.

Remember that in a neural network, each neuron is a simple classifier. The neuron takes a weighted sum of its inputs and squashes this weighted-sum in some way to produce an output, as we saw in figure 8.2. This squashing function might seem like a footnote, but it turns out to be extremely important in enabling us to train *deep* networks. For a long time, researchers' favorite squashing function in neural networks followed the S-shaped curve I show in figure 10.1a.[3] This S-shaped curve takes the weighted sum of the neurons' brightness in the previous layer and squashes it into the range 0 to 1. If the weighted sum of the neuron's

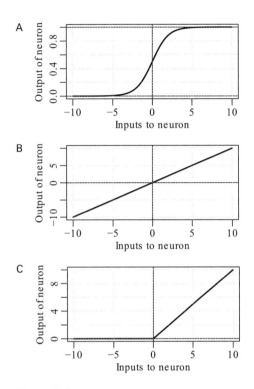

Figure 10.1
Activation functions for neural networks. The S-curve (a) (formally known as a sigmoid) was used for a long time, but ReLU activation functions (c) have become popular because they make training deep neural networks easier.

inputs is very small, the output of the neuron will be close to 0. If it is very large, the output of the neuron will be very close to 1.

The benefit of using this S-curve is that neurons' output values are all "well-behaved": no neuron will output a ridiculously high or low value, and there is a smooth relationship between the inputs and the outputs. These are good properties to have when you're training or using the network, because otherwise the edge weights could blow up to infinity when you're using the network. Having a smooth function means that you always know how much you should adjust the network weights if you adjust the network's input or output just a little bit. Researchers also liked to point out that this function was biologically inspired—but remember, using something because it's biologically inspired can sometimes be "fraught with danger."

The problem with using the S-shaped curve is that it tends to "dilute" messages passed through the network. If the weighted-sum input to the neuron is high, the neuron doesn't care whether the input is large or *really* large: it outputs the number 1 either way. It's the same at the other extreme: whether the input to the neuron is somewhat negative or *really* negative, the neuron outputs 0 regardless. This may not be a problem when we "run" the network, but it can become a problem when we're trying to train it. The message we send backward through the network to adjust the weights will become diluted as it passes through the network. One of the benefits we originally thought we had—that we know how much to adjust the weights when we're training the network—isn't much of a benefit, because the training algorithm may think it doesn't need to adjust the weights at all, when they should in fact be changed a lot. This problem is sometimes known as a "vanishing gradient." The gradient is the direction that weights in a neural network must move for it to learn from a sample of training data. If the gradient vanishes—that is, if it appears to be zero when the network training is not complete—then this means the network can't learn from its training examples: it will ignore the training example, even if the example is useful. Because of this problem, researchers continued to poke around at other activation functions.[4]

At the opposite extreme, what if we don't squash the output of the neurons at all, and instead pass the weighted sum computed by each neuron directly through as the output of that neuron, using the activation function in figure 10.1b? This doesn't have the problem we had with the vanishing gradient, and in fact it will be really easy to update the network weights if we use this squashing function. But this poses a different problem: if we use this squashing function for all of the neurons in our network, then the entire network will collapse mathematically into the equivalent of a single-layer network. Any benefits we thought we'd gained from having a deep network simply vanish. Assuming that we want the benefits of a multilayer network—and we do—this won't work either.

RELU ACTIVATION FUNCTIONS

Since about 2010, we've been seeing much better results with an activation function that's somewhere in-between these two extremes: the one shown in figure 10.1c. This activation function—used by AlexNet in 2012 and a variety of other networks since then—is called the rectified linear unit, or "ReLU" for short.[5] The ReLU is zero if the sum of the neuron's inputs is less than zero, and it's equal to the sum of the inputs if that sum is greater than zero. For a while researchers were worried that this would have the same problem as the S-shaped curve—namely, that the network would dilute a message passed through many layers. But this doesn't seem to happen in practice.[6]

Instead, the ReLU activation function appears to have some rather nice properties. For any fixed input, some subset of the network's neurons will be dark, while others will be lit up. If you vary the input a little bit in any direction, the set of neurons set to *on* or *off* typically won't change. The brightness of the *on* neurons will change as you vary the input a small amount, but the *on* ones will stay on, and the *off* ones will stay off. But more importantly, the network will behave in the small vicinity of this input exactly like a single-layer network—that is, like a bunch of weighted-average classifiers.

As you continue to vary the input to the network, moving it further from the initial input, the set of *on* neurons will begin to change. The output will still vary smoothly as you change the input smoothly—that is, it will never make a sudden jump in value as long as you don't make a sudden change in the input.[7] The relationship between the inputs and outputs, however, will change. You can think of the overall network as a patchwork of single-layer networks, stitched together to agree with the training data. Which single-layer network handles the input depends on which neurons are turned on or off by the input. In fact, it's possible for there to be an exponentially large number of single-layer networks encoded within the overall network.[8]

When I say there are an "exponentially large" number of networks, I don't mean this casually or carelessly. I mean "exponential" in the mathematical sense. The number of possible single-layer networks hidden within the overall network is described by all of the possible ways the neurons in the network can be switched on or off. For a ReLU network with just 60 neurons, the number of ways to assign its neurons to on/off—and, hence, the number of single-layer networks we could hide within it—is about the number of grains of sand on all the beaches and in all the deserts of the world.[9] A network with 270 neurons has the potential to represent as many combinations as there are atoms in the known universe.[10] And remember: modern neural networks can easily have millions of neurons. If the network only needs to use a simple function to represent its input, it can do so; and if it needs to use a more complicated function—as with a patchwork of single-layer networks—it can do that instead.[11]

Why doesn't the ReLU have the same problem the S-curve had, given that large parts of the ReLU are also flat? Let's say you have a training example you want the network to learn. Although many of the neurons will be turned off for a typical input, as long as there is at least some path of lit-up neurons from the input of the network to its output, then the network can adjust the weights along that path to learn the training example. The weights along that path will take the credit or the blame for the training example, as information from the example propagates through those lit-up neurons.[12] Later, when the network sees an input that's similar to examples it saw during training, it will "remember" those training examples by lighting up some or all of the same neurons that were lit up when it saw a similar example during training.

This benefit of ReLUs is similar to another popular trick for training deep neural networks in which neurons are temporarily "suppressed" during training. Any time a training example is used to train the network, a random subset—say, 50 percent—of the neurons are temporarily suppressed, by setting their outputs temporarily to zero.[13] The remaining neurons' weights are then updated using the training example, as if the suppressed neurons never existed. As with the ReLUs, there are an exponentially large number of ways these neurons might be suppressed—and, hence, a virtually infinite number of networks to train.

When the resulting network is used for prediction, the output of each neuron is scaled down, so that the input to each neuron becomes the average of many independently trained models. The overall network effectively becomes a giant blend of a huge number of networks that were trained, reminiscent of the model-averaging techniques that were successful in the Netflix Prize.[14]

This combination of tricks for training deep neural networks—that is, ReLU activation functions and the random suppression of neurons during training, along with having lots of data, using depth instead of width, and using convolutional layers—were some of the main factors in creating networks that could classify images as well as, or better than, humans.

Although it was technically true that neural networks have done better than humans at identifying objects in images, this fact requires a large asterisk. At least one network did indeed exceed humans' ability to recognize very fine-grained categories, but the network had an advantage in that it was trained on narrow, specific categories of objects, such as the 120 dog breeds from the training data. In many cases, the network could correctly identify narrow types of objects, such as "coucal," "Komondor," and "yellow lady's slipper," when a typical human would have only recognized these items based on their broad categories: "cuckoo," "sheepdog," and "orchid," or possibly just "bird," "dog," and "flower." The humans compared with the computer had the chance to study these categories, and the researchers behind the ImageNet Challenge found that humans did better the more they studied, but the fact remains: humans are imperfect.[15]

And neural networks have their own weaknesses. The same algorithms that beat humans can still make mistakes identifying objects in images that humans would have had no trouble recognizing.[16] It's even possible to create optical illusions for neural networks that can "trick" them into being extremely confident that they are seeing objects that aren't really there, when to a human the illusion looks like abstract art. In one case, a white background with five columns of red stitch-marks could trick a neural network into thinking it was looking at a baseball; in another, a rippling pattern of black, gray, and orange convinced a neural network that it was looking at a king penguin; and in yet another, a grid of carefully positioned rectangles convinced a neural network that it was looking at a remote control. It's also possible to construct illusions that look to humans like one object, while they look to neural networks like entirely different objects.[17] This happens because of the unique way a neural network interprets the picture.

ANDROID DREAMS

Suppose that we take a photo of your pet dog and pass that photo through a convolutional neural network like the ones we trained in the last chapter. As long as you know the network weights, the layers of the network will activate predictably, layer by layer. In each layer, some neurons will remain dark while others will light up as they respond to different patterns in the image. Since we passed a photo of your pet dog into the network, then when we look deep enough in the network—say, at the fourth or fifth level—the neurons will represent object parts that we'll likely recognize. Those neurons that respond to things like fur and parts of a dog's face will be glowing brightly. If we look at the final layer, the dog neuron(s) will be lit up, while most of the remaining neurons will be dark.

Now here's where it gets interesting. When we first trained the network in the last chapter, I glossed over some details about how we adjusted the weights of the network for each training example. Remember that the algorithm to train the network adjusted its weights based on how "incorrect" the dog neuron at the end of the network was. It used a mathematical function that measured how close the output of the network was to the training example's label. That label was just a 1 or a 0 describing whether the image did or didn't have a dog. The algorithm to train the network then calculated, using high school calculus, in which direction it should adjust the network's weights so the network could predict the output values just a bit more accurately the next time around.

What if, instead of adjusting the network's weights to agree more with the image, we instead adjusted the image to agree more with the network? In other words, once we've already trained the network, what would happen if we keep the network's weights fixed to what they are, and adjust the input image—say, a photograph of a cloud—so that the dog neuron is more bright while the other neurons remain dark?

If we adjust the image like this, adjusting the pixels a bit at a time and then repeating, then we would actually start to see dogs in the photo, even if there weren't dogs there to begin with![18] In fact, this is how some of the images in the last chapter were generated: a group of deep learning researchers took a network just like AlexNet and adjusted input images so that certain neurons—representing a great white shark or an hourglass, for example—became bright, while other neurons remained dark.[19] Google's researchers used a similar method to analyze their own neural networks. When they wrote about how they did this, they gave several examples. In one of these examples, they looked at images generated from a neuron that recognized dumbbells, the equipment that you would find in a gym. They found that the images indeed showed dumbbells; but they also showed muscular arms attached to these dumbbells. Apparently, they observed, the network learned that an important distinguishing characteristic of dumbbells isn't just the hardware itself; but also the context in which it they're used.[20]

Google created its Deep Dream images in a similar way, except that instead of forcing the network to generate pictures of dogs or other specific objects, they let the network create more of whatever it saw in the image. As the Deep Dream engineers wrote on Google's research blog:

> Instead of exactly prescribing which feature we want the network to amplify, we can also let the network make that decision. In this case we simply feed the network an arbitrary image or photo and let the network analyze the picture. We then pick a layer and ask the network to enhance whatever it detected. Each layer of the network deals with features at a different level of abstraction, so the complexity of features we generate depends on which layer we choose to enhance. For example, lower layers tend to produce strokes or simple ornament-like patterns, because those layers are sensitive to basic features such as edges and their orientations.
>
> If we choose higher-level layers, which identify more sophisticated features in images, complex features or even whole objects tend to emerge. Again, we just start with an existing image and give it to our neural net. We ask the network: "Whatever you see there, I want more of it!" This creates a feedback loop: if a cloud looks a little bit like a bird, the network will make it look more like a bird. This in turn will make the network recognize the bird even more strongly on the next pass and so forth, until a highly detailed bird appears, seemingly out of nowhere.[21]

And *that's* how the mysterious image from Imgur.com was created. You can see the results of a Deep Dream created by feeding a photograph of kittens into a similar algorithm in figure 10.2b.

Soon after Google's blog post, other researchers began using a similar idea to reimagine artistic style. They created tools that would enable anyone to transfer the style from an artist's painting to an entirely different image. If you wanted to make a photo of your family look like Vincent van Gogh painted it, you simply needed to run your photo through one of these programs.

In these programs, a style image—the Van Gogh painting—is passed through the network so that the neurons light up as usual. The neurons that light up would include some low-level edge detectors in the first few layers as well as high-level object detectors in the higher layers. Then, the style-transfer algorithm measures how the filters in each layer correlate

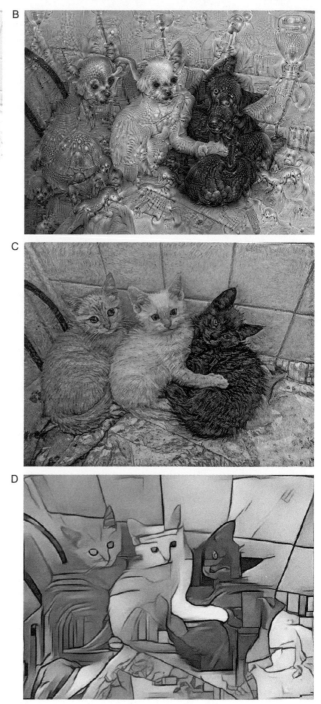

Figure 10.2
A photo of foster kittens, (a), along with a reinterpretation of the photo based on what the network sees after many iterations of the Deep Dream algorithm, (b), and style transfer algorithms, (c) and (d). Image (c) uses style from a Vincent van Gogh painting, while image (d) uses a style created from *The Simpsons*. All images except (a) were generated via https://deepdreamgenerator.com.

with one another across the entire image. This correlation is exactly how these algorithms define the style of an artist. If certain filters tend to consistently light up with each other across different parts of the image, the reasoning goes, then this indicates something important about the style of the artist. If the artist tends to use only a few, simple colors with many small dots, then the neurons that explain these small dots tend to co-occur with each other. If the artist tends to use sharp brush strokes, then any neuron that captures these sharp brush strokes will tend to occur next to itself wherever it occurs.

After this, a "content" image—your family photo—is passed through another copy of the same network, and we select a specific layer of the network to capture the essence of what's in the image. Once we've selected this layer, the algorithm adjusts the family photo so that the neurons in each layer correlate with one another in the same way they did with the style image, without allowing the neurons in the layer we've selected deviate too far from their original values. As long as we were correct in assuming that the correlation in filters expressed at each layer can capture the style of an artist, then this will cause the new image to take on the style of the first photo. This appears to be a reasonable assumption in practice, as the results of the algorithm match our intuition: when the algorithm finishes running, your family photo will have been reimagined as a Van Gogh painting—or as just about any other painting style that you used for the style image![22] I've applied this same method to some photos of the three kittens in figure 10.2c and 10.2d. As you can see, the resulting images capture the intuition we expect in different artistic styles: one of them has the intense brush strokes we associate with some of Van Gogh's most famous work, such as his self-portrait; while the other image has a style reminiscent of a cartoon image; this style was called a "Simpsons" style.

When this algorithm "reimagines" your family photo, remember that no actual "imagining" happens. The network simply processes the style image and the content image, its neurons lighting up in predictable ways for each, and then the algorithm adjusts the content image to optimize a well-defined mathematical function so that the network's activated neurons correlate in a way that agrees with the style image. The end result may seem spectacular for a computer program, but that's mostly because these networks perform their operations with higher-level abstractions than what we usually expect from computer programs. Until recently, we've come to expect computers to operate on images at a very primitive level, because that's all they've been able to do. Your home photo-editing software has tools that let you adjust the color balance of a photograph or apply softening to it. Up until recently, these operations could have been implemented with the lowest level of a convolutional neural network. But the algorithms I've described in this chapter operate on images at a much more abstract level, interpreting and adjusting images by using neurons several layers deep in the network. This is the primary strength of these networks, and it's one of the reasons they can be applied in many unique and non-intuitive applications.

In the past few chapters, we've gained some intuition for how deep neural networks can enable computers both to interpret and manipulate images in remarkably "human" ways. But up until now, our focus has been exclusively on using deep neural networks to interpret *visual* information. Is it possible to use deep neural networks to better interpret and manipulate other types of media, like audio recordings or written text? As we'll see in the next chapter, the answer is a clear yes. Deep neural networks can work well in these domains, in part because we have large amounts of data in these other domains as well. But as we'll soon see, we'll need to develop some new neural network tools—akin to convolutional filters, but for time-series data—to work with these different types of data.

11 NEURAL NETWORKS THAT CAN HEAR, SPEAK, AND REMEMBER

WHAT IT MEANS FOR A MACHINE TO "UNDERSTAND"

We've spent most of the past few chapters looking at how deep neural networks are able to recognize objects in images. I've focused on these networks largely because many of the machines in this book use vision in some form to perceive the world around them. But what if we wanted our machines to have other ways to interact with the world—to generate English sentences, or to understand human speech, for example? Would convolutional networks prove useful for this as well? Are there other neural network "primitives" that would be helpful? Popping up a level, does it even make sense to use neural networks for tasks like understanding speech?

The answer to all of these questions is yes, and in this chapter we'll take a brief look at how to do these things. Before we get into these details, however, let me be clear about what I mean when I talk about computer programs that can "understand" human speech. We're still a long way from having machines that can understand human language in the way a human does. However, we have figured out how to create computer programs that can turn a sound recording of a person speaking into a sequence of written words, a task commonly known as speech recognition. These algorithms do the same thing with a sound recording that AlexNet did with images: they classify the recording, tagging it with human-interpretable labels: words. And just as the algorithms to detect objects in images rival humans' accuracy, our speech-recognition algorithms now rival humans' ability to recognize speech.

DEEP SPEECH II

Imagine that you were given the task of designing a neural network that could transcribe human speech. Where would you begin? What would the input to the network look like, and what would its outputs be? How many layers would you use, and how would you connect these layers together? We can look at the speech-recognition system built by the web search giant Baidu to answer these questions. Baidu's network rivals humans' ability to transcribe speech; it could do this for the same reason Google's network was able to rival humans at image classification: they started with lots of data. Baidu used 11,940 hours—over a full year of spoken English—to train one of their best speech networks. And just as the creators of AlexNet did with their ImageNet data, Baidu augmented their speech dataset by transforming samples from it: they stretched their recordings this way and that, changed the recordings' frequencies, and added noise to them, so that they had many times the amount of data they started with.[1] In each case they didn't change *what* was being said; they just changed *how* it was being said. But having a lot of training data wasn't enough on its own to build a network to accurately transcribe speech: they also needed to pick the right network architecture.

We want a neural network that can take a sound recording as its input and produce a sequence of letters—a written transcription of the recording—as its output. As the input to our speech network, we can use a spectrogram of the recording. A spectrogram summarizes a sound recording by describing the intensity of different frequencies in the recording over time. You can think of a spectrogram as a black-and-white image: the x-axis is time, the y-axis is frequency, and the darkness of each pixel is the intensity of a certain frequency at a certain time in the recording. The spectrogram for a high-frequency tone would consist of a single dark bar across the top of the spectrogram, while the spectrogram for a low-frequency tone would consist of a single bar across the bottom of the spectrogram. Several pulses of sound would appear in the image as dark blobs from left to right across a white background. And just as you can turn a sound recording into a spectrogram, you can also go the other way: from a spectrogram you can reconstruct the original recording. The fact that the spectrogram encodes the recording means that we can pass the spectrogram alone as an input to the neural network.

Now that we know that a sound recording can be turned into an image, we might ask ourselves whether the network should have some convolutional layers. The answer is yes, and that's what Baidu's network used: the first few layers of their network were indeed convolutional layers. But we'll need more than just convolutional layers. We'll need an explicit way for the neural network to deal with time.

RECURRENT NEURAL NETWORKS

The most common type of neural network that interacts with time-series data—or any sequential data, really—is the *recurrent neural network*, sometimes just called an RNN. An RNN is a neural network made up of identical "units" of neurons that feed into one another in a series, as in figure 11.1. Each of these units shares the same weights, just as convolutional filters share the same weights. The only difference is that convolutional filters that share the same weights don't typically feed into one another. The very nature of RNNs, on the other hand, is that each RNN unit feeds its output directly into the next RNN unit, which, by definition, has

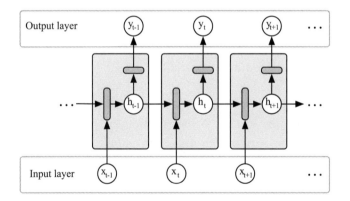

Figure 11.1
Recurrent neural network (RNN) units unfolded in time. Each unit has a state variable *h* that transitions from unit to unit. The transition is determined by the input *x* and the state of the previous unit. Each unit also produces an output *y* to share information about the state with the rest of the network. The dark boxes represent transformations—typically encoded by other neurons in the network—that may take place within the unit.

identical weights as the last unit. And each RNN unit takes its input and transforms it in various ways before outputting it. This is the magic behind RNNs: the way they manipulate data and pass it to one another enables them to keep track of *state*.

Let's briefly think back to what it was about self-driving cars that enabled them to exhibit complex behavior. Their ability to make sense of the world—that is, their ability to *perceive*—was certainly critical. But cars like Boss that drove through urban environments needed some way to make intelligent decisions as they encountered complex situations. In the middle of Boss's reasoning layer was a finite state machine (its Monopoly board), which kept track of how far along it was in carrying out its mission. As Boss made progress on its mission, it moved a virtual piece around on its Monopoly board to keep track of its state: where it is now, where it can go next, and how it should decide where to go next.

RNNs provide the same service for the neural network that the Monopoly board played for Boss. Each recurrent unit looks at its current state, does (or doesn't do) something with that state, and sometimes changes the state based on what it perceives in the world. You can think of the RNN's role as the piece-mover for the Monopoly board.

There are a few differences from Boss's Monopoly board, of course. Boss's finite-state machine had, not surprisingly, a *finite* number of states. The state of an RNN is often encoded with a vector of floating-point numbers, so the concept of a state in an RNN is more fluid: it's a point in a high-dimensional space, and its position in that space defines the semantics of the state. Another difference is that the finite-state machine in a self-driving car like Boss was handcrafted by humans, with simple rules that Boss would follow to transition from state to state.

The states and transitions in an RNN, on the other hand, are based on rules encoded into its neurons' weights; and these weights are learned from data. That said, each RNN unit is still very simple: it doesn't do much more than keep track of, and update, this state. It's just a state updater. To enable the network to do something interesting with the state, the RNN unit will typically output messages about the state to other parts of the network. For our speech network, these units output their messages deeper into the network. As you can imagine, with enough data, a chain of recurrent units in a speech network will learn states that are useful for summarizing frequency spectrograms of recorded human speech. They'll learn that certain sounds are common and which sounds tend to follow other sounds.

Now that we have RNNs, we can use them in different places in the speech network. Just as we can build RNNs that point forward in time, we can also build RNNs that point backward in time, so that they learn states and transitions that will summarize spectrograms in a different way. We can also stack sequences of RNNs on top of one another—not end-to-end in the time dimension, but placed on top of one another so that they're aligned in the time dimension, as in figure 11.2. Stacking RNNs this way helps for the same reason it helps to have multiple convolutional layers: as we go deeper, each RNN layer will summarize the previous layer by finding the most salient trends in it, building up higher and higher levels of abstraction to reason about the input to the network. Once we've stacked several layers of RNNs on top of one other, and stacked those on top of some convolutional layers, we can add a fully connected layer on top.

So a speech network takes a spectrogram as input, and processes it with a network that looks a lot like AlexNet, except that there are some RNN layers sandwiched between the convolutional layers and the fully connected layers to enable the network to model the transition between different sounds. At this point, we just need a way to predict the transcription from the output layer of the network.

The output layer of the network is a grid of neurons that represent time in one direction and letters of the English alphabet (plus gaps between these letters) in another direction. When run, the network produces a prediction of how likely each letter is to occur at any given moment during the transcription. This prediction is encoded in the output values: it's higher if the letter (at a given moment) is more likely to occur and lower if that letter is less likely to occur. But this leads to a challenge in predicting the transcription from the recorded sequence: we need to align the neurons in the output layer with the actual transcription. If we do the simplest thing, and take the most-likely letter at any given moment, then we will end up with many repeating letters, like this:

wwwhhhaattt iissss tthhe wwweeeaatthheerrrr llllikke iiinnn bboostinn rrright nnowww

One way to resolve this—at least for the task of predicting a sequence of letters—is to simply take the string of the most likely character at each

Output

Search for
alignment

Fully-connected
layers

RNN
layers

Convolutional
layers

Input

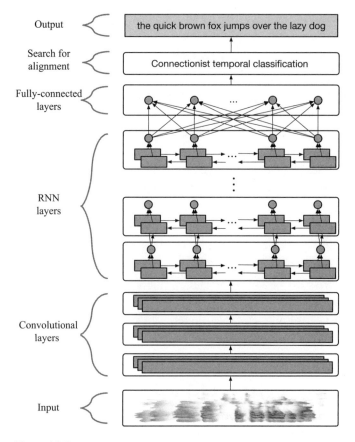

Figure 11.2
The architecture for Deep Speech 2, Baidu's speech-recognition
system. The network is trained using written transcriptions of recordings of human speech and a concept known as *connectionist temporal
classification*, which searches for an alignment between the label and
the fully connected layers. This image is adapted from Amodei et al.,
"Deep Speech 2" (cited in note 1).

moment in time, and then to remove duplicates.[2] This will often lead to a plausible, if slightly incorrect, transcription, like this one:

what is the weather like in bostin right now[3]

Note that the word "Boston" has clearly been misspelled but is phonetically correct. Sometimes the transcription is mostly phonetic but looks more like gibberish, as in this transcription:

arther n tickets for the game[4]

That should have been transcribed as: "Are there any tickets for the game?"

We can fix these transcriptions by using statistics about sequences of English words. To get an intuition for how this can help, see which of the following two phrases sounds more natural. Is it this one?:

People he about spilled thing the fun secret most of the the was blender

Or this one?:

He spilled the secret of the blender was the most fun thing about people

These phrases have the exact same words, and both of them are semantically meaningless, but you'd probably agree that the second one just sounds more natural. If you look more closely at that phrase and pick any three consecutive words in it, those words flow like you might find them in a normal sentence. This isn't the case for the first sequence of words. Baidu's researchers used this same idea, keeping track of which word collections, up to five words long, sound the most natural, based on how frequently they appeared in English text.[5] As you can imagine, using statistics about sequences of words like this can drastically narrow down the set of likely transcriptions. As another exercise, see whether you can predict the following word in this sequence:

rain fell from the _____.

Clearly this phrase ends with a word like *sky* or *clouds*. So, even if the recording objectively sounded more like "rain fell from this guy," Baidu's speech-recognition system would use language statistics to pick a transcription more like "rain fell from the sky."

Baidu's speech system then used a search algorithm to find this best-matching sequence of letters, given both the output layer of the speech network and the statistics about sequences of words it had from elsewhere. This search algorithm was a lot like the path-search algorithm Boss used to park in a parking lot, except that instead of finding a way to combine small path segments, the speech system searched for a sequence of letters; and instead of using factors like time and risk in its cost function, the speech system tried to maximize the likelihood of different letters and words in its transcription, given both the predictions from its network and the statistics of these words from its five-word language model.

GENERATING CAPTIONS FOR IMAGES

Although speech-recognition systems like the one above can accurately transcribe sound recordings, they don't understand the content of the audio recording. We're still far from having networks that can understand language, but researchers have found ways to use RNNs to make it look they can understand language. One recent breakthrough is networks that can create natural-sounding phrases to describe the content of images.

What's so spectacular about these image-captioning algorithms is that everything—from understanding the image to generating a sequence of words to describe the image—is done by neural networks (with the exception of another search algorithm, which we'll see in a moment). To put these algorithms into context, let's take a quick look at some of their predecessors, which filled in templates with the names of objects the algorithm detected in the image. The output of these algorithms was like the typical "baby talk" you might expect from a computer program:

There are one cow and one sky. The golden cow is by the blue sky.[6]

Here's another example:

This is a photograph of one sky, one road and one bus. The blue sky is above the gray road. The gray road is near the shiny bus. The shiny bus is near the blue sky.[7]

Although these algorithms do explain the scene, they're also awkward: it is true that the shiny bus is near the blue sky in the photograph, but it's semantically weird to say that the bus is near the sky. Yet this is what we've grown to expect from computers. You expect that your image-manipulation software can perform low-level image operations on an image, like adjust color balance and blurring pixels, but not more complicated things. And we don't expect computers to use language in a complicated way either.

On the other hand, the neural network approach to generating captions can create descriptions such as the following:

A group of people shopping at an outdoor market

A group of people sitting in a boat in the water

and

A giraffe standing in a forest with trees in the background[8]

The neural networks to generate captions like these use a series of transformations to convert the photograph into a series of words. In the first of these transformations, they use a convolutional neural network to process the image. This is a lot like the way AlexNet processes an image, except that instead of predicting whether different objects were in the image, the network "encodes" the image into a large vector of numbers that provide a succinct description of the scene for the rest of the network. Once the algorithm has this vector summary of the image, the rest of the network—which consists of a sequence of RNN units—generates its caption. The units, as before, are linked by their states, and each unit in the chain outputs a single word of the caption, as in figure 11.3.[9]

How could such a simple network generate coherent English captions? Remember the key feature of recurrent units: they enable a neural network to keep track of *state*. As we move further along in the chain, the state can change to keep track of what's been said and what hasn't been said. As each unit inspects its current state and outputs a new word, it updates its internal state so the next recurrent unit can do its job. And to help each unit update its state, the input to each recurrent unit is the word output by the previous recurrent unit.

You probably won't be surprised to hear that we can improve the way this network generates captions by attaching a search algorithm to the top of the network, just as Baidu did for its speech recognition system. Technically the output layer of the neural network has one neuron for each word for each time step; its output values can be combined to predict how likely each word is to appear as the next word in the sequence. From the

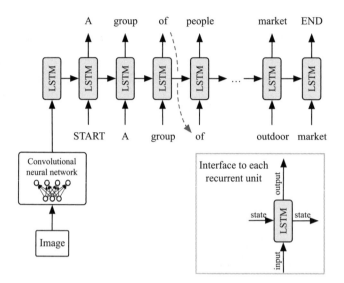

Figure 11.3
An image-captioning neural network. The state for each RNN
unit summarizes how much of the caption has been generated.
The output of each unit is a probability distribution over words;
and the input to each unit is the previously generated word. The
input to the first unit is the output of a convolutional neural
network. This image is adapted from Vinyals et al., "Show and Tell."

examples I showed a few pages ago, you can probably guess that the first
word is likely to be "A" no matter what is in the image. If there is a cat in
the image, then it's not unlikely that the next word will be "cat," and so on.

Instead of running the model once and selecting the most likely word
each time we have a choice, the search algorithm runs the model many
times to generate many sequences of words. Each time it needs to select a
word, it selects a word that's likely under the model, but the search algorithm searches in a narrow beam among the most promising candidate
captions: in some iterations it might select "furry" instead of "cat," and so
on. Once the algorithm has run the model many times to generate many
possible phrases, it evaluates each of them according to a cost function that
measures how likely each sequence of words was according to the network,
to find the best caption among many.[10]

LONG SHORT-TERM MEMORY

Because RNNs have units that feed into one another, we can think of them as deep networks when unfolded in time.[11] For a long time RNNs couldn't be built too deep because the messages that we need to send through a chain of these units during training tended to decay as they passed through the chain. The deeper into the chain of recurrent units you went, the more they tended to forget. One way the research community has gotten around this is by using "control" neurons that modify the way the unit interprets and modifies its state, as in figure 11.4.[12] You can think of these control neurons as special wires that change the way the unit behaves. These control wires work like the "set" button on a digital clock that allows you to set the time. If you hold down the set button, the clock will enter a special mode, so that when you press the other buttons, you can modify the time. When you're done, you can return the clock to its normal mode, which is to just increment the time, second by second.[13] When the control wires are set on these RNNs, their state can be updated

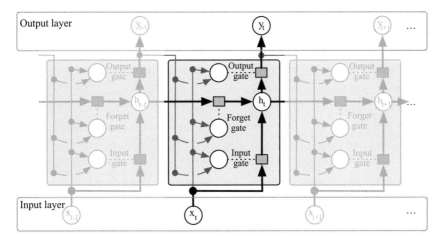

Figure 11.4
Long Short-Term Memory (LSTM) units in a recurrent neural network. This particular LSTM is the one used by Google for its image caption generator. As with a general RNN, the state can shift with each subsequent unit based on what is observed in the network. LSTMs like this one use "gates" to modify the input, the output, and the state for each unit, typically with just a multiplication. Adapted from Vinyals et al., "Show and Tell" (cited in note 8).

just like that clock; otherwise they transform the state based on their normal rules. These special units, used in Google's image-captioning network among other places, are called Long Short-Term Memory units, or LSTMs (see figure 11.4).

ADVERSARIAL DATA

Although these algorithms are getting automata a bit closer to understanding natural human language, they are still very primitive, in the sense that they can break down easily, especially if you give them inputs intended to trick them. For example, we saw in the last chapter that it's possible to create optical illusions that can trick neural networks into thinking they're seeing something that's not actually there. It would be similarly easy to trip up the caption-generating network by passing such an image to it. Researchers in the field of machine learning would call inputs like this— that is, data intended to trick a machine-learned model—*adversarial* inputs.

This idea of "tricking" neural networks with adversarial inputs is important because by understanding what sorts of images can trick these networks, we can also learn how to make them more robust. Some very recent and promising work in the field of deep learning embraces this idea to train networks that can generate realistic images.[14] One part of the system tries as hard as possible to generate images that look like the images that come from some category you care about—such as pictures of cats' faces—while another part of the system tries its best to figure out whether the generated image is from that category. Both sides of these *generative adversarial networks* (GANS) continue to improve until the generative part of the system is extremely good at creating realistic data. It's a game of cat-and-mouse, an adversarial arms race, where each side does its best to compete against the other side.

It may not seem immediately obvious why GANS are useful: why should we care about two networks that compete with each other? These networks are useful when we want to create data for some purpose: we might want a network that can generate a natural-looking picture of a horse, a bird, or a person, for example. It's possible to train one of these networks with pictures of horses and zebras, for example, to create a "generative network" that can convert photos of horses into convincing (but fake) photos of zebras; and we can train a network to produce photorealistic scenes from Van Gogh paintings.[15] And as I mentioned above, these networks can be used to generate non-image data, like sounds or realistic English sentences.

On that note, let's get back to the difficulties in building a program that can understand human language. The programs that we've discussed so far are still far from understanding human language. They can generate short sentences to describe images, but when you look closely enough at these algorithms, you'll quickly recognize their limitations.

In the first chapter of this book I mentioned IBM's Watson, which beat champions Ken Jennings and Brad Rutter in the American game show *Jeopardy!*. If we're still far from designing machines that can understand natural human language, you might wonder, how could Watson have performed so well at a game that seems to require a contestant to understand of the nuances of the English language? There was certainly some clever engineering in the project, but as we'll see in chapter 12, Watson wasn't engineered to *understand* the questions. Watson was engineered to *answer* them.

12 UNDERSTANDING NATURAL LANGUAGE (AND *JEOPARDY!* QUESTIONS)

Watson cannot be intimidated. It never gets cocky or discouraged. It plays its game coldly, implacably, always offering a perfectly timed buzz when it's confident about an answer.

—Ken Jennings, human *Jeopardy!* champion[1]

PUBLICITY STUNT OR BOON TO AI RESEARCH?

In 2006, Sebastian Thrun gave a presentation at an artificial intelligence conference about Stanley, the self-driving car he and his colleagues developed for the second DARPA Grand Challenge. The audience was electrified. Among the audience was James Fan, a graduate student at the University of Texas at Austin who was studying *question answering*, a quiet field of computer science devoted to developing computer programs that can answer written questions. As James watched Sebastian's presentation, he began to speculate.

"Wouldn't it be great," he later asked a group of his colleagues, "If there were a Grand Challenge in question answering, hosted by Alex Trebek?"[2] Alex was the host of the popular American game show *Jeopardy!*, in which contestants must have an encyclopedic knowledge of trivia, ranging from ancient history to biology to movies. During the show, Trebek poses clues to contestants in the form of an answer, and the contestants must answer these clues while phrasing their responses in the form of questions.[3]

But the colleagues laughed off James's idea. Trebek was too big a celebrity. Government pay-schedules and research grants wouldn't be able to accommodate his speaking fees. It might be great publicity for the field of question answering, they thought, but it wouldn't be a great use of taxpayer money.

IBM WATSON

Nearly five years later, on two cold days in January 2011, Ken Jennings and Brad Rutter, two of the most successful human players in the history of *Jeopardy,* faced off in a *Jeopardy* match against Watson, a computer program built by a team of researchers from IBM.[4] The game was hosted at one of IBM's research buildings, and Watson was running on racks of computers in a datacenter next door, completely cut off from the internet. The datacenter was cold and loud, as fans blew air across thousands of CPUs.[5]

The temporary studio was much warmer than both the datacenter and the winter air outside. IBM had snagged Alex Trebek to host the game; he offered the contestants clues as they selected topic categories on the game board. When the contestants knew an answer, they would buzz in. Watson also buzzed in when it knew an answer, electromechanically, its solenoid thumb hitting the buzzer with perfect timing.[6]

"Tickets aren't needed for this event, a black hole's boundary from which matter can't escape," Trebek offered.

Watson answered correctly, its screen glowing as its gentle voice—a mechanical voice of the "smooth, genial male variety" (in the words of one reporter)—rose and fell[7]: "What is *event horizon?*"

Long before the game ended, Jennings and Rutter realized they had no chance. The game had been humiliating for them. By the end of the two-day challenge, Jennings had earned $24,000, and Rutter had earned $21,600. Watson finished with a total of $77,147, a commanding lead over its human opponents.[8] Jennings wrote out a statement of surrender below his answer to the final question of the game: "I, for one, welcome our new computer overlords."

CHALLENGES IN BEATING *JEOPARDY*

Watson was miles ahead of the next-best computer program that could answer trivia questions. To see why Watson was such a breakthrough, let's look at just a few of the clues Watson was designed to answer. Here's one about the 2008 Olympics:

> Milorad Čavić almost upset this man's perfect 2008 Olympics, losing to him by one hundredth of a second.

Here's another clue:

> Wanted for general evil-ness; last seen at the Tower of Barad-Dur; it's a giant eye, folks, kinda hard to miss.

And here's yet another clue, in the category "The main vegetable":

> Coleslaw.

Take a moment to consider how a computer might answer these questions: what information it must know, how it might store that information, and how it might process the question to look up that information. And remember that IBM's researchers couldn't just program Watson to simply read the question, understand it, and recall the answer from what it had read. Its programmers needed to provide Watson with an explicit sequence of operations it could follow to answer each clue.

IBM's Watson had no human understanding of what each word—let alone each collection of words—meant. And yet still it managed to defeat two human champions. In chapters 12 and 13, we'll look more deeply at how Watson managed to do this. In this chapter, we'll start with the first piece of this puzzle: how Watson figured out what the clue was even asking.

LONG LISTS OF FACTS

On the surface, some *Jeopardy* questions might look easy for a computer to answer: *Jeopardy* is a quiz show, and quiz shows are about facts. And Watson had four *terabytes* of disk to store its databases of facts.[9] This should get us most of the way to building Watson, right?

For example, take the following *Jeopardy* clue, which appeared under the category "Who Wrote It?":[10]

> A "savage journey" titled "Fear & Loathing in Las Vegas."

Here's another example, under the category "Writers by Middle Names":

> Allan, who was "nevermore" as of Oct. 7, 1849.

To answer these questions, Watson needs to know that Hunter S. Thompson wrote *Fear and Loathing in Las Vegas*, and that Edgar Allan Poe passed away October 7, 1849—or, at least, that Poe was associated with the phrase "nevermore" or had the middle name "Allan."[11]

Facts like these can be stored in databases, and Watson did store facts like this, whenever it could. Such facts are known as *relations*. Relations are connections between people, places, and things. One such relation is the *author-of* relation, which can give us an answer to the first clue above:

Table 12.1

Charles Dickens	*author-of*	*A Christmas Carol*
Hunter S. Thompson	*author-of*	*Fear and Loathing in Las Vegas*
J. K. Rowling	*author-of*	*Harry Potter and the Sorcerer's Stone*
...	...	...

Another relation—helpful for the second clue above—is the *alive-until* relation:

Table 12.2

Edgar Allan Poe	*alive-until*	October 7, 1849
Abraham Lincoln	*alive-until*	April 15, 1865
Genghis Khan	*alive-until*	August 18, 1227
...	...	...

As you can imagine, the set of possible relations is endless, and Watson stored millions of them, to keep track of dates, movies, books, people, places, and so on.

But millions of relations alone would still leave Watson far short of being able to play *Jeopardy*. Take the clue I mentioned above, which was offered during Watson's televised match:

> Wanted for general evil-ness; last seen at the Tower of Barad-Dur; it's a giant eye, folks, kinda hard to miss.

Although Watson provided the correct response, *What is Sauron?*, it's unlikely that Watson had an *is-a-giant-eye* relation, let alone an *is-a-giant-eye-who-resided-in* relation.[12] It's unlikely that Watson had anything in its structured databases about Sauron, except that Sauron is a character in *Lord of the Rings*, and that *Lord of the Rings* was written by J. R. R. Tolkien. Just as a self-driving car couldn't anticipate rare occurrences like a woman in an electric wheelchair chasing a duck in the middle of the street—an encounter that we know happened for one self-driving car—the researchers behind Watson couldn't have anticipated all possible relations that might show up in a clue.

Another challenge Watson faced is that *Jeopardy* clues are phrased in a wide variety of ways. Take the clue above about Edgar Allan Poe, who was "nevermore" as of 1849. Watson needed some way to recognize that "nevermore" was a synonym for "dead." Watson used dictionaries and thesauri, but a typical thesaurus doesn't list "nevermore" as a synonym for "dead." The synonym is only meaningful in this context because "nevermore" is the famous line from one of Edgar Allan Poe's poems. Although relations gave Watson the ability to simply "look up" answers in its databases, only a quarter of questions had these relations to start with. To make things even worse, Watson was only able to simply "look up" answers for a mere 2 percent of clues.[13]

So how did Watson answer the remaining 98 percent of clues? It did this by systematically analyzing the clue, teasing out key information with a fine-toothed comb.

THE *JEOPARDY* CHALLENGE IS BORN

Shortly before Watson competed against Jennings and Rutter, a popular book by Stephen Baker called *Final Jeopardy* came out. The book was originally published electronically, its final chapter withheld until after the competition aired on television. Readers needed to wait to read the final chapter, which was delivered electronically after the show was broadcast (and included in the subsequent print version). Among other things, the book outlined how the team at IBM made their decision to develop a program to play *Jeopardy*, a story that unfolded as follows.[14]

In the early 2000s, IBM was looking for a Grand Challenge, a public display of the company's technical prowess. Finding such a challenge was important to IBM because the company had a lucrative consulting business, and this business depended on its customers' faith that the company was at the cutting edge in fields like big data and large-scale computing. IBM had defeated chess champion Garry Kasparov in 1997 with Deep Blue, which had been one such success; so the idea of another challenge was on everyone's mind.[15]

It's difficult to trace exactly where the original idea for a *Jeopardy* Challenge started: different employees at the company have different accounts. One version of the story holds that a senior manager at IBM got the idea when he was at a steakhouse one autumn day in 2004. He noticed other customers getting up from their untouched meals to move to a different section of the restaurant. They were crowding around televisions at the bar, three people deep, to watch Ken Jennings during his famous winning streak. After winning over 50 consecutive games, would Ken just keep on going? If the public was so fascinated by this game, the IBM manager wondered, would they be similarly interested in a game between a human and a computer?[16]

However the idea for an IBM *Jeopardy* Challenge actually started (at least one other employee at the company thought he had the idea, and James Fan, whom we met at the beginning of this chapter, also independently had the idea), once it had coalesced, it ran into plenty of internal resistance. Some saw a *Jeopardy* Challenge as a publicity stunt that could waste money and researchers' time. Even worse, it might risk the company's credibility. Despite this resistance, the head of IBM's 3,000-person research division pitched the project to some of his researchers, one of whom was David Ferrucci.[17]

Ferrucci was already familiar with the problems they might face, because one of the research teams he managed had already been working for a handful of years on a question-answering system. Theirs was among the better question-answering systems in the world, and it consistently performed well in competitions. But Ferrucci and his team also knew how far from playing *Jeopardy* these systems currently were. Still, he pitched the problem to his team. Only one of them was optimistic about the idea: James Fan, who had recently joined the team after finishing his PhD.[18] But the team concluded that the field wasn't ready yet: it would be too difficult. Ferrucci told the head of research that it would be best not to pursue the project.[19]

Before long the head of research returned to ask again about *Jeopardy*; Ferrucci and his team retreated to a conference room once again to brainstorm. As they discussed the project, their conclusions remained roughly the same: a system able to answer *Jeopardy* questions would need to be much faster than their current system; it would need to answer a much broader array of questions; and, most difficult of all, it would need to answer those questions more accurately. There were too many open research problems to address. It didn't seem possible. But in the end, inspired by the possibility of success and some hunches about how they might proceed, they relented, and Watson was born.[20]

DEEPQA

The question-answering system Ferrucci's team already had when they first began working on Watson was good by the standards of the day. IBM had already devoted a lot of resources to it—a four-person team had developed the system over the course of six years. But their existing system didn't work out of the box for *Jeopardy*, so Ferrucci's team spent about a month converting it to play the game.

Ferrucci's team also needed a way to evaluate their system. Fortunately they discovered a goldmine of *Jeopardy* clues and answers on the internet. Avid *Jeopardy* fans had created a website containing all *Jeopardy* questions and answers from televised episodes, and they had annotated the questions with detailed information.[21]

Using this site, the IBM team collected performance statistics of past *Jeopardy* winners: How often did the winners in *Jeopardy* buzz in? When they did buzz in, how often did they give the correct answer? Ferrucci's team created a scatterplot of these two numbers, a cloud of data points illustrating how accurate and how prolific at answering questions past *Jeopardy* winners were. They called this plot the "Winners Cloud," and they used it as a measuring stick to benchmark Watson.[22] If they could move Watson into the cloud, they could match the human winners' performance. If they could move it *past* the cloud, they could beat these humans.

After the team had spent a month converting their previous system to play *Jeopardy*, they evaluated it using these metrics. But their converted system performed abysmally: if it answered the 62 percent of questions Watson was most confident about—the same fraction Ken Jennings answered on average—it would only answer 13 percent of questions correctly. To be competitive with Jennings, Watson would need to answer more than 92 percent of these questions correctly.[23] It was clear to them that they would need to do things much differently.

This failure of their existing system was in fact a strategy on Ferrucci's part: the team needed to realize that their current system, with its traditional methods, had failed. By failing, they could start from scratch to reinvent a new way of looking at things.[24]

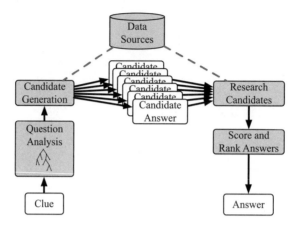

Figure 12.1
A very basic overview of the very complicated DeepQA
pipeline.

And so Ferrucci and his team experimented, implementing state-
of-the-art methods from the academic literature. After many months of
experimentation, the team finally arrived at an architecture that seemed to
work; they called it DeepQA.[25] The approach behind DeepQA was simple. Like many other question-answering systems, to arrive at an answer it
followed just a few concrete steps, which you can see in figure 12.1: *analyze the question, come up with candidate answers with search engines, research these
answers*, and *score these answers* based on the evidence it found for them. In
the rest of this chapter we'll focus on the first phase of this pipeline:
Watson's Question Analysis phase.

QUESTION ANALYSIS

The goal of Watson's Question Analysis phase is to decompose a question
into pieces of information that could be useful in finding and evaluating
answers later in the pipeline. Like most parts of Watson, the Question
Analysis phase depended heavily on the field of *natural language processing*, or
NLP. NLP gave Watson the ability to do something meaningful with the
words making up the clue: Watson used it to find the parts of speech of
the words in the clue, to search for names and places in the clue, and to create sentence diagrams of the clue.[26]

The most important task for Watson during its Question Analysis phase was to find the phrase in the clue summarizing what specifically it is asking for. Take this clue, for example:

It's the B form of this inflammation of the liver that's spread by some kinds of personal contact.

The phrase summarizing what the clue is asking for is *this inflammation of the liver.* Watson's researchers called this phrase the "focus." The focus is the part of the clue that, if replaced by the answer, turns the clue into a statement of fact.[27] If we replace the focus of the clue above by the answer, *hepatitis*, it becomes:

It's the B form of **hepatitis** that's spread by some kinds of personal contact.

Now it is a factual statement. Here's another example:

In 2005 this title duo investigated "The Curse of the Were-Rabbit."

In this clue, the focus is "this title duo." Replacing the focus by its answer, we get:

In 2005 **Wallace and Gromit** investigated "The Curse of the Were-Rabbit."

Again, that is a factual statement. By finding the focus, Watson could use that information down the road when it would generate possible answers and score them. Now let's apply this to our clue about the 2008 Olympics. Here's that clue again, with its focus in bold:

Milorad Čavić almost upset **this man's** perfect 2008 Olympics, losing to him by one hundredth of a second.

Another type of information Watson extracted from the question is a word or phrase describing the *answer type*.[28] Is the clue asking for a *president*? Is it asking for a *city*? Or maybe it's asking for an *inflammation* like hepatitis or an *ingredient* like lettuce. Again, Watson used this information to come up with candidate answers and to score them later in the pipeline. I'll describe exactly how Watson used this information in the next chapter; but for now, all you need to know is that Watson stored this information in this stage so it could select and narrow down possible answers in later stages. If the question was asking for a disease, for example, then Watson could narrow down its candidate answers in a later stage by giving higher weight to those candidate answers that were actually diseases and lower weights to candidate answers that were, for example, symptoms of diseases. The answer type is usually part of the focus, so if Watson could find the focus, it had a good chance at finding the answer type. In our clue about the 2008 Olympics, the answer type was simply *man*. So Watson would use this information later in its pipeline to narrow down its candidate answers to those were instances of *man*.

Sometimes Watson had little more than a few nouns or verbs to go on in its clue. In one of the clues we saw above, the clue was a single word: *Coleslaw*.[29] When Watson couldn't find an answer type in cases like this one, it searched the clue's category for an answer type. (Every question in *Jeopardy* is assigned to a category, and this category is visible to all players when they see the question.) The category for the clue *Coleslaw* was *The main vegetable*, so in this case Watson could set its answer type to *vegetable*, which would later help Watson to find the correct answer: *cabbage*.[30]

Watson also looked for proper nouns, dates, and relations in clues. By finding proper nouns, Watson could be much more focused as it searched for candidate answers later on. In the clue about the 2008 Olympics, it would have found the name *Milorad Čavić* and the phrase *2008 Olympics*. It would also have recognized that *2008* is a date in the clue.

And so Watson proceeded to dissect the clue, teasing little bits of useful information out of it. For some of this information, Watson used simple pattern matching. For example, it's easy to make Watson search for dates by having it search for sequences of four digits starting with 1 or 2. But for Watson to pull other information from the clue, like the clue's focus and answer type, it needed a more sophisticated suite of tools.

HOW WATSON INTERPRETS A SENTENCE

One of the most important ways our modern automata interact with the world is via perception. We've seen how a self-driving car perceives the world around it: it uses laser scanners, cameras, and accelerometers to create a model of the world. Watson didn't have laser scanners or accelerometers, nor did it have a camera to read the screen or microphones to listen to Alex Trebek. Instead, the clue was delivered to Watson electronically, in the form of a text file. When Watson looked at this text file, it saw nothing more than an ordered sequence of letters, so it used tricks from the field of natural language processing to make sense of them.

The first way Watson made sense of these characters was by interpreting the clue as a sequence of words instead of as a sequence of letters. Once Watson interpreted a clue as a sequence of words, it could then use some more interesting tricks to process the clue. The most important of these tricks was to map out the structure of the clue with a sentence diagram, just as you likely did in grade school. A computer creates a sentence diagram in a process called *parsing*; and the resulting sentence diagram is usually called a *parse tree*. You can see a parse tree for the clue about the 2008 Olympics in figure 12.2. In this clue, the subject is the proper noun

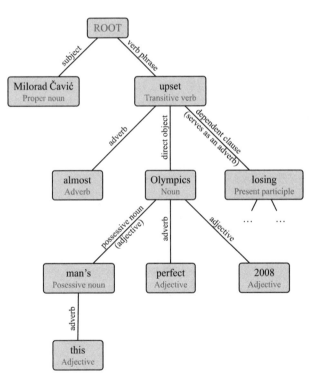

Figure 12.2
A parse tree for the sentence "Milorad Čavić almost upset this man's perfect 2008 Olympics, losing to him by one hundredth of a second." This tree is a traditional parse, much like what you might have learned in grade school. Watson didn't parse a sentence exactly like this, but it used the same idea.

Milorad Čavić, and the verb is the word *upset*; the remaining parts of the sentence modify the verb phrase. (This isn't the exact way Watson parsed a sentence, but the basic idea is the same.) Once Watson had a diagram of a sentence, it could use this diagram to perform more interesting analysis of the question, which we'll get to shortly. But first, let's look briefly at how a program like Watson could create a parse tree.

A computer can create a parse tree by using a search algorithm, a lot like the way Boss planned a path through its urban environment. Instead of searching for the best path over a map as Boss did, Watson's parser searched for the best way to create a tree out of the words in the sentence that agreed with the rules of grammar. Modern parsers use statistics about the relationships between words and parts of speech to find which parse trees are the most likely.

You probably remember from your school days that English sentences can be decomposed into a subject phrase and a verb phrase, and that each of these can be decomposed further. For example, *verb phrase* or *noun phrase* can be decomposed into two parts:

$$\text{verb phrase} = \text{adverb} + \text{verb phrase}$$

or

$$\text{noun phrase} = \text{adjective} + \text{noun}$$

We can continue applying rules like this until a sentence has been decomposed into small pieces, each of which is a single part of speech. Some sentence parsers use this fact. To parse a sentence, these parsers search for the best possible ways to split up the sentence using these rules, until they can't split the sentence into any more pieces.

Sometimes sentences have ambiguous parse trees. Here are some sentences rumored to have appeared as newspaper headlines:[31]

Juvenile Court to Try Shooting Defendant

Hospitals Are Sued by 7 Foot Doctors

You might think that these examples seem contrived. These are just the rare exceptions, right? Actually, these sorts of ambiguities can happen all the time. They're always lurking just below the surface of our language, but we don't notice them most of the time because our minds resolve their ambiguity quickly. See if you can find the ambiguity in one of the clues we saw earlier in this chapter:

> It's the B form of this inflammation of the liver that's spread by some kinds of personal contact.

In this clue, the ambiguity is around whether it's the *inflammation* that's spread by some kinds of personal contact, or whether it's the *liver* that's spread by some kinds of personal contact. While it's painfully obvious to us humans that livers can't spread by personal contact, this isn't obvious to Watson's sentence parser. There's nothing ungrammatical about that parse, even if it's semantically weird.

Here's another example, which Watson faced when it played against Ken and Brad:

> This 1959 Daniel Keyes novella about Charlie Gordon and a smarter-than-average lab mouse won a Hugo award.

In this case, the ambiguity is around whether the novella is about *Charlie Gordon and a smarter-than-average lab mouse* (the correct parse), or whether both a *novella about Charlie Gordon* and a *smarter-than-average lab mouse* won a Hugo award. (A Hugo award is an award for science fiction and fantasy books.) There's nothing syntactically or even semantically wrong with the second parse, although if you knew about the Hugo award, you would realize that it's not typically awarded to smart mice. The answer to this clue, by the way—which Watson got correct—is *Flowers for Algernon.*

There's no way for a computer to know for certain which parse tree for the statements above are correct unless it has more context about the situation; but as I mentioned before, modern parsers use statistics about words, parts of speech, and the ways they combine to form sentences. Often those probabilities are enough for the computer to find the correct parse.

Even though Watson could create these sentence diagrams, it still had no idea what they meant. To Watson, these diagrams were nothing more than data structures floating around its computer memory, some of which pointed to other ones. Fortunately for Watson, it didn't need to understand these sentence diagrams. They were merely useful tools the programmer could use to interpret the question. But how could the programmer interpret the question without even looking at it?

Remember back to the Monopoly board in the self-driving car. The Monopoly board encoded human knowledge about situations the car might find itself in, such as the etiquette around precedence at traffic stops. Just as Boss's creators handcrafted the rules for it to traverse crowded intersections when those researchers weren't around, Watson's developers handcrafted their own rules so that Watson could traverse its sentence diagrams to pull meaningful information from clues when its researchers weren't around.

Watson used these rules to inspect parse trees all through its DeepQA pipeline, starting with its Question Analysis phase. One place it used the parse tree was to find the focus of a clue. Remember, the focus is the phrase in the clue that captures what exactly is being asked for—like *this man* or

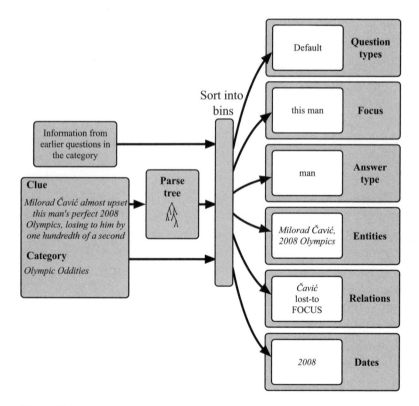

Figure 12.3
Some of the most important information Watson looks for in its clues during its Question Analysis phase.

this inflammation. To find the focus, Watson used simple rules such as *search for a noun phrase described by* "this" *or* "these."[32] Watson also looked for other information in its parse tree, including whether there were clues embedded within other clues or whether there were pairs of clues joined by a conjunction like "or." Watson also searched the parse tree for information about relations involving the clue's focus.

You can see how Watson would have analyzed our clue about the Olympics in figure 12.3. Watson has systematically dissected the clue with many rules, using the parse tree as a lens through which to inspect it. In its Question Analysis phase, Watson is an obsessive-compulsive organizer, carefully taking stock of what it finds in the sentence and putting bits of information into carefully labeled boxes. But it still hasn't come any closer to understanding what the clue was asking. Watson has blindly processed its clue so the next few phases in its DeepQA pipeline can do their work.

When Watson had finished this labeling process, its work was still far from over: it still faced the daunting task of finding the correct answer for the clue. For this, it used some of the typical data sources you might expect: dictionaries, geographic and movie databases, and even Wikipedia. But, as we'll see in chapter 13, Watson used them in a very different way than a human would use them.

THE BASEMENT BASELINE

As David Ferrucci began plotting IBM's path for taking on *Jeopardy!*, he wanted some evidence that the project wouldn't be too hard. As Stephen Baker, the author of *Final Jeopardy*, observed, there was enough internal pushback that it could be politically risky to devote many person-years of effort if there was no chance that they could succeed.[1] At the same time, he also became concerned about the possibility that it might be too *easy* to build a computer to play *Jeopardy*. What if IBM invested years of research in the project and spent millions on marketing, only to be shown up by a lone hacker working in his basement for a month? This could be a huge embarrassment—let alone a waste of time—for the company.[2]

Ferrucci and his team came up with a simple test that became known as the *basement baseline*. As most of his team spent a month converting their existing question-answering system to play *Jeopardy*, Ferrucci asked James Fan, who was the most enthusiastic member of the team about building a system to play the game, to spend that month working alone in his second-floor office, hacking together a system with whatever tools he could find. James Fan wouldn't work at all with the rest of the team during this period, except to join them for lunch and meetings. Instead, he would have to come up with his own methods. This hacker baseline would then compete with the system the other researchers were converting in order to play *Jeopardy*. If James Fan's system did better, then Ferrucci and his team needed to figure out how to address that.[3] If they couldn't demonstrate enough new ideas in this period, that would also be evidence that the problem was too hard.[4]

After a month of effort by the two teams—the regular research team and the team consisting of just James Fan—they found the basement baseline to be okay for a baseline—nearly as good as the converted system by some metrics—but it still couldn't play *Jeopardy* anywhere close to how well a human could play *Jeopardy*. At the same time, James Fan had found some promising ideas during his effort.[5] This was a relief, and the team now had some evidence that their problem had just the right amount of difficulty: it wasn't so easy that they were likely to be embarrassed, and yet they had learned that they could improve on their current approaches by applying some good old-fashioned elbow grease and throwing some extra manpower at the problem.[6]

As we saw in the last chapter, however, they faced another problem: the system they had converted to play *Jeopardy* still fell far short of where it needed to be to beat a human player.[7] Instead of trying to make their existing system work, they threw away their old assumptions and started from scratch. After months of experiments they converged on a system they named DeepQA.

Their DeepQA system began with the Question Analysis phase we saw in the last chapter. The goal of the Question Analysis phase was to pull the most salient information out of the clue, to find the people, places, and things mentioned in it; to find what type of answer the clue was looking for; and to carefully label these bits of information and package them up for later phases in the pipeline. The remaining phases in DeepQA, which we'll cover in this chapter, would enable Watson to find the correct answer.

Watson didn't find an answer to the question in the same way a human would have come up with an answer. A human might think about the question, decide on the single most appropriate source for the answer, and look the answer up in that source. If she doesn't find the answer where she looked, she might look up the answer in the second-best source, or she might adjust her research path if she finds a promising lead along the way. Once the human researcher finds the answer—very possibly from a single source—she closes her books, puts them away, and answers the question confidently.

Watson, however, treated each question as a massive research project. Its process was a lot like searching for the perfect person to hire for a job opening. The first step involves creating a detailed job description; that was Watson's Question Analysis phase, which we saw in the last chapter. Once

Watson had finished putting the together the job description, it then collected résumés for hundreds of possible people from a myriad of sources, researched many of these candidates in detail by "interviewing" them, and then carefully weighed the pros and cons of each candidate to select the best one among them all.[8] Let's begin with the first of these steps in finding and evaluating candidates: the way Watson came up with a list of candidates, a phase Watson's creators called its Candidate Generation phase.

CANDIDATE GENERATION

To fill your job vacancy, your first step at this stage would be to collect résumés of people who might be interested in the job. Your goal isn't to select the right person; it's just to put together a list of all people you should consider hiring. You would likely seek out these applicants in many places. You might list the job on a jobs search engine, you might reach out to some people in your professional network, and you might post the job opening on your company's website. You might even put a listing in the local classified ads. After some time, you will have collected a nice stack of résumés for these candidates.

Watson used the same approach to create its list of candidate answers. Watson's goal wasn't to select the correct answer; it was just to collect possible candidates for it. But Watson's problem was a bit trickier than the hiring problem: unlike a job opening—for which there might be more than one qualified applicant—clues in *Jeopardy* have exactly *one* correct answer. If the correct answer wasn't part of Watson's candidate list at the end of this stage, then Watson had no chance at answering the clue correctly. Watson therefore had a low bar to consider something as a candidate.

To be concrete, let's look at the clue about the 2008 Olympics we saw in the last chapter, to see how Watson would find candidates for it. Here's that clue again:

> Milorad Čavić almost upset this man's perfect 2008 Olympics, losing to him by one hundredth of a second.

During the Question Analysis phase described in the last chapter, Watson would have found out several things about the clue: in figure 12.3, we saw that Watson would have identified the proper nouns "Milorad Čavić" and "2008 Olympics" in the clue, that it would have found the focus, *this man,* and that it would have found the answer type, *man*. With this information about its clue, Watson could start to seek out candidate answers.

Watson looked all over the place for its candidate answers, including in news articles and encyclopedia articles. Some of its candidates came from its structured data sources, which were mostly tables with different types of relations (remember, relations were connections between people, places, and things). As a rough rule of thumb, you can assume that the relations Watson knew about were the contents of those "info-boxes" you can find on the margin of some Wikipedia pages.[9] For example, in 2010, the info-boxes on the Wikipedia pages about Milorad Čavić and the 2008 Olympics included the facts that Čavić's nationality is Serbian and that the 2008 Olympics took place in Beijing. So Watson would add "Serbian" and "Beijing" to its list of candidate answers, along with some of the other arguments to relations it found about these two. You can see some candidates I found for this clue from these relations in table 13.1.

As I mentioned in the last chapter, databases of relations only worked for a small fraction of clues. This clue was no exception: although Watson wouldn't have known this yet, none of the candidates we found from these structured databases provided the correct answer. But that's okay. Remember: Watson didn't need to select the correct answer at this stage in the pipeline. It just needed to make sure the correct answer was somewhere in its list. That's why Watson looked in many more places.

SEARCHING FOR ANSWERS

Watson continued its search for candidate answers in its vast unstructured data stores, collections of documents like encyclopedia and newspaper articles, Wikipedia articles, literary works, dictionaries, and thesauri. But how could Watson find answers from these massive collections within just a few seconds? Watson did it in the same way you find answers in large collections of text documents: with a search engine.[10]

Since Watson wasn't allowed to access the internet during the competition, it couldn't simply use a web search engine like Google. Therefore Watson's researchers collected all of Watson's documents and loaded them into their own custom search engines before unplugging Watson from the internet. These search engines then ran as part of Watson in IBM's datacenter during the game.[11] From the perspective of Watson, these search

Table 13.1
Candidate answers for the clue "Milorad Čavić almost upset this man's perfect 2008 Olympics, losing to him by one hundredth of a second"

Source of candidates	Candidate answer
Relations from Wikipedia info-boxes (DBPedia) related to "Milorad Čavić" and "2008 Olympics"	*Serbian* (Čavić's nationality)
	6'6" (Čavić's height)
	215 pounds (Čavić's weight)
	butterfly, freestyle (Čavić's strokes)
	University of California, Berkeley (Čavić's college team)
	Beijing (2008 Olympics city)
	Beijing National Stadium (2008 Olympics venue)
	August 8 (2008 Olympics opening ceremony date)
	August 24 (2008 Olympics closing ceremony date)
Candidates from Wikipedia: the titles of articles in the search results, articles that redirect to these articles, text of hyperlinks between articles, and titles of the pages linked from these results	*Grobari* (title)
	Rafael Muñoz (title, link text)
	Pieter van den Hoogenband (title)
	Aleksandar Đorđević (title)
	Milorad Čavić (title)
	Swimming at the 2012 Summer Olympics (title)
	World and Olympic records set at the 2008 Summer Olympics (title)
	Michael Phelps (title, link text)
	Le Clos (title)
	Yevgeny Korotyshkin (title)
	Beijing Olympics (link text)
	100 m butterfly world record (link text)
	voting (link text)
	Usain Bolt (link text)
	2008 Summer Olympics (title)
	2008 Olympics (page that redirects to search result)

engines worked a lot like a web search engine works for you: you enter a search query and get back a list of search results.[12]

To use these search engines, Watson just needed to come up with search queries. To make these search queries, it used the words or phrases from the clue that it found during its Question Analysis phase to be important, and it included the answer type (*president, vegetable, sense organ, duo*) in the query. If it found a relation in the clue, like the *actor-in* relation, it gave any arguments to that relation in the clue more weight. When you search for an answer on Google, you probably sometimes take a moment to think about which terms to include in your search query. Watson didn't think at all about how it crafted its queries: it just filled in blanks in simple templates created by its developers with the information it found during its Question Analysis phase.

After Watson sent these queries to its search engines, it created more candidate answers from the results. Sometimes this was as simple as adding the titles of the search results as candidate answers.[13] Other times Watson used more nuanced tricks.

One trick made clever use of Wikipedia articles. During his month of hacking on the basement baseline, James Fan discovered that Wikipedia could be exceptionally useful in generating candidate answers.[14] After researching Wikipedia a bit more, the team working on Candidate Generation discovered that an astounding 95 percent of *Jeopardy* answers were also the title of some Wikipedia article.[15]

Armed with this information, the team made Wikipedia a cornerstone in Watson's Candidate Generation phase. Any time Watson found a Wikipedia passage in its search results for a clue, it went through a checklist to generate candidate answers from that passage. First, it added the Wikipedia page title for the passage to its list of candidate answers. It also looked more closely at the passage matching the search query to find more candidates: it created candidate answers from the text of any hyperlinks (called anchor text) in the passage, as well as from the titles of any Wikipedia pages linked from those passages and the titles of any Wikipedia pages that redirected to those links.[16]

Watson's researchers also built up a list of all Wikipedia article titles so they could look for these phrases elsewhere, whether they appeared in documents from other sources—where they could become candidate answers—or in the clue itself during Watson's Question Analysis phase.[17]

This is how Watson could know, for example, that "2008 Olympics" is a proper noun in its clue: there's also a Wikipedia article titled "2008 Olympics."

Let's look back at that clue about the 2008 Olympics to see what candidates we could get out of these Wikipedia tricks. I created a search query for the clue similar to what Watson would have come up with, and I entered it into Google, restricting the search to just give results from Wikipedia .org.[18] Remember, Watson couldn't use Google since it was cut off from the internet, but its custom search engines served roughly the same role, and Wikipedia was one of the sources Watson's researchers programmed into Watson's search engines. If we go through these search results and follow the checklist Watson followed for Wikipedia—adding the text from article titles, the text of web links, and so on—then we'll come up with a lot more candidate answers, such as: Rafael Muñoz, Pieter van den Hoogenband, Swimming at the 2012 Summer Olympics, and Michael Phelps. I show these and more in the bottom half of table 13.1.

These candidates are already starting to look a lot better! This is in part because now at least some of them match the clue's answer type, which was *man*. But remember: Watson didn't know these answers were more promising. In fact, when I was collecting these answer candidates to write this chapter, I found the correct answer, with strong evidence to support the answer. But even though Watson would have come across this evidence when it was generating candidates, it didn't check whether it found the correct answer until later on. It just continued its search, looking through more and more sources, to compile its large list of candidates.

LIGHTWEIGHT FILTER

By the time Watson had finished compiling its list, it typically had several hundred candidates, and it needed to perform a deeper analysis of each of them to figure out which one was correct. Watson would need to devote considerable effort to researching each candidate—enough effort to prevent researching them all—so it narrowed its list down to a smaller set with a "lightweight filter."

You would do the same thing in your search for someone to fill the job opening. Once you had a stack of résumés for your job posting, your next step would be to perform a "deeper analysis" of your job applicants—that is, you would invite some of them onsite for interviews. If you're hiring to fill a single role and you have a few hundred applications, however, you don't have enough time to interview all of these applicants onsite. You would instead apply a lightweight filter to narrow down the résumés—for example, by eliminating those candidates lacking a college degree or experience most relevant to your job—before inviting that smaller set of candidates for an onsite interview. Out of necessity—you have a lot of résumés to review—this filter would be simple.

Watson's lightweight filter was also very simple: it might test whether the candidate answer matched the answer type—*president, city,* or *man,* for example.[19] For the clue about the 2008 Olympics, the answer type was *man,* so we could assume that Watson narrowed down its candidate list for this clue to those that match the names of people. Any candidates that passed the lightweight filter moved on to the Evidence Retrieval phase, so that Watson could spend more time collecting information about each candidate.[20]

EVIDENCE RETRIEVAL

This Evidence Retrieval phase was akin to doing onsite interviews. Whereas you might interview only a few candidates, Watson carefully researched about 100 of its candidate answers.[21] To do this, Watson again turned to its databases and search engines.

If you were interviewing a job candidate onsite, you probably wouldn't get to know the job candidate by going through the job description bullet by bullet. You would ask the candidate questions tailored to the individual's background as well as to the specifics of the job opening, hoping to find unique ways the candidate is a good fit for the job. Watson did the same thing when it researched its candidate answers. It formulated questions—search queries—specific to both the answer candidate and the clue. Again, it turned to its structured and unstructured data sources to do this research.

Watson created its search queries by combining important words and phrases from the clue with the candidate answer, treating the candidate answer as a required phrase. Here's how that might look for the 2008 Olympics clue, if we were to formulate it as a Google search query:

+"Rafael Muñoz" Milorad Čavić upset 2008 Olympics losing hundredth second

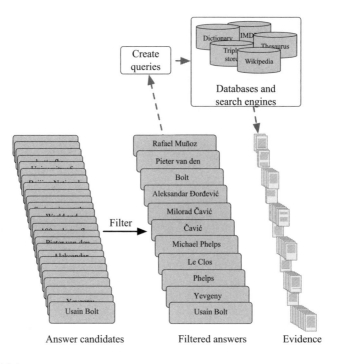

Figure 13.1
The evidence retrieval phase of Watson. Watson first filtered its answer candidates using a lightweight filter and then collected reams of evidence for each of its remaining candidates from its databases and search engines.

Watson then issued queries like this to its search engines, as in figure 13.1, so it could collect evidence tailored to both the candidate and the clue.

In doing its research, Watson collected a pile of evidence to support each of its candidates; most of this evidence was just pieces of text from its search results. For the candidate answer "Rafael Muñoz," the Wikipedia search results aren't too promising: the first result, a page about swimming in the 2008 Olympics, only references Rafael Muñoz in a table with one of his swim times. (As an aside, it turns out that evidence for the correct answer—which is not Rafael Muñoz—is actually elsewhere on this page, but again, Watson would have had no idea about this, because it was following prescriptive rules, and none of these rules told it to look at that part of the page.) The other search results for the query about "Rafael Muñoz" are similarly useless.

Of course, Watson didn't stop after researching its first candidate. It carefully researched all of the candidates that passed through its lightweight filter. Let's try this Evidence Retrieval exercise with a different candidate answer: Pieter van den Hoogenband. The search results for this query are a bit better, though they're still not great. One result is the Wikipedia page about Hoogenband, which contains the following passage:

> He returned to the Olympic Games in 2008 in Beijing and finished fifth in the 100 m freestyle.

That sentence has matches for *2008*, *Olympics*, and *100* (which is like *hundredth*), but otherwise is not a good match. The remaining results for this candidate are also underwhelming. Let's try one final candidate: Michael Phelps. The very first search result, a Wikipedia page about swimming in the 2008 Olympics, contains this passage:

> U.S. swimmer Michael Phelps set a new Olympic record of 50.58 to defend his title in the event, edging out Serbia's Milorad Čavić (50.59) by one hundredth of a second (0.01).[22]

Ah-ha! That looks much more promising. A similar passage appears in another search result, the Wikipedia page about Michael Phelps:

> On August 16, Phelps won his seventh gold medal of the Games in the men's 100-meter butterfly, setting an Olympic record for the event with a time of 50.58 seconds and edging out his nearest competitor Čavić, by one hundredth (0.01) of a second.[23]

Again, the candidate "Michael Phelps" looks very promising. If we can trust Watson's ability to evaluate the evidence for its candidates later in the pipeline, this approach for the Evidence Retrieval phase seems promising.

Wikipedia wasn't the only source Watson used in its Evidence Retrieval stage; as I mentioned above, Watson used a variety of sources, including dictionaries, thesauri, encyclopedias, newswire archives, and tables of relations, like *alive-until* and *capital-city-of*. Watson's creators made sure Watson's queries to different sources were appropriately customized. Watson created queries for each relevant source given what it had learned about the clue from the Question Analysis phase and given the candidate answer it was researching, sometimes using information from the clue's parse tree. Then it stored the results of the search to use later.

When we found the passage suggesting that "Michael Phelps" was the correct answer to the clue, we were satisfied that we had the answer and knew we could stop looking. But Watson wouldn't have stopped its research like a human would have done, because it didn't try to understand the evidence it was collecting yet. It didn't start to judge its candidates until its next phase, when it would score the evidence. As far as Watson was concerned at this point, the supporting evidence for Michael Phelps was no stronger than the evidence for Pieter van den Hoogenband; the evidence for each candidate was simply pieces of text sitting somewhere in its computer memory, similar to notes taken by the people who interviewed the job candidate. Instead, Watson simply continued its research, collecting passage after passage of evidence to support its remaining candidates. When Watson was finally done interviewing candidates, it was ready for perhaps the most interesting bit: scoring each of these candidates.

SCORING

After collecting supporting evidence for each of its candidates, Watson passed the results to a collection of scoring algorithms. Just as Watson used a variety of rules to analyze its question, its Scoring phase used a variety of rules to analyze the evidence for each candidate answer.

These scorers did most of the work you'd probably consider "interesting" in Watson: they estimated how closely each piece of evidence about each candidate answer matched the clue.

This phase would be akin to creating a giant spreadsheet to evaluate the evidence for each job candidate. To evaluate each piece of evidence for a candidate, you might use several different criteria: whether the evidence demonstrates good communication, job-related experience, culture fit, or on-their-toes critical thinking ability. Your goal in this Scoring phase is *not* to evaluate the candidates themselves: your goal is to evaluate only the candidates' responses to the questions you asked, to try to stay objective. This means you might need to separately score many pieces of evidence for each candidate. You'd then distill the spreadsheet's results into a final decision in a later stage, just as Watson waited until a later stage to weigh its own scores for each piece of evidence.

Watson used many scorers to evaluate its evidence, but each scorer tended to be fairly simple. One scorer, for example, measured the number of overlapping words between the clue and the supporting passage. It weighted each word with an approach called IDF, which gives rare words more weight, as a proxy for how much "information" the word conveys. The intuition behind this approach is that rare words convey more information precisely because they are rare: if the clue and the passage share a rare word, such as "Čavić" or "scorpion," then this should carry more weight than if they share a frequent word, like "almost" or "one."[24] The candidate answer "Michael Phelps" would have been scored well by this metric, because many supporting passages for the candidate Michael Phelps shared rare words, like "Čavić," with the clue. The passages supporting the other candidates wouldn't have fared so well for this scorer.

The glaring weakness of this word-overlap scorer is that it completely ignores the order of words in the supporting passage. For example, take this clue:

He famously became the President of China in June of 2003.

The word-overlap scorer would score the following passage highly even though it suggests the wrong answer:

President George W. Bush famously praised China in June of 2003.

Clearly this scorer would give the wrong passage too much weight, simply because it has many overlapping words.

So Watson also had some scorers that could address this shortcoming. One of them attempted to align the words in the clue and the passage sequentially, finding an alignment between the two with a search algorithm. Once aligned, matching words caused the score to be higher, while mismatching or missing words caused the score to be lower. As before, the alignment scorer gave more weight to rare words, preferring alignments that matched on rare words over those that matched on common words.

One scorer the IBM researchers added was a gender scorer; it was evident that Watson needed this scorer after Watson saw this clue during testing:

This first lady was born Thelma Catherine Ryan, on March 16, 1912, in Nevada.[25]

Watson's answer, before it had the gender scorer, was "Richard Nixon." (The correct answer was Nixon's wife, Thelma Catherine "Pat" Nixon.)

Watson also used parse trees in its scorers. One scorer was like the word-overlap scorer, but instead of measuring word overlap, it counted how often pairs of words that were connected to each other in the clue's parse tree were also connected to each other in the supporting passage's parse tree.[26] Another scorer tried to directly align the parse tree for the clue with the parse tree for the passage; if the resulting two parse trees, when aligned, matched the focus to the candidate answer, then this provided strong support for the candidate.

Some scorers checked whether dates from the clue and supporting passages agreed; others checked for geographic agreement between the clue and the passage. The list of scorers used by Watson went on and on; Watson had over a hundred scorers in all. As with the models for the Netflix Prize, any time someone in the team behind Watson found a shortcoming in the way Watson scored its answers, she could turn her intuition into a mathematical function, encode it as a scorer, test whether it improved Watson, and, if so, add it to Watson.

By the time Watson had finally finished scoring its candidates, it *still* hadn't formed an opinion about which candidate was best, although it was much closer. At this point it had lists of numerical scores for each bit of evidence for its candidates. Watson would finally form an opinion about its candidate answers in its final stage: the Aggregation and Ranking phase.

AGGREGATION AND RANKING

You might think that for Watson to select its top candidate, it could just score its answers with a simple classifier—just as we did for the children's cookbook, or just as an artificial neuron does with its inputs. But things weren't so simple for Watson. Watson did eventually use a classifier, but it needed to transform its spreadsheet of scored evidence into the right format first. Remember that when we created the spreadsheet to evaluate bits of evidence for each candidate, we might have had lots of pieces of evidence for some—and therefore lots of scores for these candidates—while we might have had little or no evidence for others—and therefore few scores for those candidates. The list of candidates was unwieldy in other ways too: there could be duplicate answers among them, and so on.

In short, this spreadsheet wasn't in the right form yet to feed into a classifier, because the things Watson was classifying—answer candidates—were heterogeneous. Weighted-average classifiers expect each item you're classifying to have the same set of features. Using a classifier on these candidates would be like trying to fit a square peg into a round hole. It just doesn't work. To resolve this mess, Watson used a sequence of seven separate transformations, each with its own classifier, before producing a final answer.[27] You can see a sketch of this in figure 13.2.

One of these transformations merged duplicate answers. In our Olympics example, the candidate answer Phelps is the same as Michael Phelps, and Bolt is the same as Usain Bolt. Sometimes Watson had a more-specific version of an answer and a less-specific version of the answer, such as a generic "sword" and "Excalibur," the name of a legendary sword. In each of these cases, Watson merged these duplicate answers into a single answer, combining their supporting evidence in the process.[28]

Another problem Watson faced was that it might have a different number of scores from each scorer across different candidate answers. So another of these seven transformations combined these scores in whichever way made sense for the scorer. Watson averaged the results of some scorers for each candidate, while for other scorers Watson took the highest value the scorer produced across all of the candidate's supporting evidence.[29] Yet other phases in Watson's ranking pipeline transformed the scores by scaling them or filling in missing feature values.[30]

Finally, a single classifier that's good at separating the best candidates from the worst candidates might be bad at differentiating between the very best candidates. So one transformation in Watson's pipeline used a classifier to filter out the very worst candidates, another selected the top five candidates, and then one more selected the best of those five.[31]

These transformations ultimately manipulated Watson's candidates until they were in a form that was conducive to applying a simple classifier, which was the final stage in the pipeline. The transformations took the square peg and shaved off its corners so that it could fit through the round hole, so that Watson could eventually feed it into that classifier.

The fascinating thing about these seven layers in Watson's final Merging and Ranking phase was that *each layer had the same architecture*. That doesn't mean that they did the same thing; as we just saw, each layer performed a different operation for Watson. But the way Watson plumbed data through each layer was identical. Each layer was composed of three basic elements: an evidence merging step, a processing step that performed

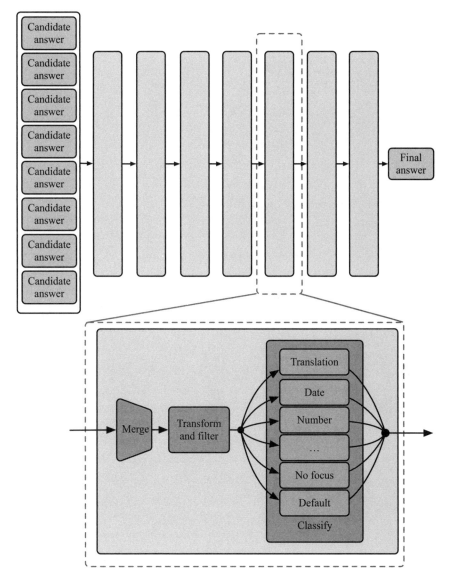

Figure 13.2
The Merging and Ranking phase in the DeepQA framework on which Watson ran. This phase consisted of seven operations, each of which had a merge step, a transform and filter step, and a linear classifier step, which used different classifiers for different types of questions. Each of the seven operations was unique in that their merge, transform, and classify steps differed (some transformations even skipped one or more of these steps), but the framework provided the capability for each step within each transformation.

whatever operation was unique to that layer—like manipulating features or filtering out candidates—and then a classification step to rescore candidates for the next phase. In some ways, these seven layers were similar to a seven-layer neural network; you can even think of this as a custom-built neural network on steroids, where the operations at the neuron level were more expressive than simple neurons, a bit like Google's Inception network.[32] The first two steps of each layer performed nonlinear transformations to the candidates, and then the third step—the classification step—was a simple linear classifier followed by the S-curve we saw in the last chapter. And the result of these transformations was a list of Watson's final answers, each with a confidence score. Watson's selected answer was the candidate from this list with the highest score.

TUNING WATSON

Watson was an absolutely massive system. In its complexity, it was also slow and difficult to tune. In an early version of Watson, which ran on a single CPU, Watson took two hours to answer a single question.[33] Fortunately Watson was also designed so that many of its stages could be run in parallel. For example, instead of researching the individual candidates separately in succession, Watson researched them all at once by farming its work out to many different CPUs. By making Watson parallel and distributing its work across about 2,880 processors, Ferrucci's team drove down Watson's answer time until it was consistently less than five seconds—and fast enough to beat Rutter and Jennings.

But how did Ferrucci and his team reason about such a complicated system? Watson was a huge software project that required the coordination of a large team of researchers—about 25 researchers working over a four-year period.[34] Changes couldn't be made in isolation. If a researcher improved her part of the system, her change might cause unanticipated problems elsewhere. To design and tune a complex machine like Watson, Ferrucci and his team used experimentation and end-to-end metrics extensively. They carefully measured every change they made, and they performed "marginal" analyses of Watson to measure how well Watson performed if they added or removed a single scorer; or how well Watson performed if they included *only* a single scorer. And all throughout, they kept careful track of where Watson was in the Winners Cloud, the scatter-plot that we saw in the last chapter, which summarized how accurate human *Jeopardy* champions were when they answered questions at differ-ent levels of confidence.

DEEPQA REVISITED

What was so special about Watson that enabled it to beat its human com-petitors at *Jeopardy*, when no other system up to that time could come anywhere close? Watson differed from its predecessors mostly in its sheer scale and in its use of DeepQA. Up to now, I've talked about Watson and DeepQA as if they were the same thing; but they were technically some-what different. DeepQA is a data-processing engine, and Watson—at least Watson the *Jeopardy*-playing program I've talked about in the past two chapters—was built on top of DeepQA. DeepQA was a more general-purpose engine that could be used for other purposes, and IBM had experimented with it in applications as diverse as medicine and gaming. Ferrucci and his team found that, when they adapted DeepQA to one of the question-answering competitions they had worked on before *Jeopardy*, it performed better than the system they'd built specifically for that com-petition.[35] Meanwhile, the converse wasn't true: when they tried to adapt the older, competition-specific system to play *Jeopardy* in that first month of work, it failed miserably.

DeepQA has nothing to do with the deep learning. The "Deep" in DeepQA refers to *deep natural language processing* or *deep question answering*, phrases IBM used to contrast it with simpler approaches to natural lan-guage processing, like the methods used in its individual scorers. Its strength came in its blending of these shallow methods, one of its core design principles, just as the best models from the Netflix Prize were blends of simpler models.[36]

WAS WATSON INTELLIGENT?

Was Watson's ability to answer *Jeopardy* questions an indication that it was truly intelligent? The answer is the same as for the other machines in this book: *not really*—at least if we're going to compare it with human intelligence. To understand why, let's think back to how Watson found the correct answer when it was presented with a clue. Watson's first step was to tease apart the clue with a variety of rules created by humans. It created a sentence diagram and used its handcrafted rules to pull out and label key bits of information that it would use to answer the clue. Watson then used these bits of information to search for the correct answer with search engines. It created a list of candidates with the result, filtered these candidates down, and searched for more evidence to support each candidate. After this it scored the evidence it had collected, and then finally it selected the best candidate with its series of transformations and classifiers.

At no point in this pipeline, however, did Watson actually *understand* what the clue was asking. It simply followed a deterministic sequence of steps, inspecting the question and scoring the supporting evidence with human-engineered rules and weights it had learned from data.

We can gain more insight into Watson's limitations by looking at where it went wrong during its live games. We already saw a case where Watson embarrassed itself by guessing that Richard Nixon was a first lady of the United States before it had a gender scorer. These problems could occur any time Watson lacked the correct scorer or filter. A related problem caused Watson to sometimes offer offensive answers.

As Stephen Baker noted in *Final Jeopardy*, Watson and some human competitors were asked during a practice session for a four-letter word in the category Just Say No. Although Watson wasn't confident enough about its answer to buzz in, its top choice, which was displayed on the screen for all to see, was "What is Fuck?" (Fortunately, a Jeopardy executive and his colleagues in the room found this funny rather than offensive.) This wasn't an isolated mishap: the team found that five percent of Watson's answers might be considered embarrassing even if they weren't outright offensive. Ferrucci put together a team to ensure Watson wouldn't say anything stupid during its live game (this team became known as the "Stupid Team"), while another team built a profanity filter with the potential to "censor" Watson during its live game.[37]

Watson was also limited by the ways it interacted with the world. For example, during one of its live games, Watson came upon a category in which it could answer clues very accurately. Watson's creators had cleverly programmed it to favor such categories when it had control of the board. Unfortunately for Watson, the clues from this category were also very short, which meant that any time Watson selected a clue from this category, its human competitors could answer more quickly than Watson, taking points for the answer and taking control of the board away from Watson.[38] In another case, Watson buzzed in after Ken Jennings answered a question incorrectly. Watson's answer was incorrect too, but it wasn't an unreasonable incorrect answer. The problem was that Watson gave the same incorrect answer Jennings had just given!

Most information about DeepQA has come from IBM itself, which has a financial incentive—and a skilled marketing team—to promote Watson as truly "intelligent."[39] In one of its white papers, for example, IBM described Watson's scorers as "reasoning algorithms," which is a bit of a stretch, when some of these scorers only do things like count up the number of overlapping words. IBM has marketed Watson to be a generically intelligent solution for a wide variety of problems.

However great Watson was at *Jeopardy*, the original version was still engineered for that one very specific task. Just as Pragmatic Theory focused on winning the Netflix Prize above all else, the team behind Watson focused on building a system that could play *Jeopardy*. And so Watson—at least the original version of Watson—couldn't do anything else, without first being retooled. And indeed, IBM has marketed Watson for a variety of other applications. Some of these other systems are likely to have been implemented so differently from the original Watson that it's difficult to judge their performance on those other applications. In fact, the Watson brand has sometimes received disappointing reviews beyond *Jeopardy*.

That said, when Watson made its initial splash, IBM published about how it worked, and this research has been accepted into the mainstream natural language processing community. No doubt that Watson's ability to play *Jeopardy* is widely seen as a truly respectable engineering achievement, and IBM set the bar considerably higher in building it.[40]

During a game of *Jeopardy*, players like Watson must make many types of decisions during the game that have nothing to do with understanding natural language. These decisions involve higher-level strategy, such as *when to buzz in, whether to buzz in, how much to wager, and which clue to select next.*

In addition to their clue scorer, the team behind Watson carefully crafted algorithms for Watson to make these strategic decisions.

These algorithms were based on models Watson had of its human opponents' behavior. We could spend an entire chapter on this topic, outlining how Watson simulated its games far into the future to make its decisions. But instead of focusing on Watson for another chapter, let's instead look in the next chapter at the more general question of how smart machines can play games of strategy.

14 BRUTE-FORCE SEARCH YOUR WAY
TO A GOOD STRATEGY

It is not being suggested that we should design the strategy in our own image. Rather it should be matched to the capacities and weakness of the computer. The computer is strong in speed and accuracy and weak in analytical abilities and recognition. Hence, it should make more use of brutal calculation than humans.
—Claude Shannon[1]

SEARCH FOR PLAYING GAMES

In the first chapter of this book we saw that the automata of the 18th century operated on the same principles as mechanical clockwork. Using only mechanical components—pulleys, gears, levers, and so on—they could perform amazing feats, like playing the harpsichord (a piano-like instrument), writing legible sentences, and making detailed illustrations with a pencil in their hand. They did this by following programs encoded within their clockwork.

Throughout this book, we've encountered computer programs that can emulate a wide variety of human-like behaviors, and in the next two chapters we'll take a closer look at computer programs that have been developed to play games like chess and Go better than the best human players. These game-playing automata were implemented as modern, digital computer programs; but, like their mechanical ancestors, modern computers still follow programs.

In fact, the computer programs that play games like chess and Go could be replicated perfectly with only physical devices. These mechanical computers, sometimes called mechanical Turing machines, can be built out of only wooden components and powered by a hand crank. Such a wooden computer might need to be extraordinarily large—so large that it might take impractically large investments to build and power—but at least in theory, it's possible.[2]

If you take a moment to ponder this, the whole premise that a wooden device powered by a hand crank could play a competitive game of chess is extraordinary. This was, after all, the appeal of the Mechanical Turk. How is it that such devices could not only play these games of strategy well; but that they could play them so well that they've beat the best human players? This is the central question you should hold in your mind throughout this chapter, as we explore the way in which machines can be programmed to play games of strategy. One of the key features of these machines is a form of foresight that they use to anticipate how the game will play out many moves into the future. To see how this works, let's start with a simple game, a game for which the program only needs to anticipate its own moves: the classic game of Sudoku.

SUDOKU

Sudoku is a game in which the sole player must fill in the blank spaces (cells) on a 9×9 grid with the numbers 1 through 9. For each game of Sudoku, the puzzle creator partially fills some subset of the cells, so that before play begins the grid looks something like the one in figure 14.1.

The goal of the Sudoku player is to place a number in each blank square, so that each row has each of the numbers 1 through 9, each column has each of the numbers 1 through 9, and each of the nine 3×3 subset grids has each of the numbers 1 through 9.

Humans approach this game by filling in one square at a time, with some combination of guesswork and the process of elimination. For example, we

4	3	5	2	6	9	7	8	1
6	8	2		7			9	
1	9				4	5		
8	2		1				4	
		4	6		2	9		
	5				3		2	8
		9	3				7	4
	4	?		5			3	6
7		3		1	8			

Figure 14.1

might notice that the third square in the first row can't be any number except 5, so we would write "5" into that square and move on.

Some cells are a bit more difficult: at first glance, the third cell in the second-from-bottom row could be 1, 2, or 8. So we might focus on some other squares first, in the hope that doing so will narrow down the possibilities by the time we come back to that cell later; or else we might pencil-in one of these numbers—say, 8—and see where that takes us. The puzzle above is relatively easy because it doesn't need much of this guesswork. In the more difficult puzzles, it's impossible to proceed without some amount of guessing.

Sudoku became popular in the 1990s largely because of a mild-mannered New Zealander named Wayne Gould. Gould designed a computer program that could develop Sudoku puzzles, which he then distributed for free to newspapers all over the world. Gould's program could develop Sudoku puzzles at different levels of difficulty: some, like the one above, were predictably easy even for novice Sudoku players, while others were predictably challenging for experienced Sudoku players. Perhaps cleverer than Gould's computer program was his marketing strategy: he gave his puzzles to the newspapers for free. In return, they advertised his computer program and his books, which the Sudoku players devoured; through this arrangement he sold over four million copies of his books.[3]

Although Sudoku can be challenging to play, it's not very difficult to write a computer program to solve Sudoku puzzles. Software engineers in Silicon Valley have been asked to do this during job interviews, and just about every introductory class in artificial intelligence teaches the key tool you need to solve a puzzle like this: search algorithms.

We've seen that self-driving cars use search algorithms to find paths through large maps and to plan ways to park in empty parking spots, and we saw that speech-recognition software uses search algorithms to find transcriptions of recorded speech. The way we would use a search algorithm to solve Sudoku is similar, except that instead of searching for a sequence of steps to take to move across a map, the program must search for a sequence of numbers to fill up the board.

In Sudoku, there are trillions upon trillions of possible board configurations. A computer program designed to solve Sudoku will search through these board configurations, iterating through many of them until it finds a fully populated board that is also a legal Sudoku layout. In the board above, there are 45 blank spaces, so the search algorithm must search through many different ways to fill all these spaces with numbers until it finds some configuration that works.

To search through these combinations, a search algorithm would reason about the Sudoku board as being in different *states*. The state of the board is described precisely by the set of numbers currently on the board. As the search algorithm fills in a certain number on the board, it moves from one state to another—to a state with one fewer blank space. At other times, the search algorithm might remove a number from the board—to a state with one more blank space.

There are many possible ways a search algorithm might wind through these states, and it's really we humans—the computer's programmers—who decide how the search algorithm should do this. We might program the computer to try every possible value for the first empty slot—the one in the top, left corner of the board—fill it in, and then consider each of these nine new states. For each of these nine states, the program would choose one of the values 1 through 9 for the *next* empty slot, and so on. Once the algorithm has filled in the 45 missing numbers, it can then test whether the board configuration is legal. If it's not legal, it will need to backtrack to change some number it set previously and then continue forward again, repeating this until it finds a combination that works.

You can think of these states as being connected in a tree structure, where two states are connected if the search algorithm can move between them by filling in (or removing) a number. I show such a "search tree" in figure 14.2, except that I've simplified the tree to search through a 2×2 grid instead of a 9×9 grid, and so that it only uses the numbers 1 through 3 to fill in the grid, instead of the numbers 1 through 9. This search tree has 81 different states at the bottom, which means the diagram is too small for you to see much detail, so I also show a subset of this tree (but larger) in figure 14.3.

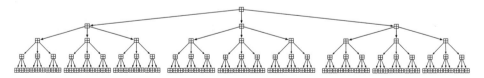

Figure 14.2
A search tree to find all ways to fill a 2×2 grid with the numbers 1 through 3. The number of states to search through grows quickly with each level of the tree, and there are $3^4 = 81$ states at the bottom of this tree. A Sudoku board with 45 empty spots would have an unfathomable 9^{45} states at the bottom of the tree.

Notice that a computer algorithm to search through a tree like this doesn't need to make any "smart" decisions. It just needs to be consistent in how it descends through the tree. At any level of the tree, the computer just tries to fill in the next empty slot with the next number it hasn't tried yet, starting from 1, and then it moves into that state to fill in the remaining squares by repeating the same process. On any given level, if it has tried a 1 for the next empty slot—and then tried all possible values for the remaining empty slots without success—it replaces that 1 with a 2 and then tries all combinations of the remaining slots again, and so on. As it tries these combinations, it essentially enumerates all of the possible ways for the 45 empty spots to be filled with the numbers 1 through 9, until it finds one that works.

I'd like to reiterate two observations I've already made. First, how exactly the algorithm moves through these states is up to the programmer. Second, a search tree like the ones in figures 14.2 and 14.3 gives the computer a methodical way to visit each state. There is no discretion an algorithm like this has in choosing which states to visit. As the computer searches through

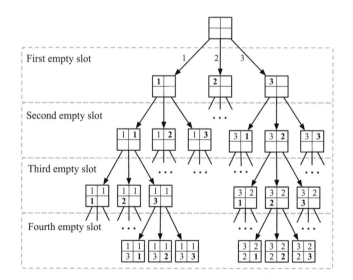

Figure 14.3
A subset of the search tree in figure 14.2, showing only selected states in the tree. At each level of the tree, the algorithm selects the next empty square and attempts to fill it in with each of the numbers 1 through 3 (shown in bold). The algorithm fills the spot with one of these values, descends to the next level, and attempts to fill in the next number.

these states, it follows a simple, prescriptive algorithm—exactly something a wooden machine with a hand crank could do.

THE SIZE OF THE TREE

Unfortunately, a "brute-force" approach like this would also be impractical because it requires the computer to consider an exponential number of states. As in chapters 9 and 10, where I discuss neural networks, I mean "exponential" in the mathematical sense: for each level deeper we go into the Sudoku tree, the number of states grows by a factor of 9. Just two levels deep, as in figure 14.4, there are 81 states in the tree. If we look 45 levels deep, the number of states is about 1 followed by 43 zeros. This would be far too many states to evaluate within a reasonable amount of time even if we had an army of people turning hand cranks on wooden machines, let alone a large cluster of computers.

Does it help that we don't need to enumerate all possible states to find the solution? For example, for the Sudoku board we saw earlier, we only need to try 36 percent of these combinations before finding one that works. Unfortunately, 36 percent of 10^{43} is $10^{42.6}$, which is still an impossibly large number.

We can fix this by "pruning" branches of the search tree, cutting the search short on a branch if we know that the branch could never lead to a valid Sudoku solution. So when we're trying to figure out which number to put into an empty spot, we still consider each of the values 1 through 9, but we only "descend" into a state if selecting that number would lead to a valid Sudoku layout. I show how a search tree for this algorithm would look in figure 14.5.

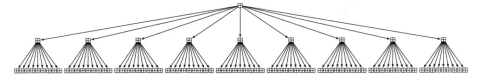

Figure 14.4
The number of states just two levels into the Sudoku search tree is $9 \times 9 = 81$. Because the number of states grows by a factor of 9 with each level in the tree, we must use a pruning algorithm to narrow the search down.

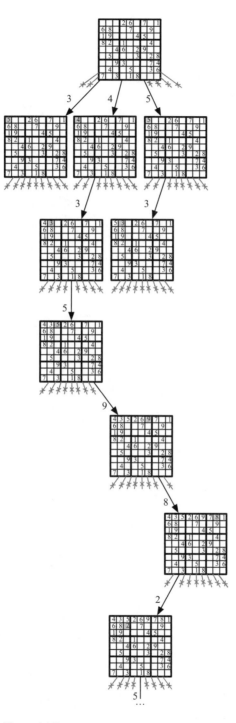

Figure 14.5
A "pruned" search tree to find the values in a
Sudoku board. Most branches are cut short
because they would lead to a Sudoku board
that couldn't lead to a valid Sudoku layout.

Figure 14.5 is hardly a "tree" all: it's more like a search "beam"! As you can see, there are a couple of false starts, but the algorithm doesn't need to branch out too much at each level. Instead of having *nine* branches at each level, the pruned search tree usually has just one. If we're lucky, we might only check about nine boards for most levels of the tree, and we could throw most of them away after finding that they're illegal. This would eliminate all but one branch at most levels before descending. This would be about 9 × 45 boards we need to evaluate—a measly 405 states. This is small enough that you could run this search algorithm quickly with a computer from the 1970s.

THE BRANCHING FACTOR

The amount by which a search tree grows at each level is sometimes called its *branching factor* or *branching ratio*. The branching factor was 9 in the first, un-pruned Sudoku search tree and close to 1 in the pruned search tree. The branching factor varies by the initial layout of a Sudoku board, and the difficulty of a Sudoku puzzle for a human depends heavily on that puzzle's branching factor. When Wayne Gould invented his program to create Sudoku boards, he was certainly aware of this: a game of Sudoku must strike the right balance in its branching factor. It can't be so low that the game feels mechanical, and it can't be so high that the game feels frustrating.

UNCERTAINTY IN GAMES

Solitary games like Sudoku tend to be less interesting from the perspective of AI research because there's no uncertainty in them: the search path and the actions the player can make are well defined from the first turn all the way to the end. One thing that makes games more interesting is *uncertainty*. Uncertainty can show up when there's some amount of randomness involved—as with any game where you roll dice—or when there's more than one player—as in a game like chess.

To see how the game play changes when there's some amount of uncertainty, let's look at a simple game, which I'll call "You-pick-this-then-flip-a-coin," in figure 14.6.

In this game, you pick a direction to go from the start position—either up or down—and then flip a coin to see where you go from there. You

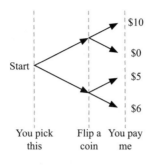

Figure 14.6

then need to pay me whatever value you end up on (sorry, but this isn't a very fun game for you). Take a moment to look at this diagram to figure out what your strategy for the first move is going to be.

To reason about this game, you might have taken an average of the two upper-most outcomes, and compared this with the average of the two lower-most outcomes, and decided that, on average, you're best off choosing the higher branch, because you would pay me less on average. If you're risk-averse, you might have reasoned differently: you would have noticed that $10 is the worst possible outcome and chosen the lower branch to avoid that outcome. Regardless of which strategy you took, the key observation is that you made your decision by looking at the end values and working your way backward to the starting decision.

Two-player games also have uncertainty, but in some sense they have *less* uncertainty for any one player because the other player's choices are somewhat predictable. Consider the game in figure 14.7, which I'll call "You-pick-this-then-I-pick-that."

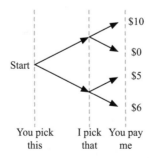

Figure 14.7

In this game, as before, you make the first up-or-down choice; then I choose whether to go up or down from there. After we've each made a choice, you again pay me the amount we end up at. Take another moment to look at the diagram in figure 14.7 to figure out your decision before you read further.

Again, this isn't a very fun game for you, because I always win; but you do have a greater ability to predict the outcome, so your choice is easier. You know that I will always choose the highest number among my options—either $10 or $6—so you would choose "down," since that will lead to you paying me only $6. As with the You-pick-this-then-flip-a-coin game, you started at the end and moved backward to decide which action to take.

In a game like chess, where the players take many turns, you would use the same approach to find the best strategy in the game, except that you must anticipate the outcome of many more decisions over the course of the game. The search tree will branch out massively within a few moves, as in figure 14.8, but even more so than can be shown in the figure. In this figure, gray dots at the end represent the outcome that *you win*, while white

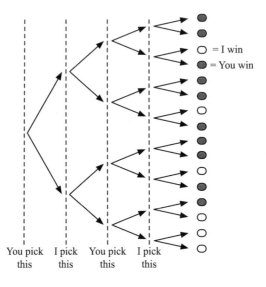

Figure 14.8
A multilayer search tree representing choices in a two-player game. Each level of the tree represents a single player's choice between two actions. Gray dots at the end represent the outcome that you win, while white dots represent the outcome that I win.

dots represent the outcome that *I win*. To figure out which move you should make on your turn, you'd again reason from the end, working your way backward. At each level, you would either predict which action *I* would take so I have the highest chances of winning, or select an action for yourself that would maximize your chances at winning. In this game, it *is* possible for you to win, provided that you make the right choices.

If we wanted to program a computer to play this game, we would use a search algorithm just as in Sudoku, but we would write the program to anticipate which moves you and I would make at each level of the search tree. It must start out by searching deep into the tree. Once the program has descended in its search to the end of the game, it then works in reverse: it looks at each move I might make as my final move, anticipates that I would only make a move that would allow me to win, if such a move exists, and assumes that that is my choice. Once it has done that, the algorithm can ignore the final layer of the tree, because it knows the outcome of my move. In the next-higher level, the algorithm anticipates which move *you* would choose. You would choose a move that guarantees that *you* would win, if such a move exists. Once the program has figured out which move you would take, it can figure out who will win from there, and it can ignore all levels of the search tree below that. And so the program would proceed, moving backward in the tree, predicting which move either one of us would make, until it hits the beginning of the search tree, which is the current layout of the board. Once it gets to the beginning, it can tell you what move you should make to guarantee that you win. We would say that this algorithm anticipates that each player will be *rational*, that is, that each will act in his or her own best interest and by thinking ahead. It is possible to assume each player is rational when we can search through the entire tree. Just as you figured out the best move for each player by starting from the end of the tree, the program would do the same, in a predictable way.

The tree above is, of course, much simpler than a game of chess. In the tree above, the branching factor is 2, with four moves (called "plies") in the game. Master chess players work through games that have, on average, a branching factor of 30 to 40 and an average of 40 moves per game.[4] This leads to a search tree that is far too large for a computer to search through without a lot more pruning.[5] The number of states we would need to search through could easily exceed the number 1 followed by 59 zeros.

Could we resolve this by using a fast-enough computer? Not really. The exponential growth rate of states as we descend into the search tree is a problem that transcends technology: it will *always* be prohibitively expensive to evaluate all of these states. Even if we could build a computer that could evaluate all board states up to 40 levels deep in a reasonable amount of time—say, over the course of two minutes—this computer would grind to a halt on searches just two levels deeper, where there are $40 \times 40 = 1,600$ times as many states to evaluate, so that the computer would need over two days to crunch through its states. And this is in a search tree that's already been pruned in the way we pruned the Sudoku tree: these 30 to 40 moves per turn in chess are *legal* moves. So we need another way to prune this tree if we're going to solve chess with computers.

CLAUDE SHANNON

If you've ever visited the quaint, Midwest town of Gaylord, Michigan, there's a good chance you've seen the bronze bust of Claude Shannon. Shannon was a mathematician well known for his work in the field of information theory, which provides an elegant way to measure the amount of information—in a very literal sense—contained in a message.

The intuition around Shannon's idea of information revolved around how *exceptional* a message is. If I told you that my cat meows, I wouldn't be giving you very much information: you know that most cats make this sound. However, if I told you that my cat barks, this would be higher-information, because most cats don't bark. And if I told you ten different (unrelated) facts like this, then I would be giving you ten times as much information.

Shannon encoded this intuition into a framework for reasoning about information. He did this by formalizing the idea of *uncertainty*: information is what you gain by removing that uncertainty. Shannon's ideas have led to a vast and beautiful branch of mathematics commonly known as information theory. Ideas from information theory have been used to help us to understand a wide variety of things, such as the theoretical limits of how much information we can send in electronic messages. This is the same idea used in the word-overlap scorer from Watson: that scorer weighted words by how much information they conveyed: words like "scorpion" and "Čavić" convey more information than "almost" and "one."

Shannon's work on information theory is extremely important in the field of machine learning, but he is less well known for an academic paper he wrote in 1949 about how to create computer programs to play chess. Years before computers were household commodities, Shannon made some simple but thoughtful suggestions about how to write algorithms to play chess that have become commonplace in the field of AI. One of his core suggestions was the idea of an *evaluation function*.

EVALUATION FUNCTIONS

An evaluation function is a test that can be applied to a game state to predict which player will win if each player plays rationally after that. A perfect evaluation function for the search tree in figure 14.8 will tell you who will win, starting from each game state. You can see what a perfect evaluation function for this game would look like in figure 14.9, where I've colored

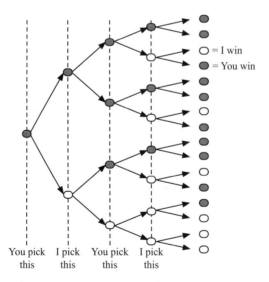

Figure 14.9
A multilayer search tree in which each state is colored with the result of an evaluation function. This evaluation function is perfect: it describes which player will win the game from each state, provided that each player plays perfectly. In practice, most evaluation functions are approximate.

each state based on who will win. A computer algorithm using this evaluation function doesn't need to search all the way to the end of the tree to
figure out which move to make: it just needs to search one or two levels
deep to peek at the evaluation function to decide which move to make.

Usually it's impossible to create a perfect evaluation function, and we
must resort to using an approximate evaluation function instead. If you've
played chess, you've probably used an approximate evaluation function to
decide your moves. Without even thinking about it, you probably assigned
a rough value to each piece on the board: a queen is worth more than a
knight, which is worth more than a pawn, and so on; and your opponent's
queen is worth more to them than their knight, and so on.

As Shannon explained, a computer's evaluation function for chess might
assign explicit weights to these pieces: a queen might be worth 9, a bishop
worth 3, a knight 3, and a pawn 1; and the value to a player of having a set
of pieces on the board is the sum of these pieces' values.[6] The numbers I've
listed here are arbitrary—and probably wrong—but they capture some of
our intuition. If you have a chance to capture your opponent's queen but
need to sacrifice a bishop in the process, it's very possibly still a good move.
If you can capture your opponent's queen without losing any pieces of
your own, that's all for the better. Formalizing this into a more rigorous
evaluation function, you might use a weighted sum of how many pieces of
each type you have, minus a weighted sum of your opponent's pieces, like
this:[7]

$$(100K + 9Q + 5R + 3B + 3N + 1P)$$
$$- (100K_o + 9Q_o + 5R_o + 3B_o + 3N_o + 1P_o)$$

If you used this—which, by the way, is an example of a classifier—as an
evaluation function, then it would help you to predict who will win the
game based on how many of each type of piece is on the board.

This is just a simple example of an evaluation function, but evaluation
functions like it can be extraordinarily powerful if you add enough features.
Deep Blue, a powerful chess-playing system built by IBM, used an evaluation function; but whereas we used 12 features in our evaluation function,
they used over 8,000 features![8]

What might some of these additional features be? Many of them were
esoteric, but they could roughly be broken up into two categories: material features—that is, features to describe *which* pieces were on the board,

like the ones above—and positional features—features that describe *where these pieces are* on the board. For example, one of your pawns is worth much more if it is near your opponent's side of the board because it is more likely to turn into a queen. And indeed, at least one version of Deep Blue preferred to advance pawns toward the opposite side of the board for this reason. Positional features are also necessary for computer chess. This became clear when Deep Blue played one of its games against the then-reigning chess champion Garry Kasparov.[9]

Kasparov is one of the greatest chess players to have ever lived. Intense and full of energy, he described playing chess as "controlling chaos."[10] When asked in 1988 whether a computer could beat a human grandmaster by the year 2000, Kasparov's answer was simple. "No way, and if any Grandmaster has difficulty playing computers, I would be happy to provide my advice."[11] In one game he played with Deep Blue, Kasparov built up a significant strategic advantage against Deep Blue. The poor computer had no idea that it was losing until it was too late: Deep Blue's evaluation function, focused on material advantage, underestimated Kasparov's own positional advantage.[12]

How would you use an evaluation function in practice? One approach is to search to a fixed depth in the tree, run the evaluation function on each game state at that depth, and then treat the result of the evaluation function as if it were the outcome of the game, as in figure 14.10. You don't need to search 40 levels deep in a game like chess: you might only search 6 or 12 levels deep, and then you'd use the evaluation function to decide which states are the most promising. Even though you may not come anywhere close to the end of the game with just six moves, the hope is that you'll have a much more accurate idea of who will have an advantage at that depth.

Evaluation functions can also be used to prune the search tree in other ways. One way to do this is with an approach called alpha-beta pruning. In alpha-beta pruning, you strategically prune based on what you've observed so far in the search tree. Let's say that you're figuring out your next move in a game of chess against me. After looking at the first move you might make—move A—you've determined that it's pretty good according to the evaluation function, considering all of my counter-moves to your move A, your counter-counter-moves, and so-on.

At this point you could stop searching, but you realize that you might be able to find an even better move, perhaps move B or move C. So you

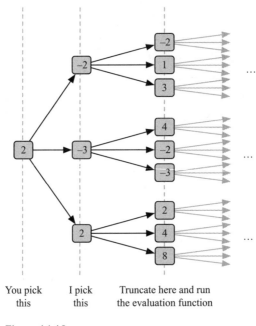

Figure 14.10
Using an evaluation function to search to a fixed depth
in a two-player game.

look at these moves too. With the very next move you consider (move B),
you immediately notice that I could make a counter-move that will let me
win the game. There's no point in looking at move B any further, since you
know that I will always choose the best move for myself. I wouldn't choose
any counter-move to move B that would be any worse than that for me.
So you can stop considering move B altogether and move on to evaluating move C. This is the essence of alpha–beta pruning: cutting your search
short when you know a certain branch on the search tree won't lead to any
better moves than one you've found already.

Alpha–beta pruning isn't limited to just the top layers of the search tree:
it can be applied at any level of the tree. Its effectiveness depends on the
order in which you search through the search tree, but it can be very effective even if you don't prioritize your search. It was also one of the methods
used by IBM's chess-playing Deep Blue.[13]

DEEP BLUE

IBM's Deep Blue was the computer that proved world chess champion Garry Kasparov wrong in his 1988 prediction that no computer could defeat a grandmaster by the year 2000. Within a year of his prediction, a computer built by a little-known team of graduate students at Carnegie Mellon defeated a chess grandmaster for the first time in history.[14] As their computer and its descendants gradually improved over the following decade, they grew more and more competitive, toppling grandmaster after grandmaster.

Deep Blue originated with this group of graduate students who had begun working on computer chess mostly for fun, largely basing their system on custom hardware designed by Feng-hsiung Hsu, the founding member of the project. Using hardware to play chess wasn't uncommon at the time, even though these chess machines could sometimes be the size of a small office refrigerator.[15] But by implementing Deep Blue in hardware, Hsu observed, they could get about a hundred-times speedup compared with the same algorithm implemented purely in software.[16] Deep Blue leaned heavily on the ability this hardware gave it to quickly search through its tree. Distributed across 30 separate computers, Deep Blue used 480 custom chess chips to blaze through about 126 million positions per second.[17]

But the team behind Deep Blue learned that brute-force search up to a certain depth with an evaluation function wasn't enough. They found that chess masters could anticipate moves in a much deeper beam than a search algorithm that searched up to a fixed depth. They did use an evaluation function with a limited-depth tree, and they did use alpha-beta pruning, but Hsu was skeptical of clever pruning methods and search tricks, at least in their hardware. Instead of using clever tricks to prune their search tree, Hsu and the team favored a different method to address the high branching factor: something called a *singular extension*.[18]

In contrast to pruning methods, which selectively cut off certain search paths, singular extensions selectively *extend* certain search paths. For example, if you move your pawn into a position that threatens my king, I will make some move to defend my king. Such moves have the property that they're clearly among best possible move I could make—sometimes the *only* possible move I could make—and when Deep Blue could identify them, it would selectively extend its search in that direction, with a branching factor of close to 1 along that extension.[19]

Unlike DeepMind's Atari-playing agent, which could play many different games, Deep Blue was designed specifically to play chess. The majority of the features in Deep Blue's evaluation function were hand-selected and hand-created, which stands in sharp contrast to most of the statistical machines in this book—although the team did use some data-driven tuning to select the weights in their evaluation function. Deep Blue also used an "opening book" to select good strategic moves near the beginning of the game and an "endgame" database to select moves near the end of the game.[20]

JOINING IBM

As Feng-hsiung Hsu began developing the chess programs that eventually culminated in Deep Blue, he began to recruit his fellow graduate students to help out.[21] A few years into the project, IBM got wind of the students' chess-playing efforts. By one account, the seed for the idea was planted with a vice president during a conversation in a men's restroom. The conversation, if you allow for some narrative liberties, went roughly like this:[22]

> *Friend:* Super Bowl commercials are an expensive way to do marketing, aren't they?
>
> *VP:* They sure are.
>
> *Friend:* Oh, by the way, have you heard about this CMU group's chess-playing computer? No? Perhaps IBM could hire this team, and they could beat the best chess player in the world. That sort of marketing could be good for business, and maybe cheaper, huh?
>
> *VP:* Interesting …

IBM eventually acquired the core group of CMU students working on the project. The students cut themselves an attractive deal when they joined IBM: they negotiated that they be given the mandate to build the "ultimate chess machine." They asked that they have the flexibility to do things on their own, without the likes of Dilbert's pointy-haired boss ordering them around.[23] They got their wish, along with some other benefits of working within IBM, including the deep pockets that would enable them to build the final version of Deep Blue and to attend competitions, and help from IBM's marketing team to manage their game against Garry Kasparov.[24]

By 1997, within a decade of Garry Kasparov's prediction that no computer could beat a grandmaster by 2000, the researchers' line of chess-playing computers culminated in the final version of Deep Blue. In a six-game match, the computer managed to defeat Garry Kasparov himself, the first professional match Kasparov had ever lost. As Hsu wrote:

> Yes, you read it right. Garry had never lost a single chess match in his professional life before the 1997 rematch. … Some were concerned that Garry would react angrily to losing a match. The IBM team was asked … specifically not to smile during the closing ceremony, especially if Deep Blue won the match.[25]

SEARCH AND NEURAL NETWORKS

So, why we didn't we use an approach like this—that is, a search algorithm— to play Atari games? Could we have designed a search algorithm to play a game like *Breakout* or *Space Invaders*? Although I'm reluctant to say the answer is a categorical no, there are a few challenges we'd face if we tried to do this.

In chess and Sudoku, the states are obvious: they describe the positions of chess pieces or numbers on the game board. The positions on the board and the rules of the game are well defined, so it's easy to encode the states and the transitions between them into a search tree. But remember that DeepMind wanted an agent that could play many different games. It's unclear what the "states" in a search tree should even look like for Atari games. Should a state in the search tree for an Atari game represent the unique arrangement of pixels on the screen? That would result in far more states than we faced for chess or Sudoku. An even bigger problem is that we have no idea how to move from one state to another as we search through the state space. It's difficult for a search algorithm to anticipate the future of the game if we don't even know how the states are connected to each other!

The role of a search algorithm when playing games is to help the agent find a path from its current state to a state with the highest likelihood of a good outcome. In chess, we search for states deep within the tree for which the evaluation function has a high value, and then we take an action that gets us one step closer to that state.

Reinforcement learning with a neural network gives us a different way to accomplish the same goal. The role of reinforcement learning when playing games is to orient the agent toward states with future rewards by telling it which actions will move it toward those states. Reinforcement learning essentially turns the problem from a search problem (which might be much harder) into a "hill-climbing" problem, where it can move, step by step, toward more promising states.

Sometimes hill-climbing algorithms don't work. They don't work well when the algorithm leads you to the top of a low hill when there are much higher hills around, separated from you by valleys. DeepMind faced this problem with games like *Montezuma's Revenge*, where it hadn't explored enough of the landscape to figure out where the bigger hills were; so it was stuck on one of these low hills.[26] A search algorithm, in contrast, might be able to search through a wider landscape, to get you past those valleys. The deeper we can search into the game tree—in theory, at least—the more likely we are to find a good action for the agent.

Is it possible to use a hybrid of these two approaches? That is, could we use a search algorithm to search deeply into the tree when possible, and then use a very sophisticated evaluation function, like the one we used for Atari, in a sort of search / neural-network hybrid?

TD-GAMMON

Gerald Tesauro, an IBM researcher who eventually worked on Watson's wagering strategy for *Jeopardy!*, used an approach exactly like this when he developed a program to play backgammon in the early and mid-1990s. Backgammon, like chess, is a two-player game in which players move their pieces around on a board. It involves a dice roll in addition to a small set of player actions, so its branching factor is a few hundred for each ply (remember, a ply is a single move by one player).[27]

Tesauro programmed his agent to use reinforcement learning, just as DeepMind did for its Atari agent. Also like DeepMind, Tesauro designed his agent to use a neural network. Its architecture was the "simple" neural network architecture we saw before, with an input layer, an output layer, and a single hidden layer:

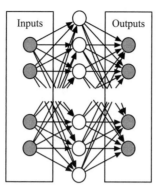

Figure 14.11

The input layer to Tesauro's backgammon network encoded the position of each player's pieces on the board as well as some handcrafted features Tesauro had created. The output layer represented the four possible outcomes the network aimed to learn: player 1 wins, player 2 wins, player 1 wins by a lot (called a "gammon"), or player 2 wins by a lot. As you can see, between the input and output layers was a hidden middle layer. In Tesauro's experiments, this hidden layer worked well with anywhere from 40 to 160 neurons.

Tesauro's algorithm was a hybrid between search and reinforcement learning, in that it searched out two or three plies before using its neural network to run the evaluation function.[28] Remember: Tesauro could use the search option because the states and transitions in backgammon are well defined. In an early version of his backgammon-playing algorithm, Tesauro trained the neural network using reinforcement learning with games played by expert humans. This "supervised" algorithm worked okay, but it wasn't great.

This changed when Tesauro let the neural network *play against itself*, which exposed it to a virtually unlimited amount of training data, the same benefit the Atari-playing agent had when it played millions of Atari games in its virtual world, the Arcade Learning Environment. After playing some 1.5 million games against itself, Tesauro's search-plus-neural-network hybrid could play competitively against the best human players. (It may very well be better than the best human players by the time you're reading this.) It has even taught the professional backgammon community new strategies, upending conventional wisdom about the game.[29]

Tesauro's pitting of the backgammon neural network against itself became a famous story in the field of artificial intelligence, but the method wasn't widely known outside of the AI and backgammon communities. The game-playing AI programs that became known to the public were the ones that made national headlines, like Deep Blue, Watson, and eventually AlphaGo, which defeated two Go world champions in 2016 and 2017.

LIMITATIONS OF SEARCH

The ideas behind Deep Blue and Tesauro's backgammon program were the foundation for the algorithms that eventually enabled AlphaGo to play the strategy game Go, but these ideas on their own weren't enough. A computer playing chess can lean heavily on brute-force search through hundreds of millions of moves per second along with a fairly simple evaluation function to prune away most of the search tree. Deep Blue's 8,000-feature evaluation function may not sound simple, but the features in it were largely interpretable by humans. These things were together enough to push a computer algorithm up to and then past the frontier of human chess-playing ability.

Go is different. The branching factor for Go is nearly 10 times as high as the branching factor for chess, and the evaluation function for Go must be much more sophisticated than the one to play chess. As we'll see in the next chapter, the ideas necessary for a computer to play Go competitively didn't even exist when Tesauro developed his backgammon-playing agent and when Deep Blue beat Garry Kasparov in 1997. It would take two decades of new ideas and hardware improvements to bring computer Go agents within reach of the best humans.

Simply scaling to more and faster processors will not be enough with current techniques. I think we need one or two further breakthrough ideas in algorithms.
—Martin Müller, Professor and Associate Chair of Computer Science at University of Alberta[1]

In spring 2011, after IBM's Watson had made world headlines for defeating world champions at *Jeopardy!*, researchers from the project toured the world to give a variety of talks on the system. James Fan, one the most enthusiastic proponents of developing the system and one of its lead researchers, visited the University of Alberta on one of these trips, where he met several leading AI researchers. One of them was Martin Müller, who had been studying computer algorithms to play the game Go. These researchers had been leading the field for some time, but the problems were difficult. As Professor Müller mused, it wasn't clear that computers could solve the problem anytime soon. The general consensus of the community was that Computer Go was at least a decade from being solved. But Müller and his fellow researchers, unfazed by a challenge, continued to work on the problem.

COMPUTER GO

The ancient game of Go has long been considered one of the greatest challenges in the field of game-playing AI. It's the oldest game still played in its original form, and it's played by tens of millions of people worldwide. As old as it is, Go has also found a strange juxtaposition with technology in the internet age. Long before the internet arrived, Go players used networked computers to play remotely with one another; and in 1992 an internet Go server was created so Go aficionados could meet up to play Go with one another online.[2] Over time more servers popped up, enabling Go players to meet up with—and play against—others throughout the world.

As the *Wall Street Journal* reported during the final week of 2016, a mysterious player named "Master" appeared on one of these servers, its avatar a wide-eyed cartoon fox. Master was peculiar, making unconventional or seemingly foolish moves, without pausing to think. But its strategies somehow worked: it defeated some of the best Go players in the world over the course of the week. In fact, Master had performed spectacularly well that week, winning all 60 of the games it played. And one of Master's games during this period was against the world's reigning Go champion, 19-year-old Ke Jie.[3]

Most players in the community had no idea who this mysterious Master was, but Ke Jie had been told in advance of his game: Master was the secret online identity of AlphaGo, an algorithm Google's DeepMind had created to play Go.

AlphaGo wasn't exactly the first program to play Go. People have been writing computer programs to play Go since around 1968. In 1985, an organization offered a prize of 40 million new Taiwanese dollars—about US$1.4 million in today's dollars—to anyone who could create an algorithm to defeat a professional Go player, kick-starting efforts at computer Go. The offer, unmet for over a decade, was eventually rescinded, and other awards began to pop up in its place.[4] Even IBM tried its hand at computer Go, where some of its researchers were working on the problem just before they were pulled away to work on Watson.[5] But for nearly half a century, a computer program that could defeat the world's best Go champions remained elusive.

This wasn't for lack of trying. Go is an extraordinarily difficult game for a computer to play. On each turn, a player must choose from about 250 possible moves.[6] An algorithm searching through just the first three plies (you make a move, I make a move, and you make another move) would already need to consider over 10 million board configurations. And these tens of millions of states barely scratch the surface of a typical Go game, which lasts about 150 moves—roughly twice the number of moves and an incomprehensibly many times the number of states in a typical chess game.[7] And so programmers tried and tried for decades, using the typical bag of AI tricks: they wrote programs to search through the game tree and developed evaluation functions—usually simple, weighted-average classifiers—to prune it. But the size of the search tree was simply too big, and their evaluation functions were too simple.

THE GAME OF GO

The rules of Go are simple. As with chess, it is a two-player game: one player controls white pieces—sometimes called *stones*—while the other controls black pieces. The players take turns setting their stones onto a 19 × 19 grid.[8] Once placed, a stone stays fixed on the board unless it is "captured" by the opponent. If the stone is captured, it's removed from the board.

The goal of Go is to "control" territory, so that at the end of the game your pieces cover as much of the board as possible. The important dynamic in the game is that each player has the ability to capture her opponent's stones, by completely surrounding the perimeter of those stones with her own. If she places a stone on the board so as to completely surround a cluster of her opponent's pieces, with no gaps to "breathe," she captures those pieces and removes them from the board. You can see an example of this in figures 15.1a and 15.b, which show a move from a game between champions Lee Sedol and Ke Jie. In 15.1b, white places a stone at D-6 to capture (and has thus removed) two black stones at D-4 and D-5. In so doing, white has gained territory for himself and further strengthened his position. The game ends when either a player resigns or both players give up their turn (that is, after they both "pass").

Despite the simplicity of its rules, Go strategy is both deep and subtle. This fact hasn't escaped the world's experts. When Ke Jie lost the match to Master, he reflected: "After humanity spent thousands of years improving our tactics, computers tell us that humans are completely wrong. … I would go as far as to say not a single human has touched the edge of the truth of Go."[9]

This is also one of the reasons Go is challenging for a computer: it can be notoriously difficult to judge the state of a Go game. The distinction between whether you capture your opponent's stones or they capture yours could depend on a single misplaced stone. For example, if the white player

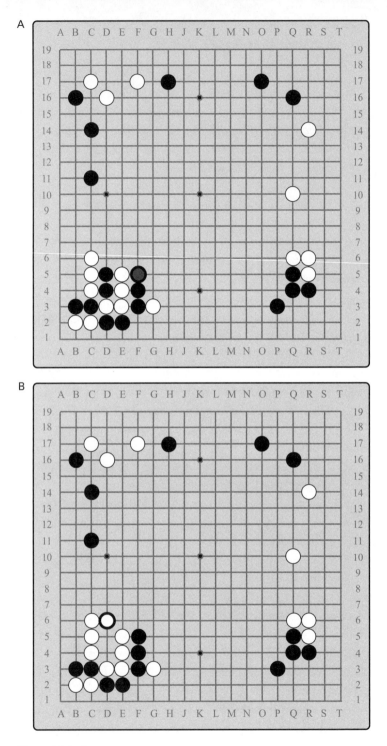

Figure 15.1a, b

An example of a Go game between Go champions Lee Sedol and Ke Jie. In the board on the bottom, which is one move after the board on the top, white places a stone that "captures" two black pieces. Game snapshots are available at https://gogameguru.com/2nd-mlily-cup-final(thisisgame 3of5oftheMLilycupfinal).

in figure 15.1b hadn't placed a white stone at D-6 to capture the black stones, then the black player could have placed a black stone at E-6 to capture the white stones.

Another reason it's difficult for a computer to evaluate Go games is that no stone is special. The value of a player's stones on the board lies exclusively in the *positions* of those stones. This is different from chess, where the evaluation function can lean heavily on the values of different pieces (what we called *material features* in the last chapter). In chess, the queen is worth far more than the pawn, so you should almost never attack a pawn if it means sacrificing your queen. In Go, the evaluation function must identify important patterns of stones on the board, which requires a pattern-matching ability that can rival a human's ability to pattern match, and which is a nontrivial task because these intuitions are often difficult even for humans to describe. This is exacerbated by the fact that the game can change quickly: the search tree below the pruning level has many outcomes that depend on the placement of a single stone, as we saw in the last paragraph.

SAMPLE MOVES TO BUILD AN INTUITION

I first played Go with an experienced friend in college. Here was his advice to me: "Download this program for your computer and play a bunch of games really fast against the computer. Don't even worry about being good at first. Just play a lot of games until you build up an intuition for how it works."

I followed his advice and quickly found that knowing the rules alone was insufficient to play well. Although I never played Go enough to become competitive, it was clear that being good at Go requires having the type of intuition humans are good at. And although I could explain some of this intuition in words, much of it was simply pattern-matching by my subconscious, hunches I had but couldn't quite put a finger on: put a free stone far enough away from the edge of the board and the opponent's stones, but not too far, and so on. That brings us to one of the key questions in developing a computer algorithm to play Go: how can we select rich enough features for an evaluation function to sufficiently capture humans' intuitions? Unfortunately, as we'll soon see, even a great evaluation function won't be sufficient to prune the search tree enough. So let's turn directly to the question we ultimately care about: how does AlphaGo traverse its search tree?

The rough intuition behind AlphaGo's strategy to picking its moves is a bit like what my college friend recommended when he suggested playing a bunch of games really fast, to build up an intuition. Every time AlphaGo needs to make a move, it simulates a bunch of games, starting from the current layout of the board. It plays through each game in its silicon imagination, digging a single path deep into the search tree, until that hypothetical game comes to an end. After it has played through this imaginary game, the program knows whether it has won or lost. It doesn't matter much that the game imagined by the program is exceedingly unlikely to ever play out. What matters is that AlphaGo can do this many thousands of times to build up an intuition for which move to make.

To build that intuition, AlphaGo bubbles up the win/loss statistics of the games it imagines to the highest levels of the search tree, where it stores counts of how often it won or lost after making different moves from its current position. Once it has run through enough games, it should have a much better sense—based on data—for which move it should play next.[10]

You can see an example of this sampling approach in figures 15.2a and 15.2b. On the top, AlphaGo plays through a single game all the way to the bottom of the tree. Then it checks which player would have won the game and sends that information back up to the top of the search tree, where it keeps count of win/loss statistics. Let's imagine that this tree has 50 layers. With the branching factor of 2 shown in the figure, there are about a *million billion* states at the very bottom of the tree. (Remember: the search tree for Go is many orders of magnitude bigger than this.)

The tricky part for AlphaGo is in simulating realistic games. It must anticipate which moves it and its opponent are likely to make on each turn. It can't just sample moves completely randomly.[11] Statistics about a game in which moves were chosen randomly wouldn't be very useful in predicting the outcome of a real game. Instead, AlphaGo needs a way to predict which moves an expert player would make.

How could AlphaGo do this? It probably won't surprise you to learn that DeepMind used the same idea for its Atari-playing agent—a deep neural network—to predict its moves. Each time AlphaGo needs to simulate a game, it makes a series of predictions—one after another—of which move each player would make, placing an imaginary stone on the board

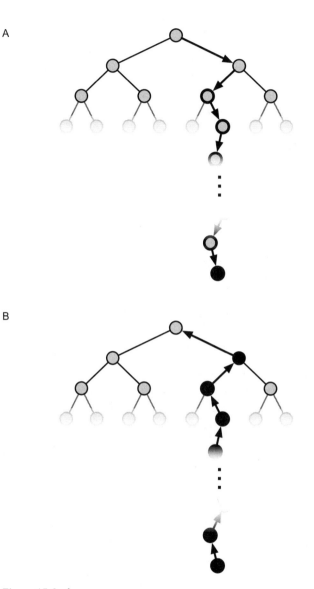

Figure 15.2a, b
An example of a simulated game in the Go search tree to be used as
a sample in its move decision (top). The sample game is run until its
end. At the end of the game, the outcome of it is known, and this
information is "bubbled up" through the tree to the top layers (bottom).
Sampled games are sometimes called "rollouts."

as it plays through the game. Each time it needs to plan a move as its imaginary game rolls out, it uses its neural network on the board with the imaginary pieces to decide the next move.

Let's call this neural network AlphaGo's *move-prediction network*.[12] This move-prediction network is very similar to the network DeepMind used to play Atari games: they both use many convolutional layers. But these networks and the ways these agents used them have some important differences.

Remember that the Atari-playing network was meant to be very general: DeepMind couldn't build any game-specific ideas into the network's architecture because the network needed to play many different Atari games. Its only inputs were the red-green-blue values of each pixel on the screen, along with the pixel values from several recent frames that showed up on the screen.

AlphaGo's move-prediction network, on the other hand, is designed specifically to play the game Go. It has lots of Go-specific logic, most of which comes in the form of features DeepMind had created to summarize how players would move. One version of AlphaGo feeds its neural network with inputs amounting to a whopping 48 copies of the game board (called "planes"); each copy of the board provides different information— that is, a different feature—about each position on the board.

Several of these feature planes summarize the board state: one plane indicates whether there is a black stone on each position, while another indicates whether there is a white stone is on each position. Some of the feature planes relay the rules of the game: *Would putting a stone here be a legal move for the player? How many of the opponent's stones would be captured if a stone were placed here?* Many of the remaining feature planes provide custom tactical features—albeit simple ones—about the position. These usually capture very simple intuitions correlated with good moves: *How many empty spots are there along the perimeter of this piece of the board? How many turns has it been since a piece was played at this location?*[13] (As we'll see later, a more recent version of AlphaGo doesn't need so many hand-built features.)

AlphaGo's move-prediction network also differs from the Atari network in its architecture. First, AlphaGo's network is much deeper: at 13 layers, it's nearly three times as deep as the Atari-playing network. Although it's deeper, it lacks a fully connected hidden layer at the end: all of its hidden layers except the output layer are convolutional layers.

A few chapters ago, we learned that convolutional layers have sets of simple pattern-matching classifiers called filters that run over small patches of neurons in their preceding layers.[14] These filters are the magical "thing detectors" that can identify interesting patterns in the previous layer— patterns that are useful in making predictions from the network. Each of these convolutional layers identifies where interesting things are happening in the input planes. AlphaGo's first convolutional layer uses about 200 separate 5×5 filters. In other words, this layer looks for 200 distinct patterns on the feature planes that would indicate something interesting is going on. Any time a filter finds an interesting pattern somewhere on the feature planes, the corresponding neuron in the next layer "lights up."

Subsequent layers in AlphaGo's move-prediction network then apply their own filters to search for *compositions of filters* from the previous layer.[15] Just as the convolutional layers deep within an image-classification neural network can find complex patterns of pixels that look for things like fur, eyes, or faces, layers deep within AlphaGo can find important patterns of Go stones on the board—exactly the patterns expert humans might look for. When the move-prediction network is run, its neurons light up, layer by layer, the layers deep within the network finding more and more complex patterns of Go pieces.

AlphaGo's move-prediction network also differs from the Atari-playing network in the form of its output. Remember that the Atari network predicts the future rewards the agent should expect for selecting different actions, and the Atari agent simply chooses the action with the highest expected reward. AlphaGo's move-prediction network produces a *probability distribution* over possible actions each player might make. AlphaGo then uses the output of this network as if it were a weighted die. When it imagines the rest of a game playing out in one of its simulations, it rolls this weighted die to select its next move, selecting actions more often if the move-prediction network says they have a higher probability of being played.

DeepMind trained AlphaGo's move-prediction network using 30 million moves played by humans from one of the internet Go servers.[16] By the time DeepMind had finished training its move-prediction network, it was able to predict these humans' moves remarkably well: in a game where players typically have to choose from about 250 possible moves, AlphaGo's move-prediction network could predict these players' moves with a respectable 57 percent accuracy.[17] This isn't perfect, so AlphaGo still had a lot of uncertainty about which moves an opponent might make. But by *sampling* players' moves as it imagined how games would play out, AlphaGo was probably being reasonable: even expert players can't predict with perfect accuracy which moves their opponents will make. Sampling would make AlphaGo more robust to its own uncertainty in how each player might move.

As accurate as it was, this move-prediction neural network was also impractically slow. DeepMind found that a full evaluation of the network took about three milliseconds.[18] This might sound fast, but a typical Go game lasts about 150 moves. This means it could take nearly half a second to simulate a single game—that is, to generate a single sample out of the thousands it might need. This would have been far too slow. For the battery of experiments DeepMind ran on AlphaGo, for example, they gave it only five seconds to plan each move. How could it run accurate simulations and still be fast enough that a single move by AlphaGo wouldn't take hours to plan?

But there was an even bigger problem AlphaGo faced. As long as the move-prediction network was imperfect—and it *was* imperfect—there was no guarantee that the win/loss statistics AlphaGo collected near the top of its search tree would tell it which move was best. This was true even if AlphaGo could collect as much data in its simulations as it needed. Even if it could run an infinite number of simulations in the blink of an eye, it still might never learn which move was best. This was the result of a subtle and nefarious bug lurking in the way that AlphaGo collected and used its statistics—at least, in the way I've explained it so far. In fact, AlphaGo *didn't* use the algorithm I've just described up to this point. AlphaGo would need to use a modified version of this algorithm that would make it robust to the limitations—in speed and accuracy—of its slow move-prediction network.

THE HAND OF GOD

The mysterious online appearance of Master, the Go player with a wide-eyed fox as its avatar, wasn't the first time AlphaGo made headlines. It became well-known in the computer Go community when it defeated the European champion Fan Hui in a five-game match, and again it made headlines throughout the world when it defeated world champion Lee Sedol in four out of five professional games in 2016.[19]

The five-day match with Lee Sedol took place in his home country of Korea, where over 8 million people play Go.[20] The five games were simultaneously gut wrenching and beautiful. Christopher Moyer of the *Atlantic* captured the atmosphere during one of the games:

> In Game 2, Lee exhibits a different style, attempting to play more cautiously. He waits for any opening he can exploit, but AlphaGo continues to surprise. At move 37, AlphaGo plays an unexpected move, what's called a "shoulder hit" on the upper right side of the board. This move in this position is unseen in professional games, but its cleverness is immediately apparent. [Go player] Fan Hui would later say, "I've never seen a human play this move. So beautiful."
>
> And Lee? *He gets up and walks out of the room.* For a moment it's unclear what's happening, but then he re-enters the game room, newly composed, sits down, and plays his response. What follows is a much closer game than Game 1, but the outcome remains the same. Lee Sedol resigns after 211 moves.[21]

After the "shoulder hit," when Lee walked out of the room, he needed almost 15 minutes to recover.[22]

Lee lost the third game as well, so he was bound to lose the match: he was at three losses out of three in a five-game match. As a representative of humans in the war against silicon, Lee addressed the world at a news conference after that game. "I apologize for being unable to satisfy a lot of people's expectations. I kind of felt powerless."[23] With that, Google won the prize of $1 million, which it donated to charities. But Lee and AlphaGo played two more games for fun, Lee hoping to regain his pride. And then something happened in the fourth game.

On the 78th move, after studying the board for 30 minutes, Lee placed a stone roughly in the middle, in a move called a "wedge," as shown in figure 15.3a. The move was equally as brilliant—and equally as unexpected—as AlphaGo's shoulder hit. Lee's wedge move became known among Go enthusiasts as the "Hand of God."[24]

As Christopher Moyer of the *Atlantic* and Cade Metz of *Wired* observed, immediately after Lee's Hand of God play, AlphaGo played a disastrous move (we might call this move its "Hand of Elephant").[25] It's possible that AlphaGo simply didn't have any good moves to play at this point, and that any move it played could have been called disastrous; but the outcome was

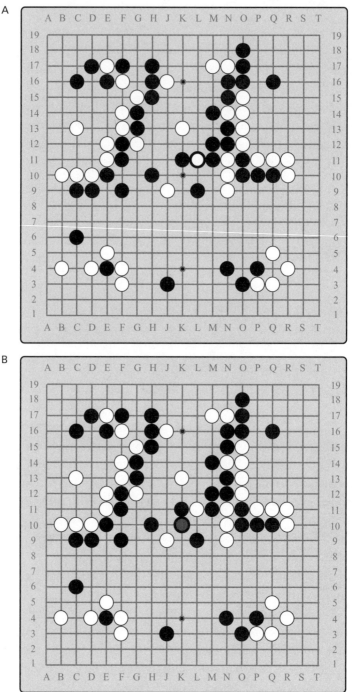

Figure 15.3a, b
The "Hand of God" move played by Lee Sedol in the fourth of their five games (L-11, top board). The "Hand of Elephant" played by AlphaGo followed immediately afterwards (K-10). Game states are available at https://gogameguru.com/lee-sedol-defeats-alphago-masterful-comeback -game-4.

the same nonetheless. Minutes later, as AlphaGo was running through its simulations, its estimate of its ability to win the game plummeted. Lee won the fourth game, and the Korean press cheered. At a post-game press conference, Lee Sedol addressed the media. "Because I lost three matches and then was able to get one single win," he explained, "this win is so valuable that I wouldn't exchange it for anything in the world."[26]

After the fourth game, AlphaGo's creators analyzed what had happened in those moves. They discovered that AlphaGo had placed too low a probability on Lee's Hand of God move, so it hadn't explored that branch of the search tree in enough detail. AlphaGo thought there was just a 1 in 10,000 chance Lee would make that move.[27]

MONTE CARLO TREE SEARCH

Over the first decade of this millennium, the algorithms related to how AlphaGo simulated its games hit an inflection point. An algorithm known as Monte Carlo Tree Search—MCTS for short—led to a paradigm shift for computer Go. If you've ever looked at a list of Go-playing computer programs, there's a good chance that the list was separated into two groups: those that came before MCTS and those that came after it. Monte Carlo Tree Search was AlphaGo's solution to both its slow move-prediction problem and its nefarious wrong-move problem.

Monte Carlo Tree Search improves on the way we simulated games earlier in this chapter: it enables an agent to run through many games, collecting statistics about which simulations end in wins, as we saw before. In contrast to the simulation algorithm we saw earlier, however, each time it simulates a game, it runs through two separate phases.

In the first phase, its "slow rollout" phase, AlphaGo descends through branches near the very top of the search tree as it did before, running the slow move-prediction neural network to find the probabilities for future moves by AlphaGo or its opponent and then rolling a weighted die with those probabilities to select which move to make, as shown in figure 15.4. This works just like the algorithm I described in the earlier section.

Once AlphaGo's MCTS algorithm descends far enough into the search tree, it then evaluates the board in two different ways. First, it evaluates the board with a neural network evaluation function that predicts the

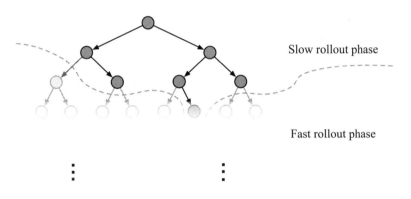

Slow rollout phase

Fast rollout phase

Figure 15.4
The boundary between the slow rollout phase and the fast rollout phase. The slow
move-prediction network and win/loss statistics from past simulations are used to
choose actions during the slow rollout phase. When a game reaches the fast rollout
phase, an evaluation function is run on the state at the boundary, and the fast move-
prediction network is used to choose actions for the rest of the simulation. As
AlphaGo runs more simulations and becomes more confident about states near the
top of the tree, it extends the envelope of the slow-rollout phase to include the states
with the most promise.

probability that AlphaGo will win the game from that state. Then—well,
rather, simultaneously—it performs a really fast rollout to simulate the rest
of the game.

The neural network AlphaGo uses for its evaluation function is nearly
identical to its slow move-prediction neural network, except that at its end
is an extra, hidden, fully connected layer, like the Atari network. This is
followed by a single output neuron that lights up brightly if AlphaGo has
a high probability of winning with that board layout.

As AlphaGo is running this evaluation function, it also runs a very fast
simulation of the rest of the game. This serves a similar purpose as running
the evaluation function, but it provides AlphaGo with an independent estimate of how the rest of the game will play out.

The simplest way to perform a fast rollout would have been to simply
choose moves at random. This is actually sometimes done with Monte
Carlo Tree Search, but Go has too large a search tree, so it would have
taken too long for AlphaGo to collect accurate estimates of win/loss statistics for this to work. Besides, DeepMind saw that it didn't work well
in practice in one of their experiments. Instead, AlphaGo chooses moves

during this fast rollout phase with—surprise!—yet another neural network. This fast move-prediction network is a lightweight version of the slow-prediction network. It has the same architecture as the slow move-prediction network but is missing a few input features that are time-consuming to compute. Without these features, the network can predict moves in about two-millionths of a second. The cost of this speedup is that the fast move-prediction network is about half as accurate as the slow network at predicting experts' moves.

Those two parts of AlphaGo's evaluation function enable it to run quickly enough to resolve the speed problem that AlphaGo faced. But they didn't address the nefarious bug lurking in the way AlphaGo selected its moves.

That bug is resolved by another feature of Monte Carlo Tree Search: the way AlphaGo chooses its moves near the top of the search tree. In addition to using the slow move-prediction network to sample its moves near the top of the tree, AlphaGo begins to prefer moves in this slow rollout phase *based on what it has learned are good moves from the games it has simulated so far*. This way, even if AlphaGo's move-prediction networks were consistently wrong in certain ways—in fact, even if AlphaGo selected random moves with its networks—AlphaGo will eventually learn to make optimal moves, because it will eventually learn from the result of its simulations which moves are the best.[28]

When it's AlphaGo's turn to select a move to play against its opponent, it chooses its move by selecting the action at the top of the search tree with the *largest* number of samples. Since AlphaGo tended to select moves during its simulations that would cause it to win the game, the move it selected to play tended to be both high-quality and very thoroughly understood by AlphaGo.[29]

Monte Carlo Tree Search sometimes assumes a fixed *time budget*—that is, it assumes that there is a fixed amount of time—and it continues to run through its simulations as long as it can, simulating game after game, until this budget is all used up. This is helpful when each player has a limited amount of time per turn: AlphaGo can run as many simulations as possible, until its time had run out. Then, when it makes its move and its opponent makes her move, AlphaGo reuses the statistics it had built up through that path of the tree.

ONE-ARMED BANDITS

AlphaGo's ability to run simulations as long as possible is deeply related to what makes Monte Carlo Tree Search so effective. Artificial intelligence researchers have been poking around at methods like MCTS for a while, but it was difficult to find an approach that guaranteed that the algorithm, as it continued to run more simulations, would eventually find the best possible action. Instead, no matter how long the algorithms crunched away, these early algorithms might still produce a non-optimal move.

The key insight that allowed Monte Carlo Tree Search to move past this limitation depended on the delicate balance between *exploration* and *exploitation*, a well-known tradeoff among artificial intelligence researchers. Imagine that you have 100 arms, and each arm can pull the lever of a different slot machine at a casino. Because you need to keep track of your arms, you can pull just one lever on a slot machine of your choice every 10 seconds. This casino is special, not just because it caters to 100-armed patrons, but also because it advertises that some of its slot machines pay out more on average than they take in.

Your goal is to come home from this casino with as much money as possible by the end of the night. So as you pull these levers, you might keep track of the payout from each of the slot machines: $1 here, $0 there, and $100 over there. The tricky bit is that this payout differs on each pull of each machine's lever, and you have no idea at the beginning how these machines will pay out. One machine might consistently pay out $10, and another might pay an average of $100 for each pull of the lever, but with high variance. You're better off pulling the arm of the second machine than the first machine, even if it pays out $0 for the first pull; but you need to try it enough times to learn that it pays out well. Machine learning researchers have studied this problem extensively; they call it the "multi-armed bandit" problem.

At what point should you give up on most of the machines and focus on just a few machines? Will you ever be satisfied to pull the lever on just *one* machine for the rest of the evening? You can recognize intuitively that you should probably try each machine at least once, and that you should gradually move to the best machines as you gather enough data to be confident about those machines. But turning this intuition into a concrete algorithm that a computer can follow—while ensuring it has the right statistical properties—is a bit trickier.

Before Monte Carlo Tree Search came around, its tree-sampling predecessors faced the same dilemma: when running simulations, they needed to explore enough of the game tree to get an accurate sense for which actions were best. The break for Monte Carlo Tree Search came around 2006, when researchers found a way to improve sampling on trees that guaranteed that the agent could find the best move eventually, provided that it had run enough simulations. This is why a random rollout policy can actually work for MCTS: an agent using MCTS starts to use the outcome statistics near the top of the search tree as it plays more games. As long as it can experiment enough that it learns the best moves, MCTS will eventually tell the agent the best possible move.[30]

How does this sampling approach work? A couple of pages ago I brushed this aside when I said, "Once AlphaGo's MCTS algorithm descends far enough into the search tree, it then evaluates the board in two different ways." The key decisions in MCTS are *where the agent decides to switch to the fast rollout policy*, and *how it samples its actions before this*.

As AlphaGo runs through its iterations high up in the search tree, remember that it adjusts its moves during the slow-rollout phase near the top of the search tree using the win/loss statistics it has gathered so far. But it also needs to spend some time exploring other moves, just as you need to spend a bit of time on each slot machine before deciding to move over to the best ones. AlphaGo's move-selection algorithm—the way it selects moves in the top of the search tree—is designed therefore to prefer moves when it doesn't have much data about them, using a formula like the one that transformed MCTS in 2006.[31]

The other key decision AlphaGo's researchers made in MCTS is where it switches to its fast rollout policy. As AlphaGo's tree search algorithm gathers more evidence that a certain path in the search tree is good, it pushes this boundary further down that path, so it can start to search more deeply along that path before switching to its fast rollout policy. This is conceptually a lot like the singular extensions Feng-hsiung Hsu and his team added to Deep Blue to play chess. Remember that those singular extensions allowed Deep Blue to search deeply into the tree along a beam of very promising moves by each player—moves the players were almost sure to make, like defending their king. AlphaGo learns these singular extensions dynamically when it sees promising sequences of moves by either player.

DID ALPHAGO NEED TO BE SO COMPLICATED?

It's worth reflecting on what made the various design decisions in AlphaGo important to its success. Some of them might seem peculiar given what we've seen with other game-playing algorithms. Did AlphaGo really need to be so complicated? For example, why did AlphaGo even bother with simulating games? Couldn't it have searched to a fixed depth and then just used a neural network evaluation function, the same way Deep Blue played chess?

Remember that the search tree for Go is orders of magnitude larger than the search tree for chess. If AlphaGo had followed Deep Blue's lead—that is, brute-force search with a custom evaluation function and some singular extensions—then it very likely would have been either too slow, or it would have searched too shallowly. On the other hand, AlphaGo managed to defeat Fan Hui while evaluating only about a *thousandth the number of* board states Deep Blue had evaluated during its game with Garry Kasparov.[32] AlphaGo's creators speculated that this was because AlphaGo selected moves during its search phase more intelligently with its slow move-prediction network, and because it evaluated these moves with a high-quality evaluation function.[33] As they speculated, AlphaGo used "an approach that is perhaps closer to how humans play."[34]

DeepMind devoted an enormous amount of resources to developing AlphaGo, with a team of about 20 employees.[35] The team experimented extensively in its design decisions for AlphaGo, and much of AlphaGo's complexity was justified by performing one experiment or another. For example, when they were deciding how many filters to use in their convolutional layers, they tried a variety of different numbers and found that it worked best with 100 or 200 filters per layer.[36]

Another experiment DeepMind ran studied how they should evaluate the board partway through the search tree after the slow rollout phase. Should they use a fast, completely random rollout? Should they use just their evaluation-function neural network? Or should they do a rollout with just a fast move-prediction network? It was from this experiment they found that random rollouts weren't very effective; and AlphaGo worked

best when it used a 50/50 mixture between the evaluation-function network and the fast move-prediction network.[37] They also pitted AlphaGo
against itself for millions of games to generate more data to improve the
evaluation-function neural network, similar to how Tesauro improved his
backgammon-playing neural network.

After its initial wins against Fan Hui and Lee Sedol, DeepMind continued to improve AlphaGo. One of its improved versions played the online
games we saw at the beginning of this chapter as the mysterious player
named Master. By the end of 2017, DeepMind had improved AlphaGo in
nearly all respects, culminating in a version they named AlphaGo Zero. It
could be trained in three days (instead of months), it required a 10th of the
processing power to play live games, and it won 100 out of 100 games
against the version of itself that had played the famous matches against Lee
Sedol. And it could do all of this although, like Tesauro's program, it learned
how to play from scratch.

How did DeepMind make these improvements? One way was by incorporating some of the improvements to convolutional neural networks
that had been discovered elsewhere over the past few years, including adding "shortcut" connections between layers and by improving the way
they trained their network. They also simplified AlphaGo's architecture,
merging the slow-move-prediction network and evaluation-function networks, and using as the network's inputs only the positions of the black
and white stones instead of the original 48 feature planes. They improved
the network's accuracy enough that they didn't need to use the fast rollouts anymore: they could simply run their evaluation function neural network once they reached the end of the slow-rollout phase.

LIMITATIONS OF ALPHAGO

Like the Atari-playing agent, AlphaGo was designed for the very specific
task of playing games. Both operated on similar principals: descend into the
search tree (just one action in the case of the Atari network) and use neural networks to evaluate the board position. Although AlphaGo demonstrated a human-like ability to recognize features on the Go board, it
could perform only a very narrow task: playing Go. As Jie Tang, a researcher
at OpenAI, pointed out, "It's not like AlphaGo is going to decide it wants
to go get a cheeseburger and try to take over the world."

One reason AlphaGo isn't about to go take over the world is that it depended on humans for everything, including its ability to place its pieces on the board. For AlphaGo to make its moves, a human operator must look at a computer screen to see which moves AlphaGo has selected and then place a stone on the board for it.

Except for its uncanny ability to recognize patterns in the game of Go and to select moves from these patterns—abilities that no doubt were impressive—AlphaGo didn't demonstrate most of the behaviors we often associate with human intelligence. It couldn't interact with a fast-changing world. Except for the statistics it aggregated in the upper levels of its search tree, it had no memory of past events; and except for the simulations it ran of how it and its opponent might move, it had no conception of future events. AlphaGo's creators, like the creators of most of the automata in this book, designed it to solve a narrow problem. For the same reason an airplane doesn't have wings that flap, AlphaGo doesn't have a memory or an ability to react quickly to a real-time environment. AlphaGo was engineered precisely to play Go, so it only demonstrates the capabilities required for that.

Soon after AlphaGo defeated Lee Sedol, DeepMind announced a new project. This next challenge was to design an agent that could play a game requiring that agent to have many more of the qualities we typically associate with human intelligence: the ability to make decisions under time constraints, to seek out the information needed to make these decisions, and to make these decisions at both a high level (planning actions that might impact the course of events far into the future) and at a low level (making lightning-quick reactions whose impact will be felt immediately). DeepMind hoped to build an agent that could play the real-time strategy game *StarCraft*.

Games are a helpful benchmark, but the goal is AI.
—Michael Bowling, professor at the University of Alberta[1]

BUILDING BETTER GAMING BOTS

Considering that the AI community has found a way to beat world champions at Go, and that Go was long considered to be one of the most difficult challenges for AI, what are the next big challenges we're trying to tackle in the field? In this chapter, we'll take a closer look at a concrete open problem that's been receiving more and more attention: the problem of building a computer program—a *bot*, in the lingo of the community—that can play games like *StarCraft* as well as the best humans can. We'll also look at which of the methods we've seen so far in this book can be useful in building *StarCraft* bots. Before going any further into the topic, I'll warn you that we haven't fully mastered the art of building these bots; so don't expect to finish this chapter knowing how to do it.

StarCraft is among the most popular games in the history of computer gaming. Released in 1998, it sold over 10 million copies within a decade of its release.[2] Of those copies, 4.5 million were sold in Korea alone, where the game is credited with starting the country's gaming craze, and where the game is played competitively and watched by large audiences in professional sports stadiums.[3] The top *StarCraft* players are idols; they receive gifts from adoring fans, and the very best ones receive lucrative contracts to play the game professionally. One of the world's top players, a 28-year-old, received a three-year contract to play the game professionally for $690,000.[4] Other players aren't so fortunate. Another 28-year-old man became so engrossed in the game that he died of exhaustion after playing for 50 hours straight in a smoky internet café.[5]

STARCRAFT AND AI

StarCraft is a game of war set in the 26th century. Like chess, each player commands an army of different types of pieces, each of which has certain strengths and weaknesses. Some pieces, like pawns, are weak and can't move very fast. Other pieces serve as tough, gnarly infantry, while yet other pieces can shoot projectiles or fly long distances (remember, *StarCraft* is played on a computer, not on a physical board). Unlike chess, *StarCraft* is a *real-time* strategy game. Instead of taking turns to move, players command individual units of their armies in real time across a large fighting area. Combat between army units is fast-paced and brutal, which gives an advantage to players who are quick with their fingers. Indeed, the top human *StarCraft* players routinely exceed five keyboard and mouse actions per second.[6]

Another feature that makes *StarCraft* interesting is that it requires each player to maintain a functioning economy. To develop their own army, players must construct and upgrade different types of buildings; and the order in which they do this matters. Different buildings allow them to create differently skilled pieces in their army or to create new buildings, so this is sometimes called the "technology tree": the deeper into the tree players build, the stronger their pieces. But to construct and upgrade these buildings, the players must acquire resources from their environment (think: the equivalent of gold, wood, and oil in the 26th century). Obtaining the resources to build this economy often requires acquiring and protecting those resources by force. So a strong economy begets a strong army, and a strong army enables a strong economy.

To make the game even more interesting, a "fog of war" obscures most of the playing space in *StarCraft*. Players can see what's happening on or near their pieces, but they can't see far beyond their pieces on the world map. This means they must send out scouts or find other ways to learn about the world. So when players make decisions, they do so with uncertainty. Players must proactively think about when and how to gather intelligence throughout the game.

Let's think back briefly to how we designed agents to play strategy games like chess and Go. In those games, the best agents searched through millions of game states and ran evaluation functions to find the states that were the most likely to lead to a successful outcome. The size of a game's search tree—and an agent's ability to search through it—depended on two factors: the branching factor at each level of the tree (how many moves the agent must choose from at a given time) and the depth of the tree (how many moves the agent might make in a game).

Go's branching factor is about 250. *StarCraft's* branching factor is much larger than this. At any given time, a player can choose to move any of one or more pieces, or she can upgrade or build new buildings. One conservative estimate of the game's branching factor pins it at 1 followed by 50 zeros (it's so high because players can move any subset of their pieces *simultaneously*).[7] The length of a *StarCraft* game is also much longer than a game of Go: while a professional Go game lasts about 150 moves, StarCraft is a real-time game. The length of a typical 25-minute *StarCraft* game is about 36,000 moves.[8] This means the search space for a typical *StarCraft* game is, very roughly, $10^{1,799,640}$ times that of a typical Go game. To make things even more challenging, *StarCraft* players have imperfect information due to the fog of war; so traditional search methods as used in chess or Go won't work for *StarCraft*.

In other words, *StarCraft* presents an awesome challenge for the field of artificial intelligence. Creating a bot that can play *StarCraft* well requires matching many qualities we believe define human intelligence, including the ability to make strategic decisions with limited information and the ability to react to unforeseen circumstances in real time. David Churchill, a professor of computer science at Memorial University of Newfoundland, called it the "pinnacle" of game AI research.

David has been organizing competitions between *StarCraft* bots since he took it over from Ben Weber around 2010, so we have some idea of how far along we are in developing these bots. From what we've seen, we're still a long way from cracking the *StarCraft* problem.[9] As of 2017, if we were to provide letter grades to *StarCraft* bots, where professional players earn an A- to an A+, and where amateur players earn a C+ to B, *StarCraft* bots fall into the D to D+ range.[10] But we have made some progress.

SIMPLIFYING THE GAME

The only way *StarCraft* bots can have even a remote chance at working is by decomposing the tasks they need to perform into manageable chunks. Some of the core ideas about what these chunks should be have come from careful analysis of how expert humans play the game.[11] I've organized some of the recurring ideas in successful bots into an architecture shown in figure 16.1. You'll probably recognize immediately that we've seen a very similar architecture when we looked at the self-driving cars at the beginning of this book and at neural networks that could play Atari games. The resemblance is partly due to the generality of the diagrams I've used (you could arguably put almost any agent into a diagram like this), but it's worth reviewing how some *StarCraft* bots fit into this architecture.[12]

At the far left of this architecture is the layer through which the agent interacts with the world. In self-driving cars, this layer contained sensors and controllers; and in the Atari agent, this layer interfaced with the Arcade Learning Environment. As of now, most *StarCraft* bots interact with their virtual world through an interface known as the BroodWar Application Programming Interface, a software library developed by a precocious young

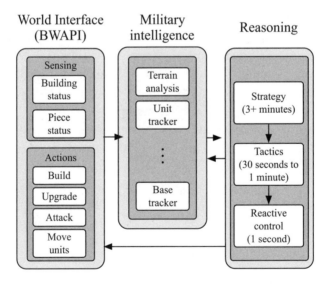

Figure 16.1
A sample *StarCraft* bot architecture, simplified.

software developer named Adam Heinermann (BroodWar is an expansion pack—that is, a specific version—for *StarCraft*). For the *StarCraft* bot, this sensing and actuation layer offers a way for bots to interact with the game itself programmatically.

In the middle layer is a perception and world modeling layer that tracks military intelligence for the agent: it summarizes information the agent has gathered about the world, including information about opponents' bases, units in the game, and the overall map. Different bots have varying levels of emphasis on this layer.

The "smart" behavior of the bot comes from the right-most part of the architecture, which we can separate into three levels. At the top level, these bots reason about *strategy*: which buildings should the bot build, which building upgrades should it perform, and when should it do these things? This strategic decision-making requires planning ahead for tens of minutes and has a direct, long-term impact on the game because the technology tree—that is, the buildings and their upgrades—directly affects the composition, strengths, and weaknesses of the bot's army later in the game. This decision-making component also requires long-term planning to develop an economy that can support the tree. At a slightly lower level, the bot reasons about tactics, which involves planning ahead for about 30 seconds to a minute: where should the agent place its buildings? Where and when should it send its troops for battle? At the lowest of these three levels is a reactive layer, which requires planning and reaction time on the order of seconds. And feeding into these three layers is information about the world, via its intelligence layer.

Now, these three-layer architectures aren't the formal three-layer architecture we saw in the self-driving cars that could navigate intersections; for example, the three layers in a *StarCraft* bot define levels of organization in a military command hierarchy or a set of buildings. As David Churchill, the computer science professor we met a moment ago, explains, "When a decision is made at the strategic level, an order is given to a tactical unit with only the information necessary to accomplish the tactical goal."[13] This is different from the formal three-layer architecture we saw in self-driving cars because there's no explicit "sequencer," or Monopoly board, layer.

PRAGMATIC *STARCRAFT* BOTS

What else has worked well in designing *StarCraft*-playing bots? Think back to the guiding principle we saw in the Pragmatic Theory team, the two guys without a clue who competed in the Netflix competition. Remember that Pragmatic Theory had exactly one goal: to win the competition. And so they aimed for quantity, combining hundreds of models and predictors, regardless of the how impractical it might be for Netflix to replicate their approach. They were pragmatic about achieving their goal.

Many of the creators of the top *StarCraft* bots have followed a similar philosophy, programming their bots with strategies that enable them to win the game, even if that means they aren't building bots that we would consider intelligent. For example, some bots are programmed to follow simple "rush" strategies, which means that they build up a small army of weak fighting units (the only units they can create without a deep technology tree) and attack their opponent before she has had a chance to build up her defenses. These rush strategies are legitimate strategies, and expert human players use variants of them. But doing this requires the agent to follow a simple set of rules with utter disregard for any long-term strategy, and the bots that implement these strategies still fall far short of beating expert humans.

Churchill designed one of the more sophisticated and successful *StarCraft*-playing bots using a variety of tools from the field of AI. But even his bot, called UAlbertaBot, would sometimes lose to these "rush" bots. At one point, he studied his opponents' bots' strategies and adjusted UAlbertaBot to be more resistant to them. This worked for a little while, getting UAlbertaBot to the top in competitions, until more competitors popped up, with their own unique rush strategies; by that time, Churchill was too busy with being a professor to adjust his bot to handle these new strategies. (Most of his work on UAlbertaBot was while he was a graduate student at the University of Alberta.)

One of the ways we can tell that even the best *StarCraft* bots are still bad is because they still have major Achilles' heels. This can sometimes lead to bizarre paper-rock-scissors cycles among some bots, as shown in figure 16.2. A few years ago, SkyNet Bot was generally very good compared to other

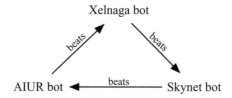

Figure 16.2
A paper-rock-scissors cycle among *StarCraft* bots from a 2011 competition. In the competition, Xelnaga usually won when it played against Skynet, Skynet usually won when it played against AIUR, and AIUR usually won when it played against Xelnaga.

bots, winning against AIUR Bot about 80 percent of the time. AIUR Bot was decent, and, like most other bots, it usually beat Xelnaga Bot. Xelnaga Bot used a "rush" strategy like the one we saw above: it attacked other players' "pawn" pieces—the ones that can create buildings and collect resources. This strategy didn't fare well against most bots, but it was also a unique weakness of SkyNet Bot, which meant that Xelnaga Bot could beat the otherwise good SkyNet Bot about 70 percent of the time![14] There's no reason such cycles couldn't happen among top Go or chess players; but its particular acuteness among the best *StarCraft* agents betrays their current weaknesses.

If you've played these games before, you've almost surely played against a computer opponent, which means you've played against a bot. So you might be wondering: If it's so difficult to create a bot to play a game like *StarCraft*, why was the computer so difficult to beat? Churchill disagrees that they're difficult. "Because real-time strategy AI is so difficult to make intelligent," he explained, "In-game bots often cheat in order to appear stronger than they really are." The goal of the bots in the software you buy off the shelf is to offer an interesting and compelling experience for the human player, not to be objectively good.[15] For example, in some cases, the computer is allowed to see the entire playing map, without the fog of war.[16] The bots might send scouts around to make it look like they don't have full visibility of the board, but this is only a trick, a form of misdirection similar to what the chess-playing Turk used, to look smarter than they actually are.[17] Their strategies are equally simple: for example, on a given level, the computer might have a scripted—that is, a predefined—build tree with very simple rules to handle exceptions.

In fact, scripted build rules are common even in the "good" bots. When Churchill and his collaborators built UAlbertaBot, they built the skeleton first, filling in its different components—like the strategy, tactics, and reactive layers—with simple, scripted rules. The idea was to have a bot that could play *StarCraft* fully even if it couldn't play well. Then, once the skeleton was in place, they could continue to improve the individual components, replacing their scripted "production module" with one that could search for an optimal order in which to develop their technology tree (they've exceeded humans at this), replacing their "combat commander" with a sophisticated combat simulation system, and so on.[18] As *StarCraft* bots continue to improve, these individual modules will most likely improve rather than their overall architectures. Or will the architectures be vastly different as well?

OPENAI AND *DOTA 2*

Many *StarCraft* players are familiar with the game Defense of the Ancients 2, or, simply, *DOTA 2*. This is a capture-the-flag style game having many similarities with *StarCraft*. To master *DOTA 2*, the player must control a "hero" character who can move about the map, attack opponents, cast spells, and so on, with a goal of destroying their opponents' "Ancient," a building to be protected at all costs.

Professional *DOTA 2* players compete annually for a $24 million prize pool. The total of past reward pools for *DOTA 2* is $132 million, far beyond that of *StarCraft* (a "paltry" $7 million) and even *StarCraft II* ($25 million). Not surprisingly, the game is challenging: a bot designed to play *DOTA 2*, as with one designed to play *StarCraft*, must be capable of making sense of a world with an extraordinarily large search space.[19]

Elon Musk, whom we briefly met a few chapters ago, launched the research lab OpenAI to "build safe artificial intelligence and ensure that AI's benefits are as widely and evenly distributed as possible."[20] In August 2017, OpenAI announced that they had created a bot that could beat some of the best *DOTA 2* players in a limited, 1-vs-1 version of the game. How did they create a bot that could search through such a large space?

The answer, as a researcher from OpenAI explained, is that they didn't. OpenAI used a combination of the tools we've seen in this chapter and the chapters about neural networks, but their architecture didn't use a search algorithm like Monte Carlo Tree Search.[21]

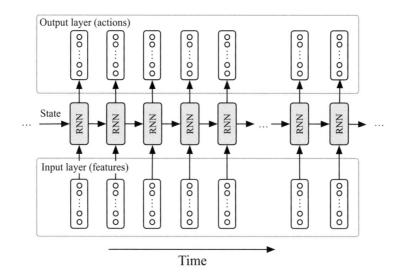

Figure 16.3
An architecture of the bot that beat some top human players at *DOTA 2*. At each epoch, the agent runs a neural network that takes in a feature vector summarizing the current world and outputs variables that determine the action the agent will select. The agent also keeps track of state, which it passes from epoch to epoch. This state serves as a sort of "memory" for the agent.

To play *DOTA 2*, a small team of researchers at OpenAI created a neural network that was like two of the networks we saw earlier in this book. At a first cut, it was a bit like the Atari-playing network. Remember that the Atari-playing agent evaluated its network over and over, selecting whichever action the network indicated would lead to the highest time-adjusted stream of rewards (i.e., chocolate). At each time step, the input to the Atari network was a vector summarizing which pixels were on the screen for the past four screenshots, while the output represented its expected future reward for taking each action. The *DOTA 2* architecture, which you can see in figure 16.3, was similar, in that its output neurons determined which actions the agent should take. Also like the Atari network, the input to the *DOTA 2* network was a list of features that encoded the current state of the game. Like the backgammon-playing neural network and AlphaGo, their neural network improved by playing games against itself.[22]

But there were some important differences between these networks. First, many of the *DOTA 2* network's input features were hand-crafted by humans, encoding things like the currently controlled piece's position on the map and details on the map. Second—and much more importantly—the *DOTA 2* network had a memory.[23]

Remember that the Atari network couldn't play certain games, such as *Montezuma's Revenge*, very well. *Montezuma's Revenge* required its agent to do two things: explore a very large environment and remember what it had done recently. But the Atari network had no memory, so even if it had a lot of experience, it would have still performed poorly at the game. How could we endow an agent with a memory?

We saw a hint at a memory unit for neural networks in chapter 11, when we looked at networks that could generate captions for images. Remember that these networks could keep track of which words they had uttered so far because they were recurrent neural networks, or RNNs. The units in RNNs are connected to one another in a series: the output-state of one recurrent unit feeds as an input-state into the next recurrent unit in the series. Each unit in the network inspects its state and any other inputs, produces some output value, updates the state, and then sends that state to the next unit in the sequence.

The *DOTA 2* network used this same idea. Like the Atari-playing network, the *DOTA 2* network was running constantly, in a loop, taking in its input features and producing some output values. *But it was also an RNN:* one of its outputs was the state, which it passed on to the next unit in the network to use. As the network was run, it "remembered" things using this state vector.[24]

The *DOTA 2* bot was far from perfect. First, having a memory alone wouldn't solve all of its problems; Atari agents that have been endowed with memories still can't beat *Montezuma's Revenge*. After its win, OpenAI hosted a session for other players to beat up their *DOTA 2* bot, and these players found some glaring Achilles' heels in the program, just as humans had already seen with *StarCraft*-playing bots. But the network's ability to defeat several of the top players in the world still moved us one step closer to creating bots that can play competitively against humans at the standard, 5-vs-5 version of *DOTA 2*—and bringing us ideas in the meantime that will also be useful in designing successful *StarCraft* bots.[25]

THE FUTURE OF *STARCRAFT* BOTS

To see one possible direction of where *StarCraft* is headed in the future, let's return to a character we've seen sporadically throughout this book: Demis Hassabis, the founder of DeepMind. Although Demis was late to join the *StarCraft* bot community, he became interested in the game some time before he founded DeepMind. When Demis discovered that one of his colleagues was a competitive *StarCraft* player, he became fascinated by this colleague's ability to consistently win the game. As another colleague recalled:

> Demis wanted to beat this guy. He would lock himself in a room with the guy night after night. He'd handicap him, by getting the guy to play without a mouse or one-handed so he could analyze exactly what he was doing to be brilliant. It was a bit like going into the boxing ring and getting beaten up, and then returning every night. It showed his incredible will to win.[26]

More recently, Demis turned some of DeepMind's efforts toward building a bot to play *StarCraft* competitively. DeepMind and Blizzard, the company behind *StarCraft*, announced a collaboration to develop and release an official interface for bots to play *StarCraft II*, as well as an environment for developers to create their own "curricula" for bots to learn in more structured ways.[27]

One of the curious things about DeepMind's decision to pivot toward *StarCraft* is that researchers at the University of Alberta had been looking at this problem for a decade beforehand. Remember: David Churchill studied there while performing pioneering research in *StarCraft* bot design. This fact in isolation might not be very interesting; but what *is* interesting is the profound impact the University of Alberta has had on the field of artificial intelligence overall, and on DeepMind's efforts in particular. As we saw in chapter 7, researchers at the University of Alberta developed the Arcade Learning Environment, which provided Deep-Mind with a way for its Atari-playing agent to interact with the world. Several key researchers from DeepMind's team that developed AlphaGo cut their teeth on computer Go at the university. And the University of Alberta has several of the world's leading experts on a variety of topics in artificial intelligence, including Richard Sutton, who has been described as the "Godfather of Reinforcement Learning." One of Sutton's contributions to the field was the very algorithm that the Atari-playing agent used to learn from its actions—the algorithm it used for off-policy learning.

If we could solve *StarCraft*, does that mean we can solve intelligence? Quite simply, no. There are many parts of human intelligence not addressed by *StarCraft*, including the ability of humans to make sense of, and draw conclusions from, entirely new and unstructured environments.

As several famous AI researchers wrote in one of the first papers about computer chess, "If one could devise a successful chess machine, one would seem to have penetrated to the core of human endeavor."[28] Now that it's been a couple of decades since we've devised a successful chess machine, it's not clear that we're any closer to the "core of human endeavor" than we were before we beat Garry Kasparov, although now we at least know how to design a system that can play an excellent game of chess. The same rough assessment applies to computer Go and *StarCraft*. Creating a bot that can play *StarCraft* competitively may to turn out to be a similarly impressive but narrow result. The tools and architectures we pick up along the way, however—the new search algorithms, new perception algorithms, and new reinforcement-learning algorithms—will be the more important accomplishments.

THE FITS AND STARTS OF AI DEVELOPMENT

Now that we've created digital automata that can outperform humans at tasks like recognizing objects in images, transcribing recordings of human speech, and playing games like Go, what can we expect to see them do in the next 50 years? Plenty. But before we speculate on where we're headed next, let's briefly look at how far we've come.

A lot of the ideas from the past 20 years that have created excitement in the AI community were the same things that drummed up excitement around AI half a century ago, in the late 1960s. Back then, the field of AI felt like it was roaring ahead, with improvements in neural networks, development of algorithms to play games like chess and Go, excitement at conferences (where AI felt like it was bursting at the seams) and hardware that was growing exponentially with the advent of microprocessors—all just before the field of AI went into a dark period known as the AI Winter. Funding for AI research dried up for several decades. AI even became "a term of derision" among some researchers.[1] The funk lasted through much of the 1980s and 1990s, before the field's rebirth over the past two decades.

In other words, the progress we've seen since just before the turn of the century is noteworthy, but it's not an isolated burst of technological advancement, even in the field of AI. It's part of a longer, sustained series of developments in AI—a series of developments that comes in fits and starts.

The automata our ancestors created in the 18th century were also part of a sustained development of technology spanning many decades. In Europe, mechanics created automata during the 18th and 19th centuries, but the trend had been going on globally for a much longer period. A trio of Persian brothers created a programmable flute-playing device as early as the ninth century, and the Greeks had developed primitive steam engines by the first century AD.[2] We should expect our modern, digital automata to follow a similarly long arc of progress, interrupted by periods of slow progress.

HOW TO REPLICATE THE SUCCESSES IN THIS BOOK

Many of the machines we've seen might look superficially different, but they have an enormous amount in common. Classifiers enabled these intelligent machines to perceive the world. Finite state machines and recurrent neural networks enabled them to keep track of what was going on around them—what they had done, what they are doing, and what they still need to do—and to focus on only the most salient parts of their environment. Search algorithms enabled them to brute-force their way to the best among millions of options. And reinforcement learning gave them the ability to learn from their experience. These "statistical elements" were then combined via remarkably similar architectures into the machines we saw, which could drive autonomously, predict humans' preferences for movies, answer *Jeopardy!* questions, and play games of strategy with stunning precision.

But the design of these statistical machines was only part of the story. All of these machines required prolonged and well-organized human effort. The smallest team in this book to "succeed" was the one that created IBM's Deep Blue; made up of only a few people, it gained and lost members here or there like a rock band over its dozen years of work. But Deep Blue attacked the problem for an entire decade. Many of the other teams we saw took less time to develop their products but were much larger—often dozens of researchers and engineers working on a project for a year or more, typically reaching tens or hundreds of person-years of research and development. And this required careful management of these teams' efforts.

Sebastian Thrun's experience in organizing the effort around Stanley the self-driving car set an excellent standard for such a high-functioning team. Sometimes he needed to make the tough but necessary decision to tell someone their part of the project, on which they might have been working for months, would not make the cut to be in the final robot. But his team members, whom he had carefully selected, recognized that this was for the good of the project.[3] For them, winning was a group effort, and everyone—including the leaders—made sacrifices. Sebastian explained:

> During this phase of the project, everyone on the core team fully understood what it meant to play with the team. Getting lunch for the team was as noble a deed as writing cutting-edge software. To the present day, I continue to be amazed by the willingness of every single team member to do whatever I asked him or her to do. And I tried to lead by example. My personal highlight was the day I spent building a tank trap out of PVC pipes. After bolting together three pipes, my team noted that the surface wasn't sufficiently similar to rusty metal. So I went back to the store to buy spray paint, and then spent hours applying a combination of paint and dirt to give the trap the look of a World War Two tank trap. This was not exactly the type [of] job for which I had come to Stanford. But it was magically gratifying to keep my hands dirty and to spend my time on mundane things of no scientific value whatsoever.[4]

These teams also couldn't have succeeded if they hadn't been embedded within larger communities of engineers and research scientists that shared their knowledge broadly. This was by design in competitions like the DARPA Grand Challenge and the Netflix Prize, but it was also true for projects like AlphaGo. Although AlphaGo was created by about 20 people in a private company, many of the ideas in AlphaGo—such as Monte Carlo Tree Search, evaluation functions, reinforcement learning, and deep neural networks—had been developed in the decades before DeepMind worked on the problem. Most of these projects succeeded not just because they were driven by a large engineering team with a clear goal and funding—but also because the ideas from which they came had been incubated by a publicly funded research community that offered the collective wisdom of decades of supporting research and experimentation. This was true even for privately funded projects: some of the core researchers on AlphaGo, for example, cut their teeth at the University of Alberta, and IBM Watson drew heavily from talent and ideas in the academic community.

Walter Isaacson came to a similar conclusion in his book *The Innovators*. He noted the difficulty in attacking an ambitious problem in a vacuum. Virtually none of the major advances in the history of the computer were the result of a lone tinkerer in his garage. The same is true of advances in AI and machine learning.

Does this mean that a lone researcher shouldn't bother to start with a project if he doesn't have a big budget and a team of researchers? Not at all, but it can still help to join or organize a larger effort down the road. Remember, for example, that the team called Pragmatic Theory started out as "two guys, absolutely no clue." But they carefully studied what the best teams did, which enabled them to rise quickly within the community and to eventually join what became the winning team. The team that created the chess-playing program Deep Blue also started out small, but eventually its members joined IBM, where they continued to develop Deep Blue over the following eight years before beating Garry Kasparov. And ultimately all of these projects started with one person who had an idea.

Sometimes the people with the ideas don't even have to solve the problem to have an impact: as we saw, they can organize a competition to encourage researchers to coalesce around a common cause. Is it possible that these competitions don't always foster advances, and instead just provide more transparency into progress that's already happening? This probably happens sometimes, but the Netflix Prize is a shining example of a competition that clearly added impetus to a field.

When Netflix planned their competition they made several important decisions that can serve as an example for future competition organizers. First, the dataset they released to the community was large enough to be valuable—it was 100 times the size of other public datasets of the same type—yet it was small-enough, and Netflix had cleaned it up well enough, that it was easy to work with. Second, they offered a large cash prize to the winners. Netflix also chose a good target for the Grand Prize: 10 percent was a difficult but not impossible target for teams to achieve.[5] They created a lively community around the project, offering an online forum where participants could share ideas and where a leaderboard could foster excitement. And finally, Netflix helped the researchers to move along by requiring winners to write reports before they could claim either a Progress Prize or the Grand Prize; these reports were widely read by members of the community.[6]

Competitions have the benefit that they can change the way a research community invests its time. One way they do this is by *standardizing* research. We've seen the same thing in financial markets: that publicly traded securities are *fungible*—that is, exchangeable with one another— means that they can be objectively evaluated, priced, and, ultimately, compared with one another. This helped with the ImageNet Challenge in 2012, where a neural network was the undisputed winner. Since all of the entrants to the competition were evaluated on the same criteria, it was clear that the network was the fair winner. Other teams immediately jumped aboard the deep-learning bandwagon, and in subsequent years the top contestants all used deep convolutional neural networks in their submissions.[7] While the 2012 team won by a large margin, nine teams in 2013 beat the best 2012 team, and progress was rapid in the ensuing years.

PERVASIVE USE OF DATA

Another recurring theme in the development of the statistical machines we've seen was their pervasive use of experiments and data. In some cases, large quantities of data were available because that data had been collected and organized by passionate gamer geeks. We saw this with games like Go (for which online games had been recorded) and *Jeopardy* (for which fans had collected questions from televised episodes). In other cases, academic researchers and companies put together comprehensive, well-labeled datasets.

In yet other cases, researchers found ways to create their own data. Sebastian Thrun and his Stanford team drove around in a car covered with sensors to collect training data for their terrain-detecting classifier. The Atari-playing neural network played millions of games in the Arcade Learning Environment to collect the data that it needed to improve its play. And the creators behind AlphaGo, the *DOTA 2* bot, and the backgammon-playing program turned their programs against themselves so they could create their own training data. The only bottleneck to how much data these game-playing programs could train on was the time it took the computers to play through their games.

WHERE WE GO NEXT

I've intentionally avoided much speculation about the future of AI in this book because I'm an engineer, not a philosopher, economist, or historian. But I do believe we've seen enough evidence in the development of these intelligent machines that I can say a couple of things about the future with fairly high confidence (although many of these things may take centuries, not decades, to occur).

First, the automata we create in the future will invariably still follow programs. This is a constraint of the media we've used to create these automata and the physical laws of the world we live in. These machines will follow programs that will grow more and more complex, and it will become more and more difficult to discern what they're doing, but it will always be possible to trace every action they perform back to a deterministic set of instructions.[8] Some philosophers have argued that this suggests that machines will never think.[9] My own belief is that humans are machines as well—we're analog machines—and if we believe that humans can think, then there's nothing to preclude us from designing digital computers that will also someday think. Rather, it's inevitable that our machines will someday think, and that they will develop emotions, opinions, and the desire for self-preservation—which will someday conflict with our own.

Second, we will continue to build machines that can replicate our intelligence and behavior more and more accurately, until there is no discernable difference between their abilities to perceive and reason and our own abilities to do these things—except that the machines will be better than us in many ways. We've been trying to do this since long before Vaucanson and his contemporaries tried their damnedest to create automata that looked and acted human.

As we continue to build better automata, these efforts will inevitably feed the perception that these machines are a threat to humanity—that they will steal our jobs and destroy our livelihoods. At the very least, these machines will make us uncomfortable in their uncanny resemblance to us. Remember: Vaucanson himself was forced to close of one of his workshops because a religious official considered it "profane."[10] And to some extent it will be true that these machines will be a threat to us: machines will take peoples' jobs precisely because they will do them more cheaply. Robots will be the "immigrants" blamed by future politicians, and their creators will market them carefully, just as IBM carefully positioned Watson. This will require our leaders to make thoughtful decisions to ensure that the benefits of improving technology are fairly distributed, and we should expect no less of them.

But however well our society can absorb these agents, we will continue to build them to meet and exceed our abilities as long as our technology—our hardware, our theory, and the software architectures behind them—continues to improve. Some of this will be driven by economics and business, but the drive to build such machines will continue long after any economic motivation has disappeared. Building machines in our image is a human endeavor, and certain qualities of human nature—curiosity, aesthetics, hubris, and vanity, but mostly curiosity and aesthetics—will compel us to continue.

NOTES

CHAPTER 1: THE SECRET OF THE AUTOMATON

1. Gaby Wood, "Living Dolls: A Magical History of the Quest for Mechanical Life by Gaby Wood," *The Guardian*, February 15, 2002, accessed February 5, 2017, https://www.theguardian.com/books/2002/feb/16/extract.gabywood.

2. Georgi Dalakov, *History of Computers and Computing, Automata, Jacques Vaucanson*, accessed March 9, 2017, http://history-computer.com/Dreamers/Vaucanson.html.

3. Tom Standage, *The Turk* (New York: Berkeley Publishing Group, 2002), xii.

4. Standage, *The Turk*, 5.

5. Wood, "Living Dolls"; Standage, *The Turk*, 5.

6. Dalakov, *History of Computers.*

7. Warren A. Marrison, "The Evolution of the Quartz Crystal Clock," *The Bell System Technical Journal* 27, no. 3 (1948): 517–536.

8. Some sources suggest that Vaucanson's duck couldn't actually digest; it had a secret chamber in it to store the incoming food and the outgoing, artificially colored feces.

CHAPTER 2: SELF-DRIVING CARS AND THE DARPA
GRAND CHALLENGE

1. Whittaker, quoted in Radha Chitale, "Red Team Falls to Its Own Offspring," *The Tartan* [CMU Student Newspaper], October 10, 2005, accessed June 15, 2017, https://thetartan.org/2005/10/10/scitech/redteam.

2. Marsha Walton, "Robots Fail to Complete Grand Challenge," *CNN*, May 6, 2004, accessed June 16, 2017, http://www.cnn.com/2004/TECH/ptech/03/14/darpa.race.

3. Joseph Hooper, "From DARPA Grand Challenge: 2004DARPA's Debacle in the Desert," *Popular Science*, June 3, 2004, accessed June 16, 2017, http://www

.popsci.com/scitech/article/2004-06/darpa-grand-challenge-2004darpas-debacle
-desert; Chris Urmson et al., "High Speed Navigation of Unrehearsed Terrain:
Red Team Technology for Grand Challenge," Technical Report, CMU- RI-04–
37, Robotics Institute, Carnegie Mellon University, 2004.

4. "Driven to Innovate," Carnegie Mellon University Homepage Archive, 2010,
accessed October 16, 2016, http://www.cmu.edu/homepage/computing/2010
/fall/driven-to-innovate.shtml.

5. Douglas McGray, "The Great Robot Race," *Wired*, March 1, 2004, accessed
June 15, 2017, https://www.wired.com/2004/03/robot-3.

6. Ibid.

7. Ibid.

8. Ibid.

9. Ibid.; Joshua Davis, "Say Hello to Stanley," *Wired*, January 1, 2006, accessed June
15, 2017, https://www.wired.com/2006/01/stanley.

10. Sometimes the controller accumulates the errors over time and adds that accu-
mulation to the signal sent to the motor; this helps if the error is consistently too
high or too low (this is called *integral control*). Sometimes the controller keeps track
of how quickly the error is changing and uses that to proactively adjust the signal
to the motor, anticipating future changes (this is called *derivative control*). This three-
rule controller is commonly known as a PID, or *proportional-integral-derivative
controller*. Technically the Humvee used only the PD parts of it for throttle control;
and they formalized it slightly differently.

11. McGray, "The Great Robot Race."

12. Ibid. Even though manual annotation of a map is time-consuming, it's actually a reasonable solution for a self-driving car, since a precise map only needs to
be created once for all self-driving cars that drive over the road, and it needs infre-
quent updates.

13. The algorithm used in many self-driving cars is called A* (pronounced
"ay-star") search, which uses approximations to improve how long it takes to
search for a good path.

14. Sebastian Thrun et al., "Stanley: The Robot That Won the DARPA Grand
Challenge," *Journal of Field Robotics* 23, no. 9 (2006): 661–692.

15. Urmson et al., "High Speed Navigation of Unrehearsed Terrain."

16. The Humvee also had several lower-power laser scanners for object detection
mounted on its sides and near the front.

17. Urmson et al., "High Speed Navigation of Unrehearsed Terrain."

18. Davis, "Say Hello to Stanley."

19. Hooper, "From DARPA Grand Challenge."

20. Chris Urmson et al., "Red Team Technology Overview," Technical Report, The Robotics Institute, Carnegie Mellon University, 2004.

21. Thrun et el., "Stanley."

22. Hooper, "From DARPA Grand Challenge"; McGray, "The Great Robot Race."

23. Hooper, "From DARPA Grand Challenge."

24. Joab Jackson, "DARPA's Desert Duel," *GCN,* March 13, 2004, accessed June 15, 2017, https://gcn.com/articles/2004/03/13/darpas-desert-duel.aspx.

25. Walton, "Robots Fail to Complete Grand Challenge."

26. Dickmanns, quoted in Davis, "Say Hello to Stanley."

27. Jackson, "DARPA's Desert Duel."

28. DARPA, "Grand Challenge 2004 Final Report," Technical Report, Defense Advanced Research Projects Agency, 2004.

29. DARPA, "Grand Challenge 2004 Final Report."

30. Walton, "Robots Fail to Complete Grand Challenge."

CHAPTER 3: KEEPING WITHIN THE LANES

1. Sebastian Thrun et al., "Stanley: The Robot That Won the DARPA Grand Challenge," *Journal of Field Robotics* 23, no. 9 (2006): 661–692.

2. Joshua Davis, "Say Hello to Stanley," *Wired*, January 1, 2006, accessed October 30, 2016, https://www.wired.com/2006/01/stanley.

3. Chris Urmson et al., "A Robust Approach to High-Speed Navigation for Unrehearsed Desert Terrain," *Journal of Field Robotics* 23, no. 8 (2006): 467–508.

4. Steve Russell, "DARPA Grand Challenge Winner: Stanley the Robot!" *Popular Mechanics,* January 8, 2006, accessed June 15, 2017, http://www.popular mechanics.com/technology/robots/a393/2169012.

5. Russell, "DARPA Grand Challenge Winner."

6. Urmson et al., "A Robust Approach."

7. This car in front of it was actually another car submitted to the race by the Red Team.

8. Russell, "DARPA Grand Challenge Winner."

9. Davis, "Say Hello to Stanley"; Joseph Hooper, "DARPA's Debacle in the Desert," *Popular Science,* June 3, 2004, accessed June 16, 2017, http://www.popsci.com/scitech/article/2004-06/darpa-grand-challenge-2004darpas-debacle-desert;

Sebastian Thrun, "A Personal Account of the Development of Stanley, the Robot That Won the DARPA Grand Challenge," *AI Magazine* 27, no. 4 (2006).

10. Davis, "Say Hello to Stanley"; Thrun, "A Personal Account."

11. Ibid.

12. Ibid.

13. Ibid.

14. Ibid.

15. Russell, "DARPA Grand Challenge Winner."

16. Davis, "Say Hello to Stanley."

17. Thrun et al., "Stanley."

18. Thrun, "A Personal Account."

19. Dean A. Pomerleau, *Alvinn: An Autonomous Land Vehicle in a Neural Network*. Technical Report, DTIC Document, 1989.

20. Thrun et al., "Stanley."

21. The line between these layers can be fuzzy; sometimes, for example, off-the-shelf sensors in the hardware layer will use things like Kalman filters: it's unclear whether this falls into the hardware or software layer.

22. Thrun et al., "Stanley."

23. Ibid.; Davis, "Say Hello to Stanley."

24. Davis, "Say Hello to Stanley."

25. Ibid.

26. Thrun et al., "Stanley"; Davis, "Say Hello to Stanley."

27. Thrun et al., "Stanley."

28. Ibid.

29. Ibid.

30. Ibid.; Davis, "Say Hello to Stanley."

31. Thrun et al., "Stanley"; Davis, "Say Hello to Stanley."

32. Red-green-blue, or RGB, is an arbitrary scale. In many cases, researchers transform RGB to a different set of numbers—such as brightness, saturation (that is, greyness), and where in the rainbow the colors fall—before using them.

33. This test made an exception for the sky, which they ruled out with a preprocessing step.

34. Thrun, "Stanley."

35. Russell, "DARPA Grand Challenge Winner."

36. Thrun, "Stanley" (note that the distance depended on the speed).

37. Ibid.

CHAPTER 4: YIELDING AT INTERSECTIONS

1. Erann Gat, "Three-Layer Architectures," in *Artificial Intelligence and Mobile Robots: Case Studies of Successful Robot Systems*, ed. David Kortenkamp, R. Peter Bonasso, and Robin Murphy (Cambridge, MA: MIT Press, 1998), 195–210.

2. Chris Urmson et al., "Autonomous Driving in Traffic: Boss and the Urban Challenge," *AI Magazine* 30, no. 2 (2009).

3. Urmson et al., "Autonomous Driving in Traffic."

4. Ibid.

5. The road map was provided by DARPA two days before the race; the mission file was provided the day of the race. DARPA, "Urban Challenge Results," accessed October 22, 2016. http://archive.darpa.mil/grandchallenge; Chris Urmson et al., "Tartan Racing: A Multi-modal Approach to the DARPA Urban Challenge," Technical Report, Carnegie Mellon University, 2007.

6. Urmson et al., "Tartan Racing." Stanford's team used a similar approach for tracking objects called a *particle filter* (see Michael Montemerlo et al., "Junior," below). Particle filters accomplish a similar goal but make slightly different assumptions.

7. Michael Montemerlo et al., "Junior: The Stanford Entry in the Urban Challenge," *Journal of Field Robotics* 29, no. 9 (2008): 569–597.

8. DARPA, "Urban Challenge Results."

9. Ibid.

10. Ibid.

11. Urmson et al., "Tartan Racing."

12. This layer was formally known as the *behavior executive*.

13. Urmson et al., "Tartan Racing."

14. Ibid.

15. Chris Urmson et al., "Autonomous Driving in Urban Environments: Boss and the Urban Challenge," *Journal of Field Robotics* 25, no. 8 (2008): 425–466.

16. Ibid.

17. Joseph Hooper, "DARPA's Debacle in the Desert," *Popular Science*, June 3, 2004, accessed June 16, 2017, http://www.popsci.com/scitech/article/2004-06/darpa-grand-challenge-2004darpas-debacle-desert.

18. It did this using an approach called *lattice search*.

19. Urmson et al., "Autonomous Driving in Urban Environments."

20. Urmson et al., "Autonomous Driving in Traffic."

21. Ibid.

22. Ibid.

23. Ibid.

24. Ibid.; Marsha Walton, "Robots Fail to Complete Grand Challenge," *CNN*, May 6, 2004, accessed October 22, 2016, http://www.cnn.com/2004/TECH /ptech/03/14/darpa.race.

25. Urmson et al., "Autonomous Driving in Traffic."

26. Chris Urmson, "How a Driverless Car Sees the Road," TED2015 Talk, accessed December 29, 2017, https://www.ted.com/talks/chris_urmson_how_a _driverless_car_sees_the_road/transcript?language=en#t-684924.

27. The motion planner could arguably be considered part of the sequencer. I have opted to place it with the controller, with the interpretation that the motion planner serves as a complex controller, itself a nearly a three-layer architecture.

28. Erann Gat, "Integrating Planning and Reacting in a Heterogeneous Asynchronous Architecture for Controlling Real-World Mobile Robots," *Proceedings of the 10th National Conference on Artificial Intelligence*, June 12–16, 1992, 809–815.

29. Ibid.

30. Gat, "Three-Layer Architectures."

31. Ibid.

32. Douglas McGray, "The Great Robot Race," *Wired*, March 1, 2004, accessed October 16, 2016, https://www.wired.com/2004/03/robot-3.

33. Urmson et al., "Autonomous Driving in Urban Environments"; Sebastian Thrun et al., "Stanley: The Robot That Won the DARPA Grand Challenge," *Journal of Field Robotics* 23, no. 9 (2006): 661–692.

34. Joshua Davis, "Say Hello to Stanley," *Wired*, January 1, 2006, accessed October 30, 2016, https://www.wired.com/2006/01/stanley.

35. Taylor Hatmaker, "Leaked Internal Uber Documents Show Rocky Self-Driving Car Progress," *TechCrunch*, March 17, 2017.

36. Johana Bhuiyan, "Self-Driving Cars Are Mostly Getting Better at Navigating California's Public Roads," *Recode*, February 2, 2017.

37. Timothy B. Lee, "Why Google and Car Companies Are About to Spend Billions Mapping American Roads," *Vox*, September 29, 2008.

38. Heather Kelly, "Google Loses Lead Self-Driving Car Engineer Chris Urmson," *CNN*, August 5, 2016.

39. Chris Urmson, The View from the Front Seat of the Google Self-Driving Car: A New Chapter," August 5, 2016, accessed June 16, 2017, https://medium.com /@chris_urmson/the-view-from-the-front-seat-of-the-google-self-driving-car -a-new-chapter-7060e89cb65f#.9kwb5jsdr.

CHAPTER 5: NETFLIX AND THE RECOMMENDATION-ENGINE
CHALLENGE

1. Steve Lohr, "Netflix Competitors Learn the Power of Teamwork," *New York Times*, July 27, 2009.

2. One year after Netflix announced the Netflix Prize, the company's streaming service began, which changed their calculations around the prize.

3. These ratings were anonymized to protect users' identities, although this became a controversy later in the competition. See Andreas Töscher, Michael Jahrer, and Robert M. Bell, "The BigChaos Solution to the Netflix Grand Prize," Technical Report, Commendo Research & Consulting (for Töscher and Jahrer) and AT&T Labs (for Bell), 2009, accessed December 10, 2017, https://www.netflixprize.com /assets/GrandPrize2009_BPC_BigChaos.pdf.

4. Formally, the rules stated that once a team improved on Netflix's algorithm by 10 percent, Netflix would issue a *last call*. The best submission within 30 days of that last call would win the prize, with ties broken by date of submission.

5. At the time, the term *data scientist* was not in wide use. Contestants came from a variety of fields (one being *collaborative filtering*).

6. Mung Chiang and Christopher Brinton, "Movie Recommendation on Net-flix" (lecture from *Networks Illustrated: Principles without Calculus*), Coursera, Princeton University, accessed March 2, 2017, https://www.coursera.org/learn/ networks-illustrated/lecture/Mx4ze/netflix-prize-the-competition.

7. James Bennett and Stan Lanning, "The Netflix Prize," *Proceedings of the KDD Cup and Workshop*, San Jose, CA, August 12, 2007.

8. The name BellKor was a combination of two of their names: Bell and Koren; it was also a play on the company name BellCore (Bell Communications Research). See Yehuda Koren and Robert Bell, "Advances in Collaborative Filter-ing," in *Recommender Systems Handbook*, ed. F. Ricci, L. Rokach, B. Shapira, and P. B. Kantor (New York: Springer US, 2011), 145–186.

9. B. T., "Underdogs in $1 Million Challenge," *Princeton Alumni Weekly Archives*, January 23, 2008, accessed April 8, 2017, http://www.princeton.edu/~paw /archive_new/PAW07-08/07-0123/notebook.html#Notebook10.

10. B. T., "Underdogs"; Lester Mackey, *Dinosaur Planet—Netflix Prize Team*, 2007, accessed April 8, 2017, https://web.stanford.edu/~lmackey/dinosaurplanet .html.

11. "Holiday Baked Alaska," Betty Crocker website, accessed March 8, 2017, http://www.bettycrocker.com/recipes/holiday-baked-alaska/c936a634-e9d5-4acc-ae6d-0127fc8d1371.

12. Clive Thompson, "If You Liked This, You're Sure to Love That," *New York Times Magazine*, November 21, 2008.

13. Ibid.

14. Ibid.

15. Ibid.

16. Jordan Ellenberg, "This Psychologist Might Outsmart the Math Brains Competing for the Netflix Prize," *Wired*, February 25, 2008.

17. Squaring the difference has many benefits. Among other things, it ensures that a difference is nonnegative. It's also a well-understood metric with nice statistical properties.

18. B.T., "Underdogs."

19. Töscher et al., "The BigChaos Solution to the Netflix Grand Prize."

20. Edwin Chen wrote an excellent blog post about these effects, which he called the Alice effect (our Scrooge effect) and the Inception effect (our *E.T.* effect). This post was *Winning the Netflix Prize: A Summary*, accessed April 21, 2017, http://blog.echen.me/author/edwin-chen3.html.

21. Todd Rose, "When U.S. Air Force Discovered the Flaw of Averages," *Toronto Star*, January 16, 2016, excerpted from *The End of Average* (New York: Harper-Collins, 2016), accessed June 16, 2017, https://www.thestar.com/news/insight/2016/01/16/when-us-air-force-discovered-the-flaw-of-averages.html.

22. Rose, "When U.S. Air Force Discovered the Flaw of Averages."

23. A rank-5 factorization would approximate the full matrix with the product of a 17,770 × 5 matrix and a 5 × 480,189 matrix. That's still a lot of numbers, but it's far smaller than the 100 million ratings we have, and it's nowhere close to the 8.5 billion cells in the original matrix. Sometimes matrix factorization assumes a 3-matrix factorization, where one factor is a square matrix and the other two satisfy certain constraints—such as that the column vectors have a fixed length and form right-angles to one another.

24. Martin Chabbert, *Progress Prize 2008,* December 10, 2008, accessed March 6, 2017, http://pragmatictheory.blogspot.com/search?updated-min=2008-01-01T00:00:00-05:00&updated-max=2009-01-01T00:00:00-05:00&max-results=6.

25. Dana Mackenzie, "Accounting for Taste," in *What's Happening in the Mathematical Sciences*, vol. 8 (Providence, RI: American Mathematical Society, 2010).

26. These matrix factorization methods include principal component analysis (PCA), singular value decomposition (SVD), and nonnegative matrix factorization (NMF).

27. In this matrix, we might set lawmakers as columns and legislation as rows, with 0 or 1 describing how each lawmaker voted.

28. Steve Lohr, "Netflix Competitors Learn the Power of Teamwork," *New York Times*, July 27, 2009; Mackenzie, "Accounting for Taste."

CHAPTER 6: ENSEMBLES OF TEAMS

1. James Bennett and Stan Lanning, "The Netflix Prize," *Proceedings of the KDD Cup and Workshop*, San Jose, CA, August 12, 2007.

2. Ibid.

3. Jordan Ellenberg, "This Psychologist Might Outsmart the Math Brains Competing for the Netflix Prize," *Wired*, February 25, 2008.

4. Clive Thompson, "If You Liked This, You're Sure to Love That," *New York Times Magazine*, November 21, 2008.

5. Dana Mackenzie, "Accounting for Taste," in *What's Happening in the Mathematical Sciences*, vol. 8 (Providence, RI: American Mathematical Society, 2010).

6. Ibid.

7. BellKor, like many of the other teams, were not particularly secretive about their methods, and their members contributed to the Netflix Prize Forum.

8. Thompson, "If You Liked This, You're Sure to Love That."

9. Ibid.

10. Ellenberg, "This Psychologist Might Outsmart the Math Brains Competing for the Netflix Prize."

11. Ruslan Salakhutdinov, Andriy Mnih, and Geoffrey Hinton, "Restricted Boltzmann Machines for Collaborative Filtering," *Proceedings of the 24th International Conference on Machine Learning,* Corvallis, OR, 2007.

12. One way they made this improvement was by creating a matrix like the star-rating matrix in figure 5.2, replacing each element with 1 if users rated a movie and 0 otherwise, and then using that matrix to estimate users' genre affinities for you, just like the one they learned from your ratings, but *based on the movies you had rated*. Their model was a bit different algebraically from the one used for matrix factorization, but it used the same basic idea. See also Yehuda Koren and Robert Bell, "Advances in Collaborative Filtering," in *Systems Handbook*, ed. F. Ricci, L. Rokach, B. Shapira, and P. B. Kantor (New York: Springer, 2011), 145–186.

13. Martin Chabbert, *Progress Prize 2008,* December 10, 2008, accessed March 6, 2017, http://pragmatictheory.blogspot.com/search?updated-min=2008 -01-01T00:00:00-05:00&updated-max=2009-01-01T00:00:00-05:00&max -results=6.

14. Thompson, "If You Liked This, You're Sure to Love That."

15. Eliot van Buskirk, "How the Netflix Prize Was Won," *Wired*, September 22, 2009.

16. Yehuda Koren, "The BellKor Solution to the Netflix Grand Prize," Technical Report, Netflix, 2009.

17. Koren, "The BellKor Solution." They modeled these with both a linear drift over time and a day-specific bias.

18. Again, they modeled these with both a linear drift over time and a day-specific bias.

19. Chabbert, *Progress Prize 2008.*

20. Note that the "average" of a movie might not be the same as its coefficient in a linear model, because it will be warped by other components in the model.

21. With the exception of users who rated movies more than once.

22. Robert M. Bell, Yehuda Koren, and Chris Volinsky, "The BellKor 2008 Solution to the Netflix Prize," Technical Report, AT&T Labs (for Bell and Volinsky) and Yahoo! (for Koren), 2008, accessed June 15, 2016, http://www.netflixprize .com/assets/ProgressPrize2008_BellKor.pdf.

23. Yehuda Koren, *The Netflix Prize Forum, Topic 799,* Netflix, 2007, accessed March 5, 2017, http://netflixprize.com/community/topic_799.html.

24. This holds true provided that these stocks aren't perfectly correlated.

25. This uncertainty can be formalized with the idea of statistical variance.

26. Robert E. Schapire, *Boosting: Foundations and Algorithms* (Cambridge, MA: MIT Press, 2014).

27. B.T., *Princeton Alumni Weekly Archives*, Princeton University, January 23, 2008, accessed April 8, 2017, http://www.princeton.edu/~paw/archive_new/PAW07 -08/07-0123/notebook.html#Notebook10.

28. Andreas Töscher, Michael Jahrer, and Robert M. Bell, "The BigChaos Solution to the Netflix Grand Prize," Technical Report, Commendo Research & Consulting (for Töscher and Jahrer) and AT&T Labs (for Bell), 2009, accessed December 10, 2017, https://www.netflixprize.com/assets/GrandPrize2009 _BPC_BigChaos.pdf.

29. Van Buskirk, "How the Netflix Prize Was Won."

30. Jeff Howbert, "CSS 490 Lecture 08a," *University of Washington Course Website,* accessed June 16, 2017, http://courses.washington.edu/css490/2012.Winter/lecture_slides/08a_Netflix_Prize.pptx.

31. Thompson, "If You Liked This, You're Sure to Love That."

32. Martin Piotte and Martin Chabbert, "The Pragmatic Theory Solution to the Netflix Grand Prize," Technical Report, Pragmatic Theory, Inc., Canada, 2009.

33. Mackenzie, "Accounting for Taste."

34. At the awards ceremony, Netflix revealed that the teams had tied up to the sixth decimal point; and BellKor's Pragmatic Chaos did in fact have slightly better predictions.

35. Xavier Amatriain and Justin Basilico, "Netflix Recommendations: Beyond the 5 Stars," *The Netflix Tech Blog.* Netflix, April 6, 2012, accessed March 4, 2017, http://techblog.netflix.com/2012/04/netflix-recommendations-beyond-5-stars.html.

36. Amatriain and Basilico, "Netflix Recommendations."

37. A large part of the discrepancy is probably that competing in the Netflix Prize requires a small capital outlay—basically just a desktop workstation—while the funding for a team developing a self-driving car could easily run into hundreds of thousands or millions of dollars.

CHAPTER 7: TEACHING COMPUTERS BY GIVING THEM TREATS

1. Quoted in Jemima Kiss, "Hi-Tech Dealing: The Connections That Led to Google Buying DeepMind," *The Guardian,* June 23, 2014.

2. Technically this score was adjusted so that it fell into a certain range.

3. Volodymyr Mnih et al. "Human-Level Control through Deep Reinforcement Learning," *Nature* 518, no. 7540 (2015): 529–533.

4. Here I use "expect" in a casual sense, but I'm actually suggesting the formal sense for the word: we use the *expectation,* or *average,* of time-adjusted rewards, where the average is taken with respect to the randomness associated with moving between states given different actions. Different applications may call for different variants than the expectation, such as a highest median time-adjusted reward.

5. Optimizing for near-term rewards can be a perfectly sensible action at times; people do this in periods of high economic inflation, for example.

6. David Churchill, Personal correspondence with author, 2017; Marc G. Bellemare et al., "The Arcade Learning Environment: An Evaluation Platform for General Agents," *Journal of Artificial Intelligence Research* 47 (2013): 253–279.

7. Some games had as few as 4 controls, while others had up to 18 different combinations.

8. There can be 36 aliens and at least 3 "shields," and the position of the space ship and flying saucers could easily be described by no fewer than 5 bits, in addition to the locations of any missiles, which could also be described with no fewer than 5 bits. This is $2^{36+3+5+5+5+\cdots} \geq 1.8 \times 10^{16}$ states.

9. At a hundred million evaluations per second, it would take five years to learn just one data point for each of these states.

CHAPTER 8: HOW TO BEAT ATARI GAMES BY USING NEURAL NETWORKS

1. Liz Gannes, "Exclusive: Google to Buy Artificial Intelligence Startup Deep-Mind for $400M," *Recode.net*, January 26, 2014.

2. Balázs Csanád Csáji, "Approximation with Artificial Neural Networks," MSc thesis, Faculty of Sciences, Eötvös Loránd University, Budapest, Hungary, 2001, 24–48, accessed November 12, 2016, http://citeseerx.ist.psu.edu/viewdoc/down load?doi=10.1.1.101.2647&rep=rep1&type=pdf. Technically, the set of functions that can be approximated are continuous functions in a compact subset of R^n.

3. On a scale where a completely random agent earns 0 points and a human earns 100 points.

4. Volodymyr Mnih et al., "Human-Level Control through Deep Reinforcement Learning," *Nature* 518, no. 7540 (2015): 529–533.

CHAPTER 9: ARTIFICIAL NEURAL NETWORKS'VIEW OF THE WORLD

1. Ellen Huet, "The Humans Hiding Behind the Chatbots," *Bloomberg News*, April 18, 2016, accessed September 25, 2017, https://www.bloomberg.com/news /articles/2016-04-18/the-humans-hiding-behind-the-chatbots.

2. Ibid.

3. This is subject to certain formal conditions, with the universal approximation theorem.

4. Tom Standage, *The Turk* (New York: Berkeley Publishing Group, 2002).

5. The Automaton has more recently been called the Mechanical Turk, not to be confused with Amazon Mechanical Turk.

6. Gerald M. Levitt, *Turk, Chess Automation* (Jefferson, NC: McFarland & Company, 2000).

7. In fact, it was operated by a variety of chess players over its time in service.

8. Huet, "The Humans Hiding Behind the Chatbots."

9. Yann LeCun, Yoshua Bengio, and Geoffrey Hinton, "Deep Learning," *Nature* 521 (2015).

10. Researchers in academia and at companies like Microsoft, Google, and Facebook have put together tools that make it simple for programmers to design networks and train them, without needing to worry about the specific math behind this technique for training a network (which is called back-propagation).

11. Or, more commonly, with batches of images at a time.

12. LeCun et al., "Deep Learning."

13. Li Fei-Fei, Rob Fergus, and Pietro Perona, "Learning Generative Visual Models from Few Training Examples: An Incremental Bayesian Approach Tested on 101 Object Categories," *Proceedings of the 2004 IEEE Computer Society Conference on Computer Vision and Pattern Recognition*, Los Angeles, CA, 2004, 178–186.

14. This time, instead of paging through a dictionary, they used categories from a source named WordNet.

15. Olga Russakovsky et al., "ImageNet Large Scale Visual Recognition Challenge," *International Journal of Computer Vision* 115, no. 3 (2015): 211–252.

16. Typically, Amazon Mechanical Turk requires more precise and detailed instructions than this.

17. Russakovsky et al., "ImageNet Large Scale Visual Recognition Challenge"; Alex Krizhevsky, Ilya Sutskever, and Geoffrey E. Hinton, "ImageNet Classification with Deep Convolutional Neural Networks," *Proceedings of the 25th International Conference on Neural Information Processing Systems,* Lake Tahoe, NV, December 3–6, 2012, 1097–1105.

18. Russakovsky et al., "ImageNet Large Scale Visual Recognition Challenge."

19. Because an image might contain multiple objects, such as a dog, the sky, land, and a Frisbee, algorithms were technically required to identify only one of the "top 5" objects in the image. The competition also had a different, more difficult challenge: to identify all objects in the image, and to describe the location of each one.

20. Russakovsky et al., "ImageNet Large Scale Visual Recognition Challenge"; *Large Scale Visual Recognition Challenge 2016,* UNC Vision Lab webpage, accessed June 16, 2017, http://image-net.org/challenges/LSVRC/2016/results.

21. Krizhevsky et al., "ImageNet Classification with Deep Convolutional Neural Networks."

22. In-between some of these layers were additional layers that shrunk the number of pixels in each layer so that downstream processing was easier and so that later filters could cover larger parts of the input image. This is called *max-pooling*. It decreased a computational bottleneck downstream in the network, made it more robust to noise, and arguably had an important role in allowing filters to match positions in an image more "softly."

23. Guido Montúfar, Razvan Pascunu, Kyunghyun Cho, and Yoshua Bengio, "On the Number of Linear Regions of Deep Neural Networks," arXiv preprint 1402.1869 (20114), accessed December 16, 2017, https://arxiv.org/pdf/1402 .1869.pdf; Sanjeev Arora, Aditya Bhaskara, Rong Ge, Tengu Ma, "Provable Bounds for Learning Some Deep Representations," *Proceedings of the 31st International Conference on Machine Learning*, Beijing, China, 2014.

24. Krizhevsky et al., "ImageNet Classification with Deep Convolutional Neural Networks."

25. Russakovsky et al., "ImageNet Large Scale Visual Recognition Challenge"; UNC Vision Lab, *Large Scale Visual Recognition Challenge 2016*.

26. Christian Szegedy et al., "Going Deeper with Convolutions," *Proceedings of the IEEE Conference on Computer Vision and Pattern Recognition,* 2015, accessed December 29, 2017, http://arxiv.org/abs/1409.4842.

27. LeCun et al., "Deep Learning."

28. Krizhevsky et al., "ImageNet Classification with Deep Convolutional Neural Networks."

29. Ibid.

30. Ibid.

31. LeCun et al., "Deep Learning"; Jürgen Schmidhuber, "Deep Learning in Neural Networks: An Overview," Technical Report, The Swiss AI Lab IDSIA, University of Lugano & SUPSI, 2014.

32. LeCun et al., "Deep Learning"; Norman P. Jouppi et al., "In-Datacenter Performance Analysis of a Tensor Processing Unit," *Proceedings of the 44th International Symposium on Computer Architecture (ISCA),* Toronto, 2017. A tensor is a generalization of a matrix used commonly in physics and engineering and used more recently in deep learning. In addition to width (one dimension) and height (another dimension), a tensor might have additional dimensions.

CHAPTER 10: LOOKING UNDER THE HOOD OF DEEP
NEURAL NETWORKS

1. Anonymous. Computer-generated image, June 10, 2015, accessed March 8, 2017, http://imgur.com/6ocuQsZ.

2. Maureen Dowd, "Elon Musk's Billion-Dollar Crusade to Stop the A.I. Apocalypse," *Vanity Fair,* April 2017, accessed June 16, 2017, http://www.vanityfair.com /news/2017/03/elon-musk-billion-dollar-crusade-to-stop-ai-space-x.

3. This is commonly known as a sigmoid function, and the formula for it is $\exp(x) / (1 + \exp(x))$.

4. Alex Krizhevsky, Ilya Sutskever, and Geoffrey E. Hinton, "ImageNet Classification with Deep Convolutional Neural Networks," *Proceedings of the 25th*

International Conference on Neural Information Processing Systems, Lake Tahoe, NV, December 3–6, 2012, 1097–1105. There are ways to still train deep neural networks if we want to use the S-shaped activation function. One common way to do this is to use *unsupervised pre-training.* This uses an idea that is conceptually very similar to the matrix-factorization methods used in the Netflix Prize, in that it finds a representation a low-dimensional representation that "explains" a lot of the variation in neurons' activations.

5. Jürgen Schmidhuber, "Deep Learning in Neural Networks: An Overview," Technical Report, The Swiss AI Lab IDSIA, University of Lugano & SUPSI, 2014. ReLUs were discussed in the literature around 2000, a decade before they became more popular for training deep networks.

6. Xavier Glorot, Antoine Bordes, and Yoshua Bengio, "Deep Sparse Rectifier Neural Networks," *Proceedings of the 14th International Conference on Artificial Intelligence and Statistics* 15 (2011).

7. This relationship is formally defined as "continuity," which is distinct from the formal definition of the word "smooth."

8. This is exponential in the number of neurons: for a network with N neurons, there are 2^N possible on/off combinations of neurons. The vast majority of these have a roughly even mix of on/off combinations, although not all combinations may be realizable given a certain set of network weights.

9. Robert Krulwich, "Which Is Greater, the Number of Sand Grains on Earth or Stars in the Sky?" *National Public Radio,* September 17, 2012, accessed June 16, 2017, http://www.npr.org/sections/krulwich/2012/09/17/161096233/which-is -greater-the-number-of-sand-grains-on-earth-or-stars-in-the-sky.

10. John Carl Villanueva, "How Many Atoms Are There in the Universe?" *Universe Today,* December 24, 2015.

11. Overfitting could become a problem in this case; some researchers, such as Glorot et al., regularize network weights, for example with an L1 penalty, which pushes network weights toward zero, to induce these weights to be sparse.

12. Glorot et al., "Deep Sparse Rectifier Neural Networks."

13. This process is called "dropout."

14. Yann LeCun, Yoshua Bengio, and Geoffrey Hinton, "Deep Learning," *Nature* 521 (2015).

15. Olga Russakovsky et al., "ImageNet Large Scale Visual Recognition Challenge," *International Journal of Computer Vision* 115, no. 3 (2015): 211–252; Kaiming He, Xiangyu Zhang, Shaoqing Ren, and Jian Sun, "Delving Deep into Rectifiers: Surpassing Human-Leven Performance on ImageNet Classification," *ICCV,* 2015.

16. He et al., "Delving Deep into Rectifiers."

17. Anh Nguyen, Jason Yosinski, and Jeff Clune, "Deep Neural Networks Are Easily Fooled: High Confidence Predictions for Unrecognizable Images," *The IEEE Conference on Computer Vision and Pattern Recognition (CVPR)* (2015): 427–436.

18. If we're not careful, the image might end up looking unnatural, as pixels might take extreme colors, and adjacent pixels might take on unnaturally different colors. Researchers have figured out that they can do to this by encouraging nearby pixels to have similar colors, and by encouraging pixels to be gray in color rather than extremely bright or dark. See also Nguyen et al., "Deep Neural Networks Are Easily Fooled."

19. Jason Yosinski et al., "Understanding Neural Networks through Deep Visualization," *Deep Learning Workshop, 31st International Conference on Machine Learning,* Lille, France, 2015.

20. Alexander Mordvintsev, Christopher Olah, and Mike Tyka, *Inceptionism: Going Deeper into Neural Networks,* June 17, 2015, accessed April 9, 2017, https://research .googleblog.com/2015/06/inceptionism-going-deeper-into-neural.html.

21. Mordvintsev et al., *Inceptionism.*

22. Leon A. Gatys, Alexander S. Ecker, and Matthias Bethge, "Image Style Transfer Using Convolutional Neural Networks," *The IEEE Conference on Computer Vision and Pattern Recognition* (2016): 2414–2423.

CHAPTER 11: NEURAL NETWORKS THAT CAN HEAR, SPEAK,
AND REMEMBER

1. Dario Amodei et al., "Deep Speech 2: End-to-End Speech Recognition in English and Mandarin," *arXiv preprint arXiv:1512.02595,* 2015.

2. To train the network, we use a special methodology called a *connectionist temporal classification* that searches for an alignment between the transcription label and the time-series.

3. Awni Hannun et al., "Deep Speech: Scaling Up End-to-End Speech Recognition," *arXiv preprint arXiv:1412.5567,* 2014.

4. Ibid.

5. Amodei et al., "Deep Speech 2."

6. Girish Kulkarni et al., "Baby Talk: Understanding and Generating Image Descriptions," *IEEE Transactions on Pattern Analysis and Machine Intelligence* 35, no. 12 (2013): 2891–2903.

7. Ibid.

8. Oriol Vinyals, Alexander Toshev, Samy Bengio, and Dumitru Erhan, "Show and Tell: A Neural Image Caption Generator," in *Proceedings of the IEEE Conference on Computer Vision and Pattern Recognition,* 2015; Kelvin Xu et al., "Show, Attend and

Tell: Neural Image Caption Generation with Visual Attention," *International Conference on Machine Learning,* 2015: 77–81.

9. Vinyals et al., "Show and Tell."

10. Ibid.

11. Yann LeCun, Yoshua Bengio, and Geoffrey Hinton, "Deep Learning," *Nature* 521 (2015).

12. Razvan Pascanu, Caglar Gulcehre, Kyunghyun Cho, and Yoshua Bengio, "How to Construct Deep Recurrent Neural Networks," *arXiv preprint arXiv:1312.6026,* 2013.

13. This analogy works up to a point: while setting your watch is an exceptional activity, the network may use the control wires on a regular basis.

14. Ian Goodfellow et al., "Generative Adversarial Nets," *Advances in Neural Information Processing Systems* (2014): 2672–2680.

15. Jun-Yan Zhu et al., "Unpaired Image-to-Image Translation Using Cycle-Consistent Adversarial Networks," *arXiv preprint arXiv:1703.10593,* 2017.

CHAPTER 12: UNDERSTANDING NATURAL LANGUAGE (AND *JEOPARDY!* QUESTIONS)

1. Ken Jennings, "My Puny Human Brain," *Slate Magazine,* February 16, 2011, accessed June 16, 2017, http://www.slate.com/articles/arts/culturebox/2011/02 /my_puny_human_brain.html.

2. James Fan, personal correspondence with author, June 9, 2017.

3. Failure to do so has lost some candidates the game: https://www.youtube.com /watch?v=YOp03rRM6Pw.

4. Larry Dignan, "IBM's Watson Victorious in *Jeopardy*; Our New Computer Overlord?" *ZDNet,* February 16, 2011, accessed June 16, 2017, http://www .zdnet.com/article/ibms-watson-victorious-in-jeopardy-our-new-computer -overlord.

5. *Jeopardy,* television broadcast, hosted by Alex Trebek, 2011; John Marko, "Computer Wins on *Jeopardy!*: Trivial, It's Not," *New York Times,* February 16, 2011.

6. Jennings, "My Puny Human Brain."

7. Casey Johnston, "Bug Lets Humans Grab Daily Double as Watson Triumphs on *Jeopardy,*" *Ars Technica,* February 17, 2011.

8. Dignan, "IBM's Watson Victorious in *Jeopardy.*"

9. Joab Jackson, "IBM Watson Vanquishes Human *Jeopardy!* Foes," *PC World,* February 16, 2011, accessed June 16, 2017, http://www.pcworld.com/article/219893 /ibm_watson_vanquishes_human_jeopardy_foes.html.

10. This clue is available on the J-Archive website, accessed June 16, 2017, http://www.j-archive.com/showgame.php?game_id=2771.

11. D. C. Gondek et al., "A Framework for Merging and Ranking of Answers in DeepQA," *IBM Journal of Research and Development* 56, no. 3.4 (2012).

12. Sauron is the evil character from *Lord of the Rings*.

13. David Ferrucci et al., "Building Watson: An Overview of the DeepQA project," *AI Magazine* 31, no. 3 (2010): 59–79.

14. Stephen Baker, *Final Jeopardy: The Story of Watson, the Computer That Will Transform Our World* (New York: Houghton Mifflin Harcourt, 2011), Kindle edition, 19–35.

15. Ibid., 20.

16. Ibid.

17. Ibid., 20–26.

18. James Fan, personal correspondence with author, June 9, 2017.

19. Baker, *Final Jeopardy*, 26–34.

20. Ibid., 34–35.

21. Ibid., 78.

22. Ferrucci et al., "Building Watson."

23. Ibid.

24. Baker, *Final Jeopardy*, 67.

25. Ferrucci et al., "Building Watson."

26. Ibid.

27. Adam Lally et al., "Question Analysis: How Watson Reads a Clue," *IBM Journal of Research and Development* 56, no. 3.4 (2012).

28. Watson's researchers called this a *lexical answer type*, or LAT.

29. This clue is available on the J-Archive, accessed June 16, 2017, http://www.j-archive.com/showgame.php?game_id=3652.

30. Lally et al., "Question Analysis."

31. These examples appeared in lecture notes for a CMU course on natural language processing in addition to newsgroup archives, and their origin story is difficult to confirm.

32. Lally et al., "Question Analysis."

CHAPTER 13: MINING THE BEST *JEOPARDY!* ANSWER

1. Stephen Baker, "Blue J Is Born," in *Final Jeopardy: The Story of Watson, the Computer That Will Transform Our World* (New York: Houghton Mifflin Harcourt, 2011), Kindle edition, 62.

2. Ibid.

3. Ibid.

4. Ibid.

5. James Fan, personal correspondence with author, June 9, 2017.

6. Baker, "Blue J Is Born," 63–66.

7. Ibid., 62.

8. David Ferrucci et al., "Building Watson: An Overview of the DeepQA Project," *AI Magazine* 31, no. 3 (2010): 59–79.

9. In fact, these info-boxes were precisely one of Watson's sources for its relations, which were part of a database it used called DBPedia.

10. Jennifer Chu-Carroll et al., "Finding Needles in the Haystack: Search and Candidate Generation," *IBM Journal of Research and Development* 56, no. 3.4 (2012).

11. Ibid.

12. Ibid.

13. Ibid.

14. Fan, personal correspondence with author.

15. Chu-Carroll et al., "Finding Needles in the Haystack"; Jennifer Chu-Carroll and James Fan, "Leveraging Wikipedia Characteristics for Search and Candidate Generation in Question Answering," *Proceedings of the 25th AAAI Conference on Artificial Intelligence* (2011).

16. Chu-Carroll et al., "Finding Needles in the Haystack." Depending on the search engine, Watson was sometimes given a list of passages instead of a list of documents. This often the case for Wikipedia.

17. Chu-Carroll et al., "Finding Needles in the Haystack."

18. We can do this with the query site Wikipedia.org and the search terms "Milorad Čavić almost upset this man's perfect 2008 Olympics, losing to him by one hundredth of a second."

19. Ferrucci et al., "Building Watson."

20. This was formally called the Evidence Retrieval phase. See Baker, "Blue J Is Born."

21. Ferrucci et al., "Building Watson."

22. Wikipedia, "Swimming at the 2008 Summer Olympics," accessed May 7, 2017, https://en.wikipedia.org/wiki/Swimming_at_the_2008_Summer_Olympics_%E2%80%93_Men%27s_100_metre_butterfly.

23. Wikipedia, "Michael Phelps," accessed May 7, 2017, https://en.wikipedia.org/wiki/Michael_Phelps.

24. J. William Murdock et al., "Textual Evidence Gathering and Analysis," *IBM Journal of Research and Development* 56, no. 3.4 (2012).

25. Julia Cort and Michael Bicks, *Smartest Machine on Earth* (PBS NOVA television episode), directed by Michael Bicks, produced by PBS NOVA, February 2011.

26. Murdock, "Textual Evidence Gathering and Analysis."

27. D. C. Gondek et al., "A Framework for Merging and Ranking of Answers in DeepQA," *IBM Journal of Research and Development* 56, no. 3.4 (2012).

28. Gondek et al., "A Framework for Merging and Ranking of Answers in DeepQA."

29. Ibid.

30. Ibid. Again, such transformations used typical tricks from machine learning and statistics to handle cases like these. For example, for a feature "is_geo_match," they might add a new feature called "is_geo_match_present," to represent when the first feature was missing.

31. Fan, personal correspondence with author.

32. It's unclear whether this could be encoded formally as a neural network, and we would need to add additional layers to handle interaction between candidates in the first two steps of each layer.

33. Ferrucci et al., "Building Watson."

34. Ibid.

35. Ibid.

36. Rob High, *The Era of Cognitive Systems: An Inside Look at IBM Watson and How It Works,* Marketing White Paper, Redbooks, accessed December 27, 2017, http://www.redbooks.ibm.com/redpapers/pdfs/redp4955.pdf.

37. Baker, "Watson Takes on Humans," 128.

38. Casey Johnston, "Bug Lets Humans Grab Daily Double as Watson Triumphs on *Jeopardy*," *Ars Technica*, February 17, 2011.

39. High, *The Era of Cognitive Systems.*

40. Daniel Jurafsky and James H. Martin, *Speech and Natural Language Processing* (Upper Saddle River, NJ: Prentice Hall, 2015).

CHAPTER 14: BRUTE-FORCE SEARCH YOUR WAY
TO A GOOD STRATEGY

1. Claude E. Shannon, "Programming a Computer for Playing Chess," *Philosophical Magazine* 7, no. 314 (1950).

2. The primary difference between a wooden Turing machine and a modern computer—and the reason you wouldn't buy a wooden Turing machine for your next computer—is that a computer can run much more quickly, and its memory can take up much less space.

3. Will Shortz, "Wayne Gould," *Time Magazine*, May 8, 2006.

4. Gerald Tesauro, "Temporal Difference Learning and TD-Gammon," *Communications of the ACM* (Association for Computing Machinery) 38, no. 3 (1995).

5. Shannon, "Programming a Computer for Playing Chess."

6. Ibid.

7. Ibid.

8. Murray Campbell, A. Joseph Hoane Jr., and Feng-hsiung Hsu, "Deep Blue," *Artificial Intelligence* 134 (2002): 57–83.

9. Feng-hsiung Hsu, *Behind Deep Blue* (Princeton, NJ: Princeton University Press, 2002).

10. Ibid., 109.

11. Ibid., 81.

12. In this game, Deep Blue also used positional features, but it believed it had a significant material advantage and still lost to Kasparov. See Hsu, *Behind Deep Blue*, 138.

13. Campbell et al., "Deep Blue."

14. Hsu, *Behind Deep Blue,* 85.

15. Ibid., 46.

16. Ibid., 24.

17. Campbell et al., "Deep Blue."

18. Hsu, *Behind Deep Blue*, 52–56.

19. Ibid., 54.

20. Campbell et al., "Deep Blue."

21. Deep Blue was preceded by Deep Thought and ChipTest. I've blurred the distinction between various versions of Deep Blue and Deep Thought; in practice, they varied in both hardware and software.

22. Hsu, *Behind Deep Blue*, 93.

23. Ibid., 133.

24. Ibid.

25. Ibid., 253–254.

26. The Atari-playing network had other limitations, such as a lack of memory, which also gave it problems in this game.

27. Gerald Tesauro. "Temporal Difference Learning and TD-Gammon." *Communications of the ACM* 38, no. 3 (1995): 58–68.

28. Richard S. Sutton and Andrew G. Barto, *Reinforcement Learning: An Introduction*, 2nd ed. (manuscript draft, MIT Press).

29. Tesauro, "Temporal Difference Learning and TD-Gammon."

CHAPTER 15: EXPERT-LEVEL PLAY FOR THE GAME OF GO

1. Kirk L. Kroeker, "A New Benchmark for Artificial Intelligence," *Communications of the ACM* 54, no. 8 (2011).

2. Sensei's Library, *Go History,* accessed April 5, 2017, http://senseis.xmp.net /?GoHistory#toc5.

3. Eva Dou and Olivia Geng, "Humans Mourn Loss after Google Is Unmasked as China's Go Master," *Wall Street Journal,* January 5, 2017.

4. Dieter Verhofstadt, *Ing Prize,* June 20, 2014, accessed February 5, 2017, http:// senseis.xmp.net/?IngPrize.

5. Stephen Baker, *Final Jeopardy: The Story of Watson, the Computer That Will Transform Our World* (New York: Houghton Mifflin Harcourt, 2011).

6. Alan Levinovitz, "The Mystery of Go, the Ancient Game That Computers Still Can't Win," *Wired,* May 12, 2014.

7. David Silver et al., "Mastering the Game of Go with Deep Neural Networks and Tree Search," *Nature* 529 (2016): 484–503.

8. Some games are played with a 9×9 or 13×13 grid.

9. Dou and Geng, "Humans Mourn Loss after Google Is Unmasked as China's Go Master."

10. Cameron Browne et al., "A Survey of Monte Carlo Tree Search Methods," *IEEE Transactions on Computational Intelligence and AI in Games* 4, no. 1 (2012).

11. That is, AlphaGo can't sample moves uniformly at random, by flipping coins.

12. DeepMind called this network a "reinforcement learning policy network."

13. Silver et al., "Mastering the Game of Go with Deep Neural Networks and Tree Search."

14. Convolutional layers need not run over all patches in the preceding layer; many times they have a step-size, or *stride*, greater than 1. AlphaGo's convolutional layers all had a stride of 1.

15. Silver et al., "Mastering the Game of Go with Deep Neural Networks and Tree Search."

16. Ibid.

17. DeepMind also trained a better move-prediction network with reinforcement learning by pitting the move-prediction network against itself. While this network performed better than the original network in head-to-head play, it didn't work as well once embedded in the full AlphaGo algorithm, "presumably because humans select a diverse beam of promising moves." Silver et al., "Mastering the Game of Go with Deep Neural Networks and Tree Search."

18. Silver et al., "Mastering the Game of Go with Deep Neural Networks and Tree Search."

19. Cade Metz, "Why the Final Game Between AlphaGo and Lee Sedol Is Such a Big Deal for Humanity," *Wired*, March 14, 2016; Christopher Moyer, "How Google's AlphaGo Beat a Go World Champion," *The Atlantic*, March 28, 2016.

20. Cade Metz, "In Two Moves, AlphaGo and Lee Sedol Redefined the Future," *Wired*, March 16, 2016.

21. Moyer, "How Google's AlphaGo Beat a Go World Champion."

22. Metz, "In Two Moves, AlphaGo and Lee Sedol Redefined the Future."

23. Moyer, "How Google's AlphaGo Beat a Go World Champion."

24. An alternative translation was "God's Touch." Metz, "In Two Moves, AlphaGo and Lee Sedol Redefined the Future."

25. Moyer, "How Google's AlphaGo Beat a Go World Champion"; Metz, "Why the Final Game Between AlphaGo and Lee Sedol Is Such a Big Deal for Humanity."

26. Metz, "Why the Final Game Between AlphaGo and Lee Sedol Is Such a Big Deal for Humanity."

27. Metz, "In Two Moves, AlphaGo and Lee Sedol Redefined the Future."

28. Silver et al., "Mastering the Game of Go with Deep Neural Networks and Tree Search."

29. Ibid.

30. Browne et al., "A Survey of Monte Carlo Tree Search Methods."

31. Ibid.; Silver et al., "Mastering the Game of Go with Deep Neural Networks and Tree Search."

32. Ibid.

33. Ibid.

34. Ibid.

35. Christof Koch, "How the Computer Beat the Go Master," *Scientific American*, March 19, 2016.

36. Silver et al., "Mastering the Game of Go with Deep Neural Networks and Tree Search."

37. Ibid.

CHAPTER 16: REAL-TIME AI AND *STARCRAFT*

1. Cade Metz, "In OpenAI's Universe, Computers Learn to Use Apps Like Humans Do," *Wired*, December 5, 2016.

2. Kristin Kalning, "Can Blizzard Top Itself with '*StarCraftII*'?" *NBC News*, May 31, 2007.

3. Ibid.; Alex Bellos, "Rise of the E-sports Superstars," *BBC Click*, June 29, 2007.

4. Cory Barclay, *The 15 Richest Online Gamers in the World,* February 24, 2015, accessed March 17, 2017, http://www.therichest.com/rich-list/world/the-15 -richest-online-gamers-in-the-world/.

5. *BBC News.* "S Korean Dies after Games Session." August 10, 2005; John Anderson, *Spot On: Korea Reacts to Increase in Game Addiction,* September 12, 2005, accessed March 17, 2017, http://www.gamespot.com/articles/spot-on-korea -reacts-to-increase-in-game-addiction/1100-6132357/.

6. Josh McCoy and Michael Mateas, "An Integrated Agent for Playing Real-Time Strategy Games," *Proceedings of the 23rd AAAI Conference on Artificial Intelligence* 8 (2008): 1313–1318.

7. Santiago Ontanón et al., "A Survey of Real-Time Strategy Game AI Research and Competition in *StarCraft*," *IEEE Transactions on Computational Intelligence and AI in Games* 5, no. 4 (2013): 1–19

8. Ibid.

9. David A. Churchill, *A History of* StarCraft *AI Competitions (and UAlbertaBot),* 2016, accessed March 18, 2017, https://declara.com/content/ng0ynE75 (origi- nally http://webdocs.cs.ualberta.ca/~cdavid/starcraftaicomp/history.shtml).

10. Ontanón et al., "A Survey of Real-Time Strategy Game AI Research and Competition in *StarCraft*."; David Churchill, "UAlbertaBot," *Github*, September 11, 2014, accessed March 18, 2017, https://github.com/davechurchill/ualbertabot /wiki; StarCraft *Rating System,* accessed April 20, 2017, http://iccup.com/starcraft /sc_rating_system.html.

11. McCoy and Mateas, "An Integrated Agent for Playing Real-Time Strategy Games."

12. See e.g., the entry on SkyNet in Ontanón et al., "A Survey of Real-Time Strategy Game AI Research and Competition in *StarCraft*."

13. David Churchill, "Heuristic Search Techniques for Real-Time Strategy Games," PhD thesis, Department of Computer Science, University of Alberta. 2016.

14. Ontanón et al., "A Survey of Real-Time Strategy Game AI Research and Competition in *StarCraft*." An alternative explanation might be that the *StarCraft* game dynamics, and not the bots, are flawed.

15. Santiago Ontanón et al., "RTS AI: Problems and Techniques," in *Springer Encyclopedia of Computer Graphics and Games*, 2015, accessed December 29, 2017, https://www.researchgate.net/publication/311176051_RTS_AI_Problems_and _Techniques.

16. Ibid.

17. Ibid.

18. Churchill, "Heuristic Search Techniques for Real-Time Strategy Games."

19. *DOTA 2 vs StarCraft II,* accessed January 27, 2018, https://www .esportsearnings.com/comparisons/vvbb-dota-2-vs-sc2; *StarCraft: Brood War,* accessed January 27, 2018, https://www.esportsearnings.com/games/152-starcraft -brood-war/largest-tournaments-x400

20. *Elon Musk,* accessed October 10, 2017, https://openai.com/press/elon-musk.

21. Jie Tang, personal correspondence with author, August 25, 2017.

22. Ibid.

23. Ibid.

24. Ibid.

25. Ibid.

26. Tom Rowley, "Demis Hassabis: The Secretive Computer Boffin with the £400 Million Brain," *The Telegraph,* January 28, 2014.

27. Most *StarCraft* gamers today play on *StarCraft BroodWar,* a prequel to *StarCraft II.* Oriol Vinyals, *DeepMind and Blizzard to release* StarCraft II *as an AI Research Environment,* November 4, 2016, accessed April 16, 2017, https://deepmind.com /blog/deepmind-and-blizzard-release-starcraft-ii-ai-research-environment/.

28. Feng-hsiung Hsu, *Behind Deep Blue* (Princeton, NJ: Princeton University Press, 2002), 4; Allen Newell, John Calman Shaw, and Herbert A. Simon, "Chess-Playing Programs and the Problem of Complexity," *IBM Journal of Research and Development* 2, no. 4 (1958): 320–335.

CHAPTER 17: FIVE DECADES (OR MORE) FROM NOW

1. Stephen Baker, *Final Jeopardy: The Story of Watson, the Computer That Will Transform Our World* (New York: Houghton Mifflin Harcourt, 2011), 35.

2. Teun Koetsier, "On the Prehistory of Programmable Machines: Musical Automata, Looms, Calculators," *Mechanism and Machine Theory* 36, no. 5 (2001): 589–603.

3. Sebastian Thrun, "A Personal Account of the Development of Stanley, the Robot That Won the DARPA Grand Challenge," *AI Magazine* 27 (2006).

4. Ibid.

5. Yehuda Koren, "The BellKor Solution to the Netflix Grand Prize," Technical Report, Netflix, 2009.

6. Xavier Amatriain, "Netflix Recommendations: Beyond the 5 Stars," *The Netflix Tech Blog,* Netflix, April 6, 2012, accessed March 4, 2017, http://techblog.netflix.com/2012/04/netflix-recommendations-beyond-5-stars.html.

7. Olga Russakovsky et al., "Imagenet Large Scale Visual Recognition Challenge," *International Journal of Computer Vision* 115, no. 3 (2015): 211–252.

8. This will be true up to physical limitations of the hardware we use to build these automata. It may become more difficult to trace actions due to quantum effects, if and when we develop viable quantum computers.

9. This is known as the Chinese Room Argument.

10. Gaby Wood, "Living Dolls: A Magical History of the Quest for Mechanical Life by Gaby Wood," *The Guardian*, February 15, 2002. https://www.theguardian.com/books/2002/feb/16/extract.gabywood.

INDEX